AFRICANS IN THE OLD SOUTH

Mapping Exceptional Lives across the Atlantic World

RANDY J. SPARKS

Harvard University Press

Cambridge, Massachusetts

London, England

2016

Library of Congress Cataloging-in-Publication Data

Sparks, Randy J., author.
Africans in the old South : mapping exceptional lives across the
Atlantic world / Randy J. Sparks.
pages cm
Includes bibliographical references and index.
ISBN 978-0-674-49516-6 (alk. paper)
1. African Americans—Southern States—Biography. 2. Blacks—Atlantic
Ocean Region—Biography. 3. Slaves—Southern States—Biography. 4. Slave
trade—History. 5. Southern States—History—18th century. 6. Southern
States—History—19th century. I. Title.
E185.615.S695 2016
305.896'073075—dc23   2015030866

For Judith Lee Hunt

AFRICANS IN THE
OLD SOUTH

Contents

Maps

All maps by Rebecca Wren

"We do not take a journey,
but rather a journey takes us."

—John Steinbeck

Introduction

Is it not the chief disgrace in the world, not to be an unit;—not
to be reckoned one character;—not to yield that peculiar fruit
which each man was created to bear, but to be reckoned in the
gross, in the hundred, or the thousand . . . ?

—EMERSON

O F ALL THE DISGRACES that darken the history of humanity, the Atlantic slave trade must rate near the top. The largest forced migration in human history, its far-reaching toll is all but incalculable. Most
of its estimated 12,500,000 victims, a number almost as difficult to grasp
as the sands on a beach or the stars in the heavens, are nameless and
faceless men, women, and children whose lives cannot be reconstructed
from the remaining historical record. It is important, even crucial, then,
to reconstruct as many of those lives as possible, and this collection of
biographies of Africans in the Old South and the Atlantic World adds to
the growing number of biographies of those caught up in the slave trade.
The subjects of the chapters that follow share one thing in common—all
of them were natives of West Africa who lived in the American South
between 1760 and 1860. Beyond that, however, they have surprisingly
little in common, and that very diversity lies at the heart of this book
and complicates our understanding of both Southern and Atlantic history. Of the millions of victims of the slave trade brought to the Americas,
only an estimated 389,000 came to the American South, about 79,000
of those after 1800.[1] Many of the Africans whose life narratives are presented here were victims of that trade. Others, however, were directly
engaged in the slave trade. That trade cannot be understood by looking

only at its victims, and this volume contains life narratives of both the enslavers and the enslaved for members of both groups made their way across the Atlantic to the American South during this era.

Particle physics has taught us that the Romantics were not entirely wrong to think that you could understand the world through a grain of sand. Is it best to understand the universe by viewing it through a telescope or through a microscope? Both are essential. The universe looks different when viewed at the sub-atomic level, and the laws once thought to govern the universe operate differently at that level. The way we view history likewise changes with scale. In the life narratives of Africans in the Old South presented here, I use the tools of microhistory to challenge the dominant portrayal of native Africans in the region. Macrohistories of plantation slavery seek to give readers an idea of the life of the "typical" slave. No field of historical study has been more rich or productive than that scholarship, and yet these broad overviews by their very nature tend to flatten out the human experience, to narrow the range of the possible, and to distance readers from the real people whose lives lie behind the generalities. Microhistory seeks to complicate that picture through the lives of individuals whose experiences defy the dominant narrative. Microhistorians make no claim that their subjects are "typical," and, in fact, microhistorians look for outliers, for individuals who leave some substantial trace in the historical record and whose experiences do not fit neatly into the picture historians have drawn. Microhistorians search for stories that cut against the grain, and follow their subjects on the ground, paying close attention to the world they lived in, the options before them, and the choices they made from among those options.[2] This book attempts to capture the unfamiliar, the exceptional, the lives of men and women who defy our expectations of what their lives should have been like. I have strayed off the beaten path, but I hope that offers a fresh perspective, a novel view, of times and places that have been extensively studied and that we think we understand perhaps better than we do.

The book is also situated in the Black Atlantic World, and the concept of the Black Atlantic functions here as both methodology and subject. The Atlantic World paradigm has reshaped our understanding of the Early Modern World and the radical transformation brought about by the multi-faceted connections between Europe, the Americas, and Africa that sprang up in the wake of Columbus's voyages to America.

Much of that literature has focused on the European Atlantic World, and particularly the British Atlantic, opening the field up to criticisms that it is largely a reworking of traditional European imperial history. Scholars of the Black Atlantic are well positioned to broaden the field of Atlantic History and to emphasize the role Africans played within that world.[3] Of course, Africans have figured in that history, but largely as victims of the Atlantic slave trade. That emphasis is understandable and appropriate given the scale of the trade. That history was long dominated by the "numbers game," by an attempt to arrive at some reasonable estimate of the number of victims of the trade. That historiography was incredibly rich and significant, but it often obscured the lives of individuals. That trend has been challenged in recent years by a number of microhistories of the Black Atlantic in the Early Modern era. As Carlo Ginzburg suggested in his landmark microhistory *The Cheese and the Worms,* "if the sources offer us the possibility of reconstructing not only indistinct masses but also individual personalities, it would be absurd to ignore it. To extend the historic concept of the 'individual' in the direction of the lower classes is a worthwhile objective."[4]

This project embraces what has been called the "biographical turn" in the scholarship of the Black Atlantic, and it speaks to a growing effort to record the life histories of individual African slaves and their descendants. *Slave Biographies: The Atlantic Database Network,* for example, seeks to provide biographical data on individuals enslaved around the Atlantic World. They are restoring to history the identities of men, women, and children who would otherwise be lost, hidden in archives and legal and ecclesiastical records scattered across continents. Paul Lovejoy is directing an ambitious project called the SHADD Biography Project which aims to collect biographical information on as many as 100–200,000 Africans in the New World. Historians Lisa Lindsay and John Wood Sweet edited an important collection focused on biographies of African and African-descended individuals in the eighteenth- and nineteenth-century Black Atlantic. In his essay in that collection, Joseph Miller, one of our most distinguished scholars of African history, wrote, "the so-called 'biographical turn' in the 'Black Atlantic' . . . is a historiographical advance that I find as profound as the 'quantitative turn,' the sweeping research of pan-disciplinary proportions a half-century ago that generated the scholarship that has now crested in the launch of the Voyages database." Like Miller, I see the reconstruction of individual lives as an important corrective to quantitative studies of the slave trade that have largely ignored the lives of individuals. Studying the life experiences of individuals allows us to better understand the diversity of the African experience in the Atlantic World and in the Old South. Not all Africans crossed the Atlantic as slaves, not all voyages across the Atlantic were one-way, not even for enslaved Africans. It is important to see Africans as individuals with complex lives, as men and women who enslaved and who suffered enslavement, who moved from freedom to slavery and back again, who defy any easy categorization.[5]

Prince Sneed, a former slave on St. Catherine's Island, fifty miles south of Savannah, Georgia, recalled a story he heard by the fireside from his grandfather. Jacob Waldberg owned the entire island which he divided into two plantations producing Sea Island cotton and worked by over 250 slaves. Among those were new Africans who were being acculturated and taught to work raising Sea Island cotton. The driver was working the Africans hard, having them hoe in the fields. When the driver came out to check on their progress, he found two of the Africans resting under a shade tree while their hoes continued to work by themselves. The shocked driver challenged the men, who responded with a chant, " 'Kum buba yali kuni buba tambe, Kum kunka yali kum kunka tambe,' quick like." Then they rose off the ground and flew away, and no one saw them again. Sneed reported, "Some say dey fly back tuh Africa. Muh gran see dat wid he own eye." Wallace Quarterman of Darien, Georgia, told a very similar story of native Africans working under an overseer named Mr. Blue who put the men in the field but, as Quarterman put it, "he couldn do nuttn wid em. Dey gabble, gabble, gabble, an nobody couldn unduhstan um an dey didn know how tuh wuk right." Blue whipped the Africans "with a long whip," and after that abuse, the men got together, stuck a hoe in the field, and repeated a chant. They rose up in the sky, turned themselves into buzzards, and flew back to Africa, leaving nothing but a hoe standing in the field. The tropes of winged Africans taking flight back to Africa and hoes working magically in the fields are widespread in the Lowcountry and the Caribbean, and have been adopted by novelists like Toni Morrison. What do these magical tales reveal about the lives of Africans in the Old South? The stories always refer to newly arrived Africans, not yet fully acculturated, who are capable of working powerful magic, who escape bondage and punishment and return to their homeland. The stories also echo African trickster tales featuring Anansi the spider or other animals that morphed into Brer Rabbit tales in the U.S. South. The Africans are powerful shape-shifters, able to change their identities and gain their freedom. These folktales challenge the dominant perception of newly arrived Africans in the historical literature.[6]

When writing about Africans in the Old South, historians have rightly emphasized their victimhood. Most of those enslaved Africans who stepped off the slave ships in the Americas were from the interior of Africa, fearful of Europeans, unable to speak European languages, ignorant of the fate that awaited them, and sometimes preferring death by starvation or suicide to enslavement. They were more likely than creole slaves to run away in groups with others from their African nation on a quixotic quest to return to Africa. These new Africans endured a difficult period of acculturation, forced to perform the backbreaking labor expected of them while slowly learning a broken English that enabled them to communicate with their fellow slaves as well as their masters and overseers. Historian Ira Berlin has paid close attention to African or "saltwater" slaves and the challenges that confronted them in the plantation South. He compares their experience with the first generation of slaves, the "Charter Generation," whom he identified as "Atlantic creoles." These Atlantic creoles first emerged on the West Coast of Africa as Europeans and Africans came into close contact. They were familiar with Atlantic trade and culture, often fluent in its languages, cosmopolitan. They had spent time in the Americas and were more likely to gain their freedom than those that came after them.[7]

The plantation revolution, which got underway in the late seventeenth century in the Chesapeake and later in colonies like South Carolina, brought massive imports of Africans drawn more deeply from the interior and, unlike the Atlantic creoles, they were more provincial. The percentage of African-born slaves in the population rose steadily in the South; however, the majority of Virginia's slave population was native-born by 1720 and in South Carolina by 1750, and by 1780 three-fourths of Virginia's and two-thirds of South Carolina's enslaved populations were creole. The proportion of African-born slaves in the South stood at around 22 percent by 1810, but declined sharply thereafter.[8] Berlin observed that for them, "the Atlantic was a strange, inhospitable place, a one-way street to oblivion." Tied to the inland villages, to their families and clans, they were ignorant of the vast trade networks of the Atlantic. Culturally, they were not as sophisticated as the Atlantic creoles; they "lacked the linguistic range and cultural plasticity of the charter generation." Once caught up in the slave trade, they endured the horrors of the Middle Passage. On the tobacco and rice plantations of the South, to which the overwhelming majority of them were bound, these Africans "worked harder and died earlier" than the creoles. Their family lives were "more truncated," and they knew "little about Christianity and European jurisprudence." They accumulated little property, they seldom gained their freedom, and their slave names "reflected the contempt in which their owners held them."[9] The life narratives presented here challenge these generalizations at almost every turn. That is not to say that Berlin's brilliant and sweeping depiction of colonial slavery is inaccurate, only that these microhistories reveal a range of experience broader than portrayals of "typical" Africans would suggest. Berlin's generational model is certainly useful for understanding the collective experiences of Africans in the South, but it does not account for the complexities of individual experience.

The radicalization of freedom in the Age of Revolution created greater opportunities but also greater complexities for the enslaved. More free territories sprang up around the Atlantic World during the late eighteenth and nineteenth centuries, even in Africa itself, and so for enslaved Africans the most meaningful boundaries were those that separated freedom from slavery. As we will see, Africans became very adept at navigating these waters, finding the legal loopholes and juridical fissures that could gain them the liberty they struggled to achieve. Life narratives offer a compelling window into this quest for freedom that allows us to see individuals as they maneuvered through this world, as they tried and failed and changed their strategy, learning at every step. Through their lives, we see this history set in motion, as real individuals experienced it. This perspective emphasizes human agency and demonstrates that individuals are not simply puppets manipulated by historical forces they cannot see or comprehend, but active individuals and conscious actors. It is only at the level of lived experience, as Carlo Ginzburg and Carlo Poni argued, that we do not risk "losing the complexity of the relationships that connect any individual to a particular society."[10]

Some readers may be frustrated by certain aspects of the book, particularly my intention to take seriously narratives that cannot be fully proven given the passage of time. It is my conviction that listening to the voices of Africans or other "subalterns" is necessary to tell a more accurate and whole history than can be told otherwise.[11] By their very nature, these sources cannot always be verified, and they are often fragmentary. That does not mean that I have read these narratives uncritically. In some cases, I raise serious doubts about the version of events presented in the narratives, but even in those cases the inaccuracies and deceptions are themselves important to an understanding of the narrators and their life strategies. I have attempted to verify the details of each of the life stories presented here. When that has not been possible, I have made my best evaluation of the events described in the narratives, but I recognize that these are matters of interpretation, and some readers may draw different conclusions.

Rather than hide those gaps and question marks that hang over these life narratives, I have attempted not only to highlight them, but to probe them and their origins. Were they created intentionally by the individuals as a part of a strategy to gain their freedom? Are they inherent in the study of the enslaved whose voices are often mediated and silenced in the historical record? More and more, historians are questioning the very nature of archives themselves, and our reliance on them as historians who rely on the written record.[12] Research into the lives of these individuals illustrates that relations of power, gender, class, and race are powerfully reflected in the historical record, and we must make conscious decisions about how the very nature of the historical record shapes our ability to access the voices of the enslaved.

Michel-Rolph Trouillot refers to the limitations imposed on historians by the written record as "archival power . . . the power to define what is and what is not a serious object of research, and, therefore, of mention." He argues that silences enter the historical record "at four crucial moments: the moment of fact creation (the making of *sources*); the moment of fact assembly (the making of *archives*); the moment of fact retrieval (the making of *narratives*); and the moment of retrospective significance (the making of *history* in the final instance)." Both presences and absences in the archives are created; they cannot be natural or neutral.[13] Ann Laura Stoler reminds us that the silences in the archives arise from several different sources; some things went unrecorded because they were considered common knowledge, while in other cases a thing was unwritten because "it could not yet be articulated" or "it could not be said." These silences and gaps in the historical record lead to what Stoler refers to as "disabled histories," and several of the life narratives presented here fall into that category.[14] I believe that these fragmentary histories still have value, but that is one reason I think of these as life narratives rather than traditional biographies. Since the historical record related to Africans in the Old South is often woefully incomplete, this volume defies the usual convention that a book's chapters be of roughly equal length. In some cases, a rich documentary basis allows for a much fuller treatment of a life, while in others the records are so fragmentary that only a short snapshot is the most that can be reconstructed. I have let the sources dictate the length of the chapters.

Several themes run through these narratives and shape my analysis of them. One is the question of identity formation among Africans in the American South. I use "African" or "Africans" here to refer to individuals born anywhere on that continent, not as a cultural identifier. Historians of African American history have grappled with the issues surrounding African identities among victims of the Atlantic slave trade for generations with increasing complexity, and those discussions have usually taken a corporate rather than an individual approach to that topic. Two main schools of thought have dominated that literature, generally divided between those scholars who have emphasized cultural continuity and Africa-centered models and those who have focused on discontinuities and a creolization model. Taken together, these narratives illustrate the difficulty in locating a collective "African" identity that could link these divergent individuals together. They point to the remarkable diversity that characterized Africans bound for the Americas, and the highly individualized struggle that confronted every African who arrived in the South. These cases raise a more fundamental question of an individual's sense of identity.[15]

For these men and women, self-identification was both situational and relational, heavily dependent on where individuals found themselves, and shifting over a lifetime characterized by movement and changes in age and status. Joseph Miller suggested that one common feature of an African worldview is that Africans think of time as cumulative, as "ongoing compositions of experiences (and relationships), all retained to form the lived present as a compound . . . compilations of selves constituted through the experiences and relationships of a lifetime."[16] Self-identification is not an abstraction, then, but something deeply personal, shaped by an individual's place in a community, their relationships with the people around them, and their own sense of belonging. A consideration of any of the life narratives presented here will demonstrate just how complex this question could become, and how many-layered and rich their own self-identities must have been. Historian Michael Gomez is not unaware of these variables and complexities, but he suggests, for example, that "the African-born, despite the length of time spent away from their homeland, retained a psychic attachment and orientation to Africa," a generalization that glosses over the full range of the experiences of individuals. Recent scholarship focused on individual Atlantic Africans offers a more nuanced view of identity formation. Historian Lisa Lindsay suggests that "we should be thinking about diasporic African identities not so much as based on specific locations or ethnicities—when they can even be known—as on particular constellations of subjectivities, goals, and contexts." I endorse her view that biography can help us "reframe" African identity in the Atlantic World, and see it not as something fixed but rather as "a strategy, and a potentially flexible one at that." I do not wish to discount the importance of the African ethnic identifications that Gomez chronicles, but ethnic identifications appear to be relevant in only one of the cases presented here and apply best to the lives of enslaved Africans in the plantation districts. That is not to say that Africans in the South underwent what James H. Sweet described as "a sort of untrammeled civilizing process in which individual rights" replaced African epistemologies. Rather, as Sweet so powerfully argues, what we see is the "fragmentation" of European ideologies and African communal ones and the remaking of those into an Atlantic worldview.[17]

Frederick Cooper, a scholar of African history, has observed that of the many key concepts that drive current scholarship, "identity" easily wins the prize as the most frequently employed term in scholarly articles over the past couple of decades and, as a result, its meaning has become somewhat slippery. He points out that, as scholars, we have been asking the concept of identity to do a lot of heavy lifting. The term is often used to connote a "*sameness* among members of a group or category" that is then said to express itself in group solidarity or collective action. This use of the term is common in studies of race, gender, ethnicity, and social movements. It is also understood as a product of social and political action as well as the foundation for future action. The term is also used to describe the core of the self, something fundamental to all social beings. The characterization of identity as a deep aspect of selfhood to be prized and preserved is a usage that frequently appears in studies of race and ethnicity. As employed in postmodernism and other schools of thought influenced by Foucault, identity is understood as growing out of "multiple and competing discourses . . . invoked to highlight the *unstable, multiple, fluctuating, and fragmented* nature of the contemporary self." Cooper points out that while there are points of convergence here, more often these various understandings of the term veer off in different directions. He proposes that scholars find a more nuanced language to distinguish these very different meanings from one another and to do the theoretical work that the overburdened term was meant to do.[18] I have attempted to do that here.

Michel-Rolph Trouillot has also emphasized that historians must be aware of the specific context in which their subjects operate. He suggested that we must consider individuals in three capacities: "1) as agents, or occupants of structural positions; 2) as actors in constant interface with a context; and 3) as subjects, that is, as voices aware of their vocality." Agents include such things as class and status, slaves and masters, mothers and fathers. People have agency, but they can only act within certain confines specific to time and place; "both their existence and their understanding rest fundamentally on historical particulars." To consider individuals as subjects calls on us to try to understand not only what people did, but why they did it, to ask what objective they thought they were pursuing.[19]

As the book's title suggests, another common theme in these life narratives is movement. In myriad ways, the Africans who journeyed around and through the Atlantic World and the American South saw their lives, their self-identifications, and choices shaped by their locales. Their mobility is such a salient feature of their lives that it is useful to think of these narratives as "life geographies." In that sense, geography is not simply a location or a stage set for life, but rather a significant factor in shaping identity, relationships, and opportunities. The places where people live their lives, the spaces through which they move, allow us to measure a life with a different yardstick.[20] To emphasize the importance of geography, each of the following chapters opens with a map showing the routes these individuals traveled around the Atlantic. These graphics illustrate that geography and movement play critical roles in the lives of these individuals, and those pathways reveal what Tony Ballantyne referred to as a webbed spatiality, a "complex mesh of networks," that crosses the ocean's surface and helps define the Black Atlantic.[21] Each individual life in this book can be thought of as a strand connecting one place contingently to another, a thread taking new forms and embodying "loose ends and on-going stories." As these individuals moved they made new links and broke old ones, and their individual identities were shaped by these changing locales.[22] Changes in personhood came from dwelling in different spaces—over time most Africans put down roots, engaged in their local society, and created new friendships and family networks, though they may still have had feelings of loss and nostalgia for their African home. Ann Laura Stoler has argued that "research that begins with people's movements rather than with fixed polities opens up to more organic histories that are not compelled by originary narratives designed to show the 'natural' teleology of future nations, later republics, and future states."[23]

Salman Rushdie has referred to people who have been "borne across the world" as "translated men and women" (he noted that the word "translation" derives from the Latin for "bearing across"). These migrants, he observes, lose both language and home, they are defined by others and often become either invisible or a target. They are forced to learn new languages, build new homes, and form new relationships. "Uprooting, disjuncture and metamorphosis," according to Rushdie, define the migrant experience, and this is true whether those migrations were voluntary or involuntary.[24] All of these narratives speak to this "'decentering,' of the autonomous individual and unified life," a process described by Stephen Daniels and Catherine Nash, which has "emphasised the intersection of the geographical and biographical, in overlapping domains of self and place, positionality and identity, spatiality and subjectivity." Daniels and Nash observe that "the self became something made and remade in different situations," and that a biographical approach can best reveal the highly complex and contextualized nature of migration and its consequences.[25]

Chapter 1 explores the lives of Elizabeth Cleveland Hardcastle and her niece Catherine Cleveland, members of a prominent mixed-race slave trading family from the area now known as Sierra Leone, who immigrated to South Carolina in 1740. Elizabeth was about twenty-five years old while Catherine was a child of five, and their experiences highlight the importance of race, age, and gender in the migrant experience. Elizabeth had been educated in Liverpool before her move to South Carolina where she invested in plantations and slaves, married an Englishman, and lived her life as a member of the white planter elite. Her niece, however, could not pass as white and was regarded as a free woman of color. Thanks to a twenty-year legal battle over Elizabeth's considerable estate, their life histories are the best documented of those presented here.[26] Their lives are a reminder of the importance of class in colonial America—they had wealthy and prominent relatives in England, Africa, and South Carolina—and the complex interplay between race, class, and gender. They also remind us that not all Africans—even in the South—can be considered subalterns. They may have been the most exceptional Africans to arrive in the colonial South, but the fact that Elizabeth Cleveland lived her life as a member of the slave-owning planter elite illustrates that not all Africans came to colonial America as slaves. Elizabeth had no children, but Catherine became the matriarch of a large and prosperous family of free blacks. Differing racial categories within this single family raise important questions about shifting identities in the Atlantic World.

Chapter 2 explores the lives of the members of the Holman family whose story suggests that the Cleveland's experience was not entirely unique. Historians on both sides of the Atlantic have written about them, but their family history looks somewhat different when compared to and contrasted with other Atlantic Africans in the South. The Holmans came to the South Carolina Lowcountry from the same region in West Africa as the Clevelands and, like them, had been elite, Anglo-African slave traders there. John Holman, the British founder of that family, sought to secure a safe haven for his family and a secure investment for some of his considerable profits from the Atlantic slave trade. By the 1790s Holman could envision a transatlantic commercial enterprise where the family would control slave factories on the Rio Pongo and invest in slave voyages to transport those slaves across the Atlantic where they were to be sold in partnership with slave traders in South Carolina. In addition, the family would own rice plantations on the Rio Pongo where hundreds or even thousands of slaves labored to produce rice during the rainy season. These slaves could be sold into the Atlantic slave trade during the dry season after the crop was harvested. Similarly, the family would own and operate rice plantations in the South Carolina Lowcountry, manned by the very slaves who had gained expertise growing the crop on the Rio Pongo. Counterfactual history is a questionable enterprise, but had the United States not abolished the Atlantic slave trade in 1808, it is possible to imagine that Holman's scheme, which was embraced by other slave traders based in Charleston and on the Rio Pongo and Rio Nunez, might well have come to fruition and made Charleston the primary port for an African slave trade that could have fueled the rise of the Cotton Kingdom. A model for just this sort of transatlantic slave trade enterprise existed in the Southern Hemisphere where West African and mixed-race traders moved back and forth between Brazil and West Africa. Unlike Elizabeth Cleveland, the Holmans did not join the ranks of the white planter elite, but rather forged relations with the region's elite free people of color. Through those marriages, the Holman daughters joined secure and prosperous households and a wealthy extended family; however, the Holman sons failed to prosper in the Lowcountry and returned to West Africa and the slave trade business there.

Chapter 3 analyzes the narrative of Robert Johnson, a member of the Kissi ethnic group, who was kidnapped as a child and sold into slavery in Savannah, Georgia, in 1797. His narrative originated from a speech he gave at an 1837 abolitionist meeting in Boston, published in the abolition press, and more recently in John Blassingame's collection of narratives, though it has not received much attention from historians. His experience is a reminder of the enslavement of children, which became increasingly important in the late eighteenth- and nineteenth-century slave trade, and the unique challenges that confronted them. Johnson's speech recounted his own story of enslavement, but he also told a dramatic story of the murder of an enslaved girl named Delia on an isolated Georgia plantation early in the nineteenth century. I attempt to verify his story, which raises important questions about the nature of sources from the enslaved and the silences of the archives. Johnson's owner, Jabez Bowen, a native of Rhode Island who became a federal judge in Georgia, was driven out of the state for condemning slavery from the bench and calling for abolition. Bowen took Johnson with him to Rhode Island where Johnson was eventually manumitted.

Johnson, enslaved as a boy, mastered English, left the slave South for free territory in the North, won his freedom, became a physician, and joined the movement against slavery in the United States. I have traced Robert Johnson's journey from slavery in Georgia to freedom in Rhode Island and Massachusetts.

Chapter 4 explores the life narrative of Dimmock Charlton, also from the Kissi nation, who was enslaved illegally in Savannah around 1813. Charlton claimed to have been liberated when the British captured a Spanish slave ship during the War of 1812. He had joined the crew of the H. M. S. *Peacock*, a British warship sunk by an American warship off the coast of Demerara during that war. He and most of the crew survived and were rescued by the American ship and imprisoned in New York. Known on board the ship as John Bull, he was somehow taken to Savannah, enslaved there, and given the name Dimmock Charlton. He eventually bought his freedom, but was unable to purchase the freedom of his wife, his children, or grandchildren. He traveled north to try to raise the necessary funds from northern abolitionists when the women of the family who owned his young granddaughter brought her with them on an extended stay in New York City. Charlton learned that his granddaughter was now on free soil, and sued for her freedom. He won that case, and sent her to Canada where she was adopted. He claimed British citizenship based on his service on the *Peacock*, and traveled to Britain in an attempt to gain that citizenship and to continue his efforts to raise the funds to free his family. Not everyone believed Charlton's story and questioned whether or not he actually served on the British naval vessel. I attempt to verify his story, a quest that raises important questions about the enslaved voice, the nature of the archives, and the shifting identities that Charlton embraced as he moved from Africa, to a British warship, to Savannah, to the North, and then to England.

Chapter 5 takes up the case of three Africans who were picked up in a canoe in the Caribbean by a British merchant ship in 1829. The ship was en route to Mobile, Alabama, and when the ship arrived with the three Africans on board, the Collector of Customs jailed them and threatened to seize the vessel for violating U.S. laws against the African slave trade. The British consul in Mobile attempted to gain custody of the men, but they escaped before their case could be resolved. They were captured in Mississippi, sold by the sheriff, and appeared as runaways again in Baton Rouge, Louisiana, when the British consul in Mobile convinced American authorities to recognize the men as free and under British protection. They were sent to Liverpool and from there were returned to their homeland by British authorities. Their case is the most fragmentary of the cases presented here and, though I follow their archival trail to the British archives, they are never even named in the records. Still, their case is a revealing one. Their own remarkable efforts to resist enslavement against enormous odds were successful and took them on a dramatic circuit around the Atlantic World. Their case also shows how far the British authorities would go to protect Africans that fell under their care and the tensions that arose between the U.S. and Britain as a result of British efforts to abolish and police the African slave trade.

Chapter 6 follows the narrative of Charles Smith, liberated by the British from a slave ship off Old Calabar (in modern-day Nigeria), and resettled first in Sierra Leone and then on the Gambia. He became a sailor and traveled on a merchant ship to New York City and then to Mobile in 1838. When he went into a bar in Mobile his free status was challenged, and he was arrested and sent to a plantation outside the city while his case was under investigation. There, he met another African named Sack N'Jaie, a former merchant in Sierra Leone, who told him that he had been illegally enslaved after being picked up by a Portuguese ship off the African coast and sold in Mobile. Once Smith was freed, he returned to Sierra Leone, tracked down Sack N'Jaie's father, Pharaoh Moses, and told him that his son was illegally enslaved in Alabama. Moses himself had been enslaved on the Gambia as a young man. Forced to leave his wife, son, and daughter behind, he was sold into slavery in Charleston, South Carolina early in the nineteenth century. He married, had a second family, and eventually purchased freedom for himself and his family. With the help of the American Colonization Society, he returned to Africa with his entire family and was even reunited with the son he had left behind in Africa, Sack N'Jaie, who was now enslaved outside Mobile. Moses went to the British authorities in Sierra Leone, who contacted their superiors in London, who then demanded that U.S. officials investigate the matter and free Sack N'Jaie. American authorities investigated Smith's own story and raised enough questions to cast doubt on Smith's version of events.

The full story of the African slave trade could only be known with biographies of each of its 12,500,000 victims, but that sort of complete record is lost to us forever. This great loss, one of the world's chief disgraces, serves to highlight the importance that should be attached to every individual story that can be retrieved. And in order to be fully understood, the tragic history of the slave trade must embody its perpetrators as well as its victims, for they, too, have a history. These life geographies of individual Africans, both enslavers and enslaved, remind us of the human and individual dimensions of the Atlantic slave trade and its impacts on individuals and families as well as on the American South. It was the slave trade that literally gave birth to the mixed-race slave trading families on the Sherbro and the Rio Pongo, and that trade propelled them and millions more across the Atlantic and, in some cases, back again. By reckoning these single characters, as Emerson urged, I have attempted to uncover the connections that crisscrossed the Atlantic World, to link the personal and individual experiences to historical developments that existed across space and time, and thereby to render those momentous changes more intelligible.

1

Anglo-African Women Join a Plantation Society

I N AUGUST 1764, in the sweltering heat of the Lowcountry summer season, a London ship called the *Queen of Barra* sailed into Charleston harbor. Two of its passengers, Elizabeth Cleveland, a young woman of twenty-five, and her niece Catherine Cleveland, a girl of five, waited anxiously for their new home to come into view. The city lay along the flat peninsula between the Ashley and Cooper rivers, which met there, Charlestonians claimed, to form the Atlantic Ocean. The city's Cooper River waterfront was lined with elegant homes occupied by the merchant and planter elite and by the stores and warehouses that profited from the city's lively trade, but the church steeples of St. Michael's and St. Philip's would have been the first feature to greet anyone approaching from the sea. A bustling port, Charleston handled 90 percent of the South Carolina colony's trade which was expanding rapidly during the 1760s, fueled by the growth in exports of rice and indigo and by the importation of enslaved Africans that accompanied the expansion of plantation agriculture. Slave imports grew from a couple of hundred a year in 1720 to 2–3,000 a year in the 1760s, making Charleston by far the largest slave market on the North American mainland. When Moses Lopez returned to Charleston from Rhode Island in 1765 after a twenty-year absence, he was awed by the changes; he found the city "twice as big as when I was here in 1742. It has increased with sumptuous brick houses in very great number. One cannot go somewhere where one does not see new buildings and large and small houses

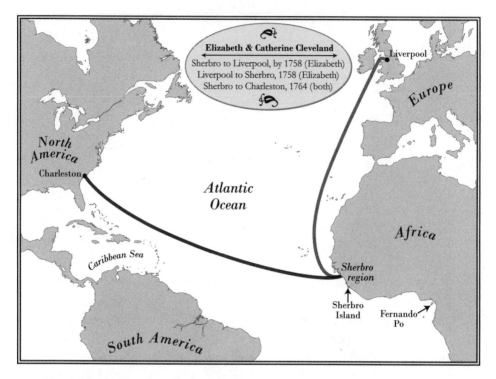

Map 1. Elizabeth and Catherine Cleveland

started, half-finished, and almost finished. To me who comes from poor, humble Rhode Island, it seems . . . a new world."[1]

It was, in many respects, an African world. By the time the Clevelands arrived, Charleston had a small black majority, but in the rural parishes Africans overwhelmed white residents; all but three rural parishes were over 70 percent black. That African presence was not lost on anyone; as early as 1737 a Swiss emigrant, Sameul Dyssli, remarked that "Carolina looks more like a negro country than like a country settled by white people." By 1790 that black majority seemed so entrenched that South Carolina historian David Ramsay concluded, "Providence intended this for a negro settlement." The *Queen of Barra,* owned by London merchant Richard Oswald, was one of the many slave ships arriving in the 1760s from Sierra Leone, and she carried in her stinking holds 300 slaves for the bustling Lowcountry market. The ship unloaded its surviving human cargo on Sullivan's Island, where slaves were quarantined before being sold at auction. The ship proceeded to Charleston where it tied up along the city's bustling docks. The 1760s saw a spike in the number of slaves arriving in South Carolina and in the number from the Windward Coast, which included Sierra Leone.[2] There was nothing particularly unusual about the ship in August 1764, aside from the Clevelands.

The busy trade networks between Charleston and Sierra Leone help explain the Clevelands' unusual arrival as passengers on an African slave ship. Of all the tens of thousands of immigrants who arrived in colonial Charleston, they were among the most exceptional. They were natives of the Sherbro River region of Sierra Leone where their family operated one of the most successful slave trading depots along the coast. Elizabeth's father was an Englishman, her mother, a mixed-race Anglo-African, while Catherine's father was Anglo-African and her mother an African. Like so many immigrants to the Americas, they came to build new lives for themselves in South Carolina, but unlike almost every other African, they came to Charleston voluntarily and as free people. Their experiences challenge many of our preconceptions about the eighteenth-century Atlantic World and the place of Africans, and especially African women, within it. Their long and rich lives in South Carolina complicate our understanding of the constructions of race and gender, slavery and freedom in the Lowcountry.

While many of the mixed-race slave trading families along the coast of Sierra Leone traced their ancestry back to the Portuguese, there were very few Afro-Portuguese in the region around the Sherbro River for the *lançados*, the Portuguese men who lived in African communities, had not settled there. Instead the region was dominated by Anglo-African families, especially the Corkers, the Rogers, the Tuckers and the Clevelands, all of whom except the Clevelands traced their origins to Englishmen employed by royal trading companies. Zachery Rogers and John Tucker were employees of the Gambia Adventurers who arrived on the coast in 1665. Thomas Corker, who was employed by the Royal African Company, arrived in 1684. Following a pattern established by the Portuguese along that coast, all these men took the daughters of prominent local African rulers as their wives. These women lived with their husbands inside the factories, they were supported at the company's expense, and their sons were employed by the company often

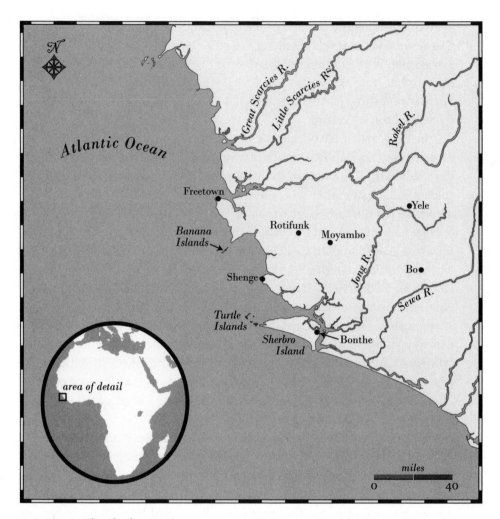

Map 2. The Sherbro Region

after they had been educated in England, an expense the company resisted. In 1692 the company ordered that "the children of Mr. Rogers and all others that doe the Company noe service be discharged," an order the company found hard to enforce. The company continued to complain about some members of these families in their employ, but others filled important functions like interpreter for which they were well qualified while others served as factors in the company's trading posts outside Sherbro. The Tuckers became a powerful family, and by the mid-eighteenth century, Henry Tucker was the wealthy and influ-

Anglo-Africans, it was important to be able to function in either of the worlds they inhabited. That ability to operate comfortably in both worlds was essential to their success as Atlantic merchants and traders and as local traders and political leaders.[7]

William Cleveland died in 1758, a loss that forced his children to return to the Sherbro where John, as the eldest son, took over the family business. An English trader who knew him reported that after being educated in Liverpool, John returned to Africa and "carried on the slave trade with more than common expertise and success." Making his headquarters on the Banana Islands, he proved himself to be a master at exploiting his dual heritage. The Banana Islands were located between Freetown and the Sherbro River, and provided a convenient stop for ships too large to navigate the shallow Sherbro. The island had some high ground and fertile lands. Notoriously fair in his business dealings, he soon prospered, and he used his profits strategically. As his wealth increased, "he dealt it out in credits to the neighbouring chiefs, whom by this means he always retained in a state of dependence." Most of the petty chiefs in the area turned to the slave traders for European goods which were advanced to them on credit. As the chiefs fell further into his debt, town after town came "under his subjection" and he thereby acquired the right to seize the chiefs and all their dependents should they not be able to repay the debts. He acquired his slaves for sale in part through this means, by breaking up towns and enslaving all the inhabitants. He "laid waste town after town on the river Sherbro," and extended his own authority over the region. Though Cleveland's tactics were harsh, he retained his reputation for fairness, "for in all his transactions . . . he had never been known to deviate from the established customs of that country." Here again, his understanding of local customs enabled him to out maneuver other local chiefs and traders. Unlike some unscrupulous slave traders, he made it a policy never to "catch" or kidnap "the inhabitants of any town . . . without previously having previously acquired the right to do so." For this reason, he was regarded as "a good and humane man."[8]

A description of the home of his brother James probably also describes John's lifestyle and further illustrates the Clevelands' cultural hybridity. An officer in the Royal Navy, John Mathews, who visited with him described his house as being built in the "Country Manner," that is, in the local African style, though larger than most. James's "manner of living is a nearly comfortable to the European Custom as Circumstances will admit," Mathews reported, and he also observed that his house was "also furnished in the English Style." Mathews tried to discover if Cleveland believed in the African religion practiced around him, and while James laughed at some of "their ridiculous superstitions," he was unwilling to fully discount the "predictions of the Conjurers and Sandcasters" whose forecasts, he claimed, were often realized. Mathews noted that Cleveland was motivated by his "Interests" as a merchant, and added, "To sum up his Character is a few Words: With a White Man he is a White Man, with a Black Man a Black Man." That description is probably the best summation of the abilities of these Anglo-Africans to move between two worlds.[9]

Elizabeth probably returned from school in Liverpool to Africa with her brothers. Her situation there may have been similar to that of her relative, Miss Norrie, also a mulatto descendant of an English trader, a Mr. Norrie, and a woman from the Corker family. John Mathews reported that like Elizabeth, Miss Norrie was educated in England, and "on her Return to her native Country, she continued to dress in the English Fashion, and appears to be a sensible and intelligent woman, and still retains the Address of the Europeans. She lives as the Natives do, but that I believe is the Effect of Necessity, not Choice." Did Elizabeth yearn for a different, more comfortable, life than she had on the Banana Islands? Did she and her brother see financial advantages in Elizabeth's relocating? Or did rising tensions in the region cause her to seek safety elsewhere? The records are silent on these questions, but somehow Elizabeth and John made the remarkable decision that she would relocate to South Carolina where she and John would invest some of the family fortune in land and slaves. John sent his daughter, Catherine, along as a companion to live with his sister abroad.

Elizabeth and Catherine sailed from the Bananas on the *Queen of Barra*, carrying 368 slaves for the Charleston market. No doubt some of those slaves were sold by John Cleveland to the ship's captain, Alexander Taylor. The voyage would have been a difficult one for Elizabeth and Catherine, but their discomfort paled beside the sufferings of the enslaved men, women, and children sweating and retching below deck, sixty-eight of whom died during the voyage. The horrors of the slave trade and the Middle Passage would have been on full display, and even though Elizabeth and Catherine came from a slave-trading family, it is unlikely they had ever encountered the grim reality of the trade at such close quarters. It is also likely that some of those slaves belonged to the Clevelands. The ship arrived in August 1764, at the height of the summer heat.[10]

Even the hot, humid summer weather must have been a relief from the slave ship, and the Clevelands were received by their relatives, Anne Isabella Cleland and her husband Francis Kinloch, Sr. One compelling reason that the Clevelands chose South Carolina was that they had wealthy and prominent relatives in the colony. John Cleland, a native of Scotland and a relative of William Cleveland, moved to South Carolina in 1735 with his wife, Mary Perry, who had inherited considerable property in the colony, including the site of Georgetown. Cleland quickly rose to prominence and became a member of the Royal Council in 1740 and served until his death in 1760. The couple's only daughter, Anne Isabella, married the only surviving son of James Kinloch, another prominent South Carolinian, a native of Scotland, and member of the Royal Council from 1720 to 1757. That union made the couple almost unimaginably rich; both Anne and Francis inherited vast properties, and they owned a number of the Lowcountry's finest rice plantations including the Rice Hope, Kensington, Rosemont, Willow Bank, Winyah, Weehaw, and Boone Hall plantations and property in Charleston. Elizabeth and John must have reasoned that such eminent connections would gain them entry into South Carolina's white slaveholding society.[11] Why the Clelands welcomed their mixed-race African relatives is a more complicated question.

No doubt Elizabeth's access to her brother's riches facilitated her acceptance in her new home. Cleland advised her on the purchase of a plantation, and she looked for land in his neighborhood and eventually made her first purchase from James Keith, a planter, physician, and member of Cleland's network of Scotsmen. On November 19, 1768, she bought Brick House Plantation, containing 750 acres, and Wampee Plantation, containing 600 acres, from Keith at a cost of £5,420 with funds supplied by the firm of Ross & Mill in London, a slave-trading firm with extensive contacts on the coast of West Africa and in South Carolina. The plantations were located four miles from the village of Monck's Corner in St. John's Parish. The parish was twelve miles wide and fifty miles long, between the Cooper and Santee Rivers and running along the Santee. It encompassed some of the best land in the Lowcountry,

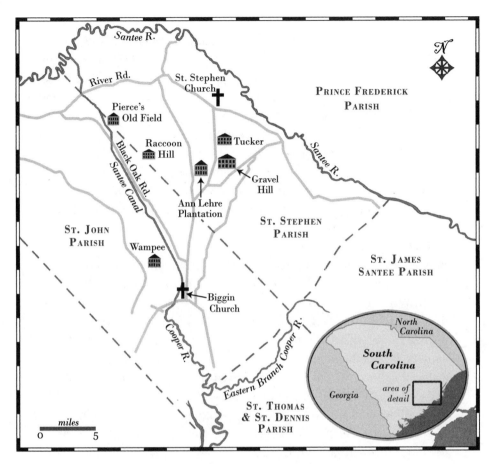

Map 3. Elizabeth Cleveland Hardcastle's and Catherine Cleveland's Lowcountry Neighborhood

rich rice lands along the lower rivers and land in its upper reaches suitable for indigo and, later, for cotton. F. A. Porcher, whose family owned plantations there, described it as "the garden spot of South Carolina" and a "second Egypt." He wrote, "A breadth of three or four miles of swamp as fertile as the slime of the Nile could have made it, was safe for cultivation; and its margins were thickly lined with the residences of as prosperous a people as ever enjoyed the blessings of God." Some of the Lowcountry's most prominent planter families lived in the parish—including the Laurens, Ball, Harleston, Cordes, and Prioleau families. Keith advertised the plantations for sale in 1768, claiming that ill health required him to consider leaving the colony. He described Wampee Plantation as having 300 acres of rice land, "a good dwelling house, kitchen and wash house, dairy and store house, chair house, stable, corn house, fowl house, smith's and carpenter's shops, all built within these seven years; also a barn, 68 feet by 46, with a pounding machine, that has, and will now, beat out 3400 lb of rice a day, and is but four years old, a cart house 30 feet by 20, one year old, like wise two straw houses, and negro houses sufficient to accommodate 70 slaves, a very good garden, paled in the best manner. The buildings are all of the best stuff, and were erected without any prospect of ever selling them.—On the *Brick House* plantation is a brick house, and Sundry outbuildings." He also advertised forty slaves for sale.[12]

These plantations were a sizable investment, and their purchase suddenly thrust Elizabeth into the role of a plantation mistress with sole responsibility for managing the complex operation of a large rice plantation. While it was not uncommon for women to manage plantations in the Lowcountry, they were usually widows, or in the unusual case of Eliza Lucas, the daughter of an absent owner. Like almost all rice planters, Elizabeth employed a white overseer who, with the assistance of enslaved drivers, would have supervised the planting, flooding of the fields, harvesting, and processing necessary to produce the valuable staple. Elizabeth came from a rice-growing region and, in fact, in 1790 Thomas Jefferson acquired a large cask of seeds containing three varieties of rice through James Cleveland who sent it from the Bananas along with careful descriptions about the growing habits of the different varieties which included both upland and lowland.[13] It is doubtful that Elizabeth would have shared her half-brother's understanding of rice cultivation, though it is possible she had some familiarity with the crop and its cultivation.

She also began to integrate herself into the active life of her fellow planters, and into the world of the South Carolina planter gentry. Her English education, her wealth, her family connections, and her plantations and slaves gained her acceptance into that class. It was a small, self-conscious group. The elaborate system of hereditary nobility created by the Fundamental Constitution of Carolina with its peculiar titles of nobility never functioned as intended, but the colony was one firmly grounded in class as well as race. Historian Robert Olwell wrote, "Like the English elite on whom they modeled themselves, the 'gentry' of the mid-eighteenth-century low country saw themselves as a ruling class at the top of a rigidly hierarchical society." She became a member of St. John's Anglican Church, commonly known as Biggin Church, located two miles north of Monck's Corner, where the local plantation gentry gathered. Lowcountry Anglican churches were not only houses of worship, they were also outposts of the government. Representation in the colonial assembly was defined by the Anglican parishes, and the churchwardens conducted elections, the dates for elections were posted on the church door, polling took place there, and results were announced there as well. The church's architecture, along with pew rentals and seating, was intended to reinforce order and to mark distinctions of deference, rank, and even race. Elizabeth's rented pew marked her as a member of that elite. Elizabeth's niece Catherine was baptized there by the Reverend Mr. John Hockley sometime between 1765 and 1767.[14] One local resident, Mrs. Prioleau, recalled seeing Elizabeth at Keithfield Plantation; Mrs. Prioleau was a girl at the time, who played with Catherine, "and retained a vivid recollection of her admiration of the finery with which the little mulatto stranger, presented to her as a playfellow, was arrayed." Sometime around 1770 Elizabeth began a courtship with William Hardcastle, a surgeon in the British Army who relocated to the Lowcountry, and the couple decided to marry in 1771.[15]

That year was one of joy and of sorrow, for her brother John died around the same time, and his death, along with her marriage, brought dramatic changes to Elizabeth's life. Her plantations were advertised for sale at auction in 1771 by David Deas, James Gordon, and Charles Mill. They also advertised twenty slaves for sale, including a boatman, a cooper, and two "handy boys." Mill was the younger brother of James Mill of the firm of Ross & Mill who had advanced John Cleveland the funds to purchase the plantations. John Cleveland died in 1771, and the sale indicates that he had not paid off that debt before his death. Further evidence of that debt comes in the marriage agreement between Elizabeth and William. That agreement specified that Elizabeth was "possessed of interest in & entitled to a Considerable personal Estate Consisting of Several very valuable Negro Slaves[,] a large stock of Cattle. . . ." Clearly, Elizabeth was protecting her own interests, and Hardcastle gave up his claim to her personal estate. As a part of the agreement, Elizabeth transferred twenty-one slaves and her herd of cattle into the hands of two trustees, William Loocock and William Clarkson. Elizabeth and William were to have the use of these assets which would be inherited by any children that the couple might have or by the surviving spouse.[16] This trust would have protected her valuable property in slaves and cattle from her brother's creditors.

In June 1771 Elizabeth and William transferred ownership of Wampee and Brick House Plantations to Charles Mill, acting as the agent for Mill & Ross. That agreement, finalized in December 1771 after the sale of the lands, made it clear that Elizabeth had purchased the plantations in her own name with "moneys belonging to her brother John Clevland of the Bananas on the windward coast of Africa who then was & still is largely indebted unto Gilbert Ross & James Mill of London. . . ." Elizabeth and William continued to live at Wampee; they must have leased the plantation after its sale.[17] Dr. Hardcastle engaged in his medical practice, and apparently Elizabeth also became a skilled and respected healer. Frederick Porcher recalled that his grandfather, Isaac DuBose, died in her home in 1773 after having gone to her for "the benefit of her surgical skill; for she had the reputation of having learned a great many of the secrets of surgery from her husband and had a reputation for skill which gave her a large practice." The respect many of her neighbors held for her is also evidenced by her appearing as witness on several of their wills.[18]

William died in 1777, and Elizabeth acted as administratrix of his estate along with his business partner James Bolton. He left a substantial estate valued at over £5,500, including mahogany furniture, a backgammon table, china and glassware, silver plate, books, a flute, wearing apparel valued at the considerable sum of £100, two slaves, and a dozen horses. At this time, an estate valued at over £1,000 was considered an indication of wealth. In a move perhaps prompted by her husband's death, in 1780 Elizabeth purchased a plantation called Raccoon Hill located partly in St. John's Parish with most of the property's 750 acres in St. Stephen's Parish.[19]

When the Revolution began St. Stephen's Parish, with one of the largest populations outside Charleston, mustered one hundred twenty-six men in its militia, rank and file, while over 5,000 slaves labored on its plantations. Among those plantations was Burnt Savanna, the residence of Revolutionary War hero Francis Marion. St. Stephen's and

St. John's parishes suffered during the war. Almost immediately, the out-break of war divided the close-knit community as some planters cast their lot with the Patriots, while others remained Loyalists. Planters like John Peyre tried to remain neutral, though after the fall of Charleston to the British in May 1780 that became more difficult. The British issued a proclamation ordering men to take up arms in support of the king, a call that Peyre obeyed. He and his brother Charles joined "a strong body of Tories" in the Williamsburg district, a group defeated by Marion. John and Charles were marched overland to Philadelphia where they were imprisoned and where Charles died. The British fortified Biggin Church and General Cornwallis made his headquarters near there at Silk Hope Plantation. Brothers John and Joseph Palmer, too aged and ill to fight, were both known to be fervent Patriots. They were captured, taken to Biggin, thrown into the Colleton family crypt and imprisoned there. At Henry Laurens's Mepkin Plantation, not far from Wampee, British soldiers looted the place and robbed the overseer and his wife. In July 1781 British frigates sailed up the Cooper River and troops marched to Biggin Church. With a force of 600–700 men, the British burned the church and laid waste to nearby plantations, and at the Battle of Quenby Bridge defeated 700 Patriots led by Marion and General Thomas Sumter. As Frederick Porcher later wrote, "about us armies were encamped, houses were burned, men were imprisoned and brutally murdered. . . ." Resistance largely collapsed in the area, and many Patriots cast their lot with the British who were in the ascendancy.[20]

Since the Revolution began, rumors had circulated in Charleston that the British intended to free and arm slaves in the South. So pervasive were these rumors that "massacres and insurrections were words in the mouth of every child." While the British did arm some black refugees, the fears of armed slave battalions and insurrections did not materialize. Still, over 5,000 South Carolina slaves fled to the British lines, many of those from St. John's and St. Stephen's parishes, and when the British made their final evacuation from Charleston in 1782, the black Loyalists went with them. This must have been a trying time for Elizabeth, recently widowed and alone with Catherine as war waged around them. Her decision to purchase Raccoon Hill and leave Wampee was no doubt tied to the events around her. Wampee was close to Biggin Church and to the road between Charleston and Georgetown which made the area a locus of conflict. Raccoon Hill was farther removed from the worst of the conflict in the parish, and the war had caused a drop in the price of land and slaves. Her move in 1780 proved to be a timely one.[21]

Once the Revolution ended, the work of rebuilding the community began, though economic problems plagued those efforts. Some Loyalist planters had their estates confiscated, particularly those who supported the crown from the beginning of the conflict. Those planters who had joined the British only after their occupation were more likely to be forgiven for acting under duress. As Frederick Porcher recalled, "with a few exceptions, the confiscated estates were generally restored to their owners. In this noble work of pacification none labored more zealously than General Marion." That rapprochement was an important part of the reintegration of the community. An economic downturn followed the Revolution, and the loss of the British bounty on indigo and naval stores hurt South Carolina's economy. Some formerly valuable plantations were abandoned as worthless, and valuable investments in stocks and securities had been paid in depreciated continental currency. Porcher summed up the gloomy prospects, "When peace was restored every planter was in debt; no market crops had been made for years; and where the river swamp was their sole dependence, even provisions had not been made. It was not a season therefore merely of embarrassment; ruin stared many in the face."[22]

The fact that Elizabeth survived these travails when many planters did not is a testament to her skills and clever management. Not only did she survive, she prospered and expanded her holdings considerably. In 1797 she purchased Pierce's Old Field Plantation containing 700 acres for £200 sterling, and in 1804 she purchased Tucker Plantation containing 1200 acres for £400 and made that her home. In 1792 construction began on the Santee Canal running through St. Stephen's Parish to link the Cooper and Santee rivers. Construction of the project took eight years and required the hire of up to 1,000 enslaved laborers. Elizabeth was probably among those who profited by hiring out her slaves since Pierce's Old Field bordered the canal. Frederick Porcher noted that "every one availed himself to a greater or less extent of this opportunity of hiring their negroes; for men they received thirty and for women twenty pounds sterling per annum, besides their food." While it operated at a loss, it did help promote the economic recovery of the parish. A few planters in the parish experimented with cotton as a commercial crop in the mid- to late 1790s, but the difficulty in separating the seeds from the lint prevented it from becoming economically viable. Eli Whitney's invention of the cotton gin in 1793 solved that problem, and in 1799 Elizabeth's neighbor James Sinkler was the first planter in the parish to grow a profitable crop of the fleecy staple. He planted 300 acres of cotton, made 216 pounds per acre, and sold the crop for from fifty to seventy-five cents per pound, a gross of between $32,400 and $48,600.[23] Tucker Plantation bordered Sinkler's, and Elizabeth probably purchased it to capitalize on the new money crop. She planted about eighty acres of cotton on the plantation, and if her yields were similar to her neighbor's, that would have brought her a gross of at least $8,500.[24] Her estate inventory shows that she owned six foot gins, an early model of the cotton gin, yet another example of her innovative management. Samuel DuBose wrote, "The gin first used for cleaning cotton of the seed was a clumsily constructed foot gin without the wheels, as now used, but instead, two cross-pieces with clubs at their ends, to give the necessary power. The greater part of the crops was either ginned early in the morning, or after task-work at night, a hand doing four or five pounds at each time." These machines cost up to $250 each.[25]

Back on the Banana Islands, Elizabeth's half-brother James, who had taken over the family's slave trading business, also found his operations impacted by the conflict. The American Revolution broadened to a wider Atlantic conflict between the British and the French that "almost completely interrupted" the Atlantic slave trade. James responded by expanding his farming operations, experimenting with cotton, for example, at virtually the same time as South Carolinians. He even brought two Europeans, skilled agriculturists, to the island to train his people in the best practices of the day. As one Englishman familiar with trade on the coast noted, "Slave Factories [have] a great Advantage even in the Trade of Produce, for a Trade in Produce can be carried on by one who deals in Slaves at a trifling additional expense. . . ." For Cleveland, slaves awaiting sale could be employed as productive laborers on his lands, and that produce could be used to feed his captives and to sell to the slave ships which needed to stock up on supplies to feed their captives as they crossed the Atlantic.[26]

Elizabeth owned around thirty slaves at any given time, and only about ten of those were considered full hands, a small workforce by the standards of the parish. Very little information survives about the men, women, and children she owned or her treatment of them. She did not directly supervise the field hands herself but, like most planters, she employed overseers over the years, including Orasha Bass, Stephen Clarke, and William Kennedy. Three lists of her slaves survive: the first in her 1771 marriage agreement with William Hardcastle lists twenty-two slaves, the second from 1812 lists twenty-eight slaves, and one from 1818 lists thirty-two slaves. The remarkable overlap between these lists suggests that her slaves lived in stable families and that her holdings grew by natural increase. An 1821 advertisement for the sale of Tucker Plantation noted that there were thirty-three slaves there, "mostly good workers; three of whom are prime single Fellows, and the remainder in small families." Several slaves in both the 1812 and 1818 lists were identified as old, and by 1818 four of the older slaves were valued at only $1, compared to $800 for a prime hand.[27]

No advertisements for runaway slaves from her plantations appeared during Elizabeth's lifetime, and only one appeared a few years after her death, in 1813. That advertisement offers a few additional clues about life on her plantation. The advertisement for Lucy appeared in April 1813, but she had been gone for a year by that time. She ran away to Georgetown "in company with an old Wench, her mother, who has since returned." Lucy was one of Elizabeth's trusted house slaves, and she sometimes kept the keys to the house. Lucy was "tolerably well known in Georgetown" and had been there several times, which suggests that it was not unusual for the slaves to spend time in the town. Lucy made little effort to hide there. Thomas Palmer, who placed the advertisement, noted that she "conceals herself only when sent for by the subscriber." He noted that she was so well known there that no "particular description" was necessary. Despite her long absence, Lucy's mother's return to the plantation and Lucy's very public presence around town suggests that this was not an attempt to escape completely, but rather an extended stay in town. Even Palmer seemed to take her behavior in stride; "should she return of her own accord," he wrote, "no notice will be taken of her offense."[28] The picture is one of a small but stable slave community, one with a number of interrelated families who could expect to live long lives among several generations of their kinfolk.

Elizabeth integrated herself into her new community as she had her previous one. She joined St. Stephen's Anglican Church where her name appears on the Vestry Minutes of 1800–1801 as one of twenty-eight members contributing to the church's support, and she acted as witness of several wills for her neighbors. Catherine does not appear in census records as being a part of the household, and it is likely that she remained at Raccoon Hill with her own growing family. At about the time of her move, Elizabeth took in Jasper Scouler, a deserter from the British army, who remained with her until his death in February 1806. He was a watchmaker and a carpenter, and he may have first been her employee—he built several houses and outbuildings on her plantation—but evidence suggests that he became her partner, though they never married. Many of their neighbors testified to the nature of their relationship. Dr. William Chisolm reported that "they lived together . . . as man and wife . . . I was frequently at Mrs. Hardcastle's House, (it was sometimes called Mrs. Hardcastle, sometimes called Scouler Home), and saw Mr. Scouler there acting like the Master of the House. . . ."[29] Archibald Kenedy who was "intimate with them" and visited at their home once a week, agreed that "they lived as man and wife . . . he lived as Master of the House."[30] Maurice Cooper agreed that Scouler acted "as master of the House, ordering the servants, & setting at the table."[31]

Even more compelling evidence of their relationship is that they invited Scouler's nephew, Thomas, to move from Scotland to join their household. Jasper's brother had written his friend John Kirkwood asking for his help in locating his brother in South Carolina. In April 1796, John wrote Scouler in London to tell him that he had located Jasper. As luck would have it, Elizabeth purchased a lock from Kirkwood and the two struck up a conversation. When she heard where he was from in Scotland she asked about Jasper's family, and she asked Kirkwood to write Scouler and invite his son Thomas to move to South Carolina. In his letter, John informed Scouler that his brother was "in very good Surcomstances in deed and wants Thos. very much to come out. . . . He hast been in good health for this many years but being up in years and Mrs. Hardcastle's older than he is he thinks that you may as well come and have the property which is very considerable as to let it fall to Strangers & Mrs. Hardcastle told me herself that all she had should be his or yours if you will come and if you come you may keep yourself easy for Life. . . ."[32] Additional evidence of the affection Elizabeth had for Scouler is provided by her 1784 will leaving her entire estate to Jasper Scouler and his heirs.[33] Scouler predeceased Elizabeth after sharing over twenty-five years together, and his death in February 1806 deprived Thomas of the fortune he had hoped to inherit. Scouler may not have been the last romance of her life. Frederick Porcher alleged that "the last of the regular rectors of St. Stephens church was an Irishman who lived notoriously as the paramour of Mrs. Hardcastle." It is significant that these rumors continued to circulate a generation after her death and, in fact, the Reverend James Connor, rector of St. Stephen's, did live with Elizabeth in the last year of her life, apparently on intimate terms. He reported that he lived in her house for a year, and was "never absent from her two days at once."[34]

Frederick Porcher wrote that Elizabeth's "position in the parish was a curious and anomalous one. Many of the people asserted the prejudice of race, and would hold no intercourse with her; among these was my father's family; others on the other hand visited her and were visited by her; and among these were some at least of my mother's family." There is much evidence to confirm that Elizabeth was accepted as white by many people in the parish and by the parish officials who recognized her as a witness on legal documents, a recognition that would have been denied blacks. She was legally wed to an Englishman, she was listed along with other whites as a member of the parish church, and in the federal censuses taken during her lifetime she was identified as a white head of household. Porcher added that she lived near his uncle Thomas Palmer and Frank Peyre, "and as she had a considerable estate and no children, these gentlemen hoped by their attentions to be paid for their compliances in her will." Elizabeth was apparently well aware of their interests in her estate. Connor reported that on one occasion the two of them saw a carriage approaching the house, and Elizabeth asked him who it was. When he told her it was the Palmers, she said, "O, my God, the Turkey [buzzards] are flying about, but the old Cow is not yet dead."[35]

When Elizabeth fell seriously ill in December 1808, the buzzards began to circle. She had drawn up a will in 1804 to replace her 1784 instrument leaving everything to Jasper Scouler. Thomas Scouler was not forgotten in her new will—he received a plantation—but the bulk of her estate went elsewhere. She had taken care not to die intestate, in part out of her determination to see that Catherine was provided for. Catherine was "the principal object of her Solicitude, and of her Bounty . . . who tho' her nearest Relation would on account of some legal impediments, have received nothing, and would have been in a State of Want, in Case of an Intestacy." Those legal impediments were simple; while Elizabeth was recognized as white, Catherine was not. While no physical description of Elizabeth survives, it is likely that the problem was simply one of phenotype. Frederick Porcher, who knew Catherine or "free Kate," as he called her, described her as "a dark bronzed mestiza." Elizabeth did all she could to protect Catherine's freedom. In 1807 she drew up a Certificate of Freedom for Catherine, outlining the circumstances of her birth and her free status, a document witnessed by her neighbors Francis Peyre and Thomas Palmer. At that time Catherine had eight children and three grandchildren of her own, and since the status of the children followed that of the mother, the freedom of the entire family was at stake. The following December as her health began to fail, Elizabeth drew up a Deed of Gift transferring Raccoon Hill Plantation to Catherine upon her death, additional evidence that Catherine made her home there.[36] She chose to transfer Raccoon Hill to Catherine outside the will she wrote at about the same time; she must have feared that Catherine might not be able to protect that prize from the buzzards circling around her.

On December 11, 1808, Elizabeth sent for Thomas Palmer and for her neighbor Ann Lehre. Ann's father, the Reverend Alexander Findlay, served as rector of St. Stephen's parish from 1771 until his death in 1783, and she was also related to Elizabeth's old friend and neighbor William Keith. Ann's plantation adjoined Elizabeth's, and the two were close friends. A few hours after Ann arrived, Elizabeth took her hand and begged her to befriend Catherine. She told Ann that Catherine had some papers she wanted to see executed. She selected Thomas Palmer to write her new will. His Gravel Hill Plantation also adjoined Elizabeth's, and she was close to him and his entire family. Thomas Brent, one of the witnesses to Elizabeth's will, described the "great intimacy between Mrs. Hardcastle and Mr. Palmer's family." His father, John Pamor (a Huguenot planter who insisted that his descendants Anglicize their name to Palmer), had owned a plantation adjoining Brick House Plantation, Elizabeth's first home, so she had known the family since her earliest days in South

Carolina. Thomas was not at home when she called for him, but he arrived the next morning.[37]

When he went into her room, she was sitting in her favorite chair
near the fire. She called for a small trunk where her old will was stored.
She took it out and showed him where she had made several changes
to the document. She asked for a pen and ink and erased her legacies
to Mrs. Mary Allison Dudley Hillen and to Thomas Scouler. She asked
him to take notes on the back of the old will, then make the final copy
at his home. She left twenty-two bank shares to Catherine, the interest
to be paid annually until her death at which time they were to be divided between Catherine's sons, Joseph and Isaac. Her sheep and hogs
were to go to Catherine along with five slaves: Dick, Bess, Tom, Nelly,
and Johnny, two married couples and a son. The transfer of Raccoon
Hill to Catherine was also recorded in the new will, an additional effort
to guarantee that transfer. She wanted Pierce's Old Field Plantation left
to Thomas Scouler, and four slaves to James Dudley, Mary Hillen's
son. The other changes were minor. She left her friend Mrs. Lehre a
bond of $160 and six cows and calves to be taken from Pierce's Old
Field Plantation. She left $50 to her friend Mrs. Query and six cows and
calves, because, she said, Mrs. Query was so fond of butter. Her remaining
goods were to be sold and the money divided between Palmer's children. He went home, rewrote the will, and returned to read it to her.
Her legacy to Scouler was worded "to her friend," affectionate language
that she asked to be removed, since, she said, he was not her friend. She
asked for her spectacles, read the rest of the will and was satisfied with
it. Palmer called in three witnesses, and she asked that Connor be included among them since he might be offended if he was excluded. After
the will was signed she remembered that she had not left anything to
Mrs. Roxanna Madray, another friend and neighbor, and she requested
that a codicil be added giving her "a young Negro wench" to be purchased from the proceeds of her cotton crop, which was done, witnessed,
and signed.[38]

Elizabeth's decision to write Mrs. Hillen out of her will had disastrous
consequences. Mrs. Hillen was descended from the South Carolina Clelands and was Elizabeth's distant cousin. When she married Dudley she
had "a handsome fortune," but her husband squandered it and everything was sold at public auction to cover his debts. Her friends bought
some slaves for her, and she had a house and garden in Georgetown

thanks to the generosity of her friends. Everyone agreed that "her case was considered a hard one. . . ." She had married Dr. Ebenezer Hillen only in November. Elizabeth and Mrs. Hillen had been close for many years, and Mrs. Hillen was a frequent guest in her home and lived there for a time, but apparently the relationship had cooled. Harriet Palmer, Thomas, Sr.'s wife and a friend of Elizabeth's, recalled that Mrs. Hillen, then Mrs. Dudley, had visited with Elizabeth during the previous summer and that Elizabeth "was much disgusted with her," so much so that she took out her will and scratched out her generous legacy to her. She reported that Elizabeth was further outdone when she received a letter from Mrs. Dudley announcing her upcoming marriage, in which she added that she had secured her property except for what she expected to inherit from Elizabeth, a presumption that made Elizabeth so angry that she threw the letter out of her bed and swore that Mrs. Dudley would get nothing from her. Elizabeth's closest friend, Ann Lehre, told much the same story. Elizabeth had not received Mrs. Hillen's letter giving the news of her approaching marriage until after the fact. She recalled the same language in the letter about settling her future inheritance and added that Mrs. Hillen had asked that the letter not be shown to the Reverend Connor. She said that Elizabeth was "very angry" and said that "she was determined to disappoint her." She alleged that Hillen had only married his bride because of that future inheritance and that he would not have it.[39]

In the days that followed, her friends Ann Lehre, Honoria Query, another neighbor, Mrs. Palmer, and Mrs. Madray took turns sitting up with her; she insisted that they sometimes go home and rest, "saying she would tire them all out before they were done with her." Mrs. Palmer came every day, and stayed with her once every three nights. On December 20, Dr. and Mrs. Hillen arrived. Mrs. Palmer said that Elizabeth was uneasy about their arrival, and noted how glad she was to have made her will before they arrived. The morning after their arrival, Mrs. Hillen was in Elizabeth's bedroom with her and Mr. Palmer. Elizabeth was looking toward her clothes press, which was locked, and Mrs. Hillen asked her if she wanted the keys. "Fetch them," Elizabeth replied, and she brought the keys to Elizabeth who was too weak to take them. Mr. Palmer told Mrs. Hillen to leave the keys on the table, but she refused and put them in her pocket instead. Later that afternoon Mr. Palmer demanded the keys or the will, and the scene became somewhat heated. He "had dined that day in company and was a little merry," that is to say, a little intoxicated. He said to Elizabeth, "Put me in possession of the Will, I demand it of you." The Reverend Connor pleaded with Palmer to stop arguing, saying, "Don't disturb her in the last agonies of death." Palmer and Connor left the room. Elizabeth was offended and said, "No person has a right to my Will while I live."[40]

Mrs. Query sat with Elizabeth that night until about 1:00 A.M. when Mrs. Hillen relieved her, and she went to another room to sleep. Elizabeth was blind and failing. When Mrs. Query went back in the room the next morning about 8:00 o'clock, she asked Mrs. Hillen how Elizabeth was doing. She responded, "Almost gone. There will be a fine fuss here, by-and-by. The Will is destroyed." Mrs. Hillen claimed that Elizabeth had read the will then destroyed it, though the Palmers and others doubted that Elizabeth was in any condition to have read the will, much less to have thrown it in the fire as Mrs. Hillen claimed. Just as Elizabeth's corpse was being taken from the house, Mrs. Hillen said that she knew nothing of a will, and "frequently contradicted herself." Palmer challenged her version of the events of the night before, and the exchange became heated.

The Reverend Connor conducted Elizabeth's funeral service at St. Stephen's Church, one so moving that her friends published a notice in a Charleston newspaper which read: "The friends and acquaintances of the late Mrs. Elizabeth Hardcastle, particularly request the Rev. Doctor James Connor, for a copy of his truly pathetic and well adapted discourse delivered at St. Stephen's Church on that occasion." The Charleston newspapers published a notice of Elizabeth's death, a mark of her elite status and her whiteness, since such notices would not be published for a person of color. The notice, which may have been based in part on Connor's remarks at her funeral, urged readers to imitate her character. It praised her "candour of sentiment, her purity of manners, her integrity of heart, her social disposition, her shelter from the storm, her stretched out hand to relieve the way-faring and the weather-beaten traveler," traits that "commanded the unfeigning esteem of all those with whom she was connected as a relation or acquainted as a friend."[41]

Inventories of Elizabeth's personal property, excluding the value of her plantations, showed her to be a wealthy woman. Her estate was valued at $13,401.74; the bulk of that, $13,254, was in human property, the value of her thirty-two enslaved men, women, and children. Her personal effects showed that she lived a life of comfort and fashion. Her home was furnished with mahogany tables, bedsteads, and chairs. Mahogany was the most fashionable wood for furniture during the eighteenth century, so much so that the period has been dubbed the "age of mahogany." It was a tropical hardwood from the Americas, and the taste for it was an Atlantic phenomenon since rich sugar planters in the West Indies helped popularize it. She played games on card tables and slept on featherbeds. Her collection of books was stored in a bookcase. She enjoyed coffee and tea, and had the necessary coffee grinder, tea and coffee pots and cups, a tea strainer, sugar canister, a tea table, and teaspoons to enjoy those luxuries in style. She had two liquor cabinets and wine glasses, and she dined on a set of Queen's Ware plates and dishes. Queen's Ware was a popular creamware that earned its name after Josiah Wedgwood designed a set of the dishes for Queen Charlotte in the 1760s. In his catalogue Wedgwood bragged that "it is really amazing how rapidly the use of it has spread almost over the whole Globe," including to America where men of taste like Thomas Jefferson owned a set.[42]

Connor had urged those mourners at Elizabeth's funeral to imitate her virtues, but those noble sentiments were in short supply as her friends and relations prepared to do battle over her considerable estate. As the Hillens predicted, the will was indeed contested in court—for the next twenty years. The courts ruled in favor of the Palmers, then the Hillens, and each party appealed every decision. In 1810 Thomas Scouler, Jasper Scouler's nephew, petitioned the state senate arguing that he had moved to South Carolina from Scotland because of promises made to him by both Elizabeth and his uncle and that her 1784 will had made him the primary beneficiary. Scouler wrote, "To have his hopes blasted, his family to suffer and property, the hard earned labor of his Uncle Jasper, to pass into the hands of strangers must by your honorable Body be considered distressing," and he requested that he be granted the portion of the estate that "his Uncle Jasper should have been entitled to devise away at the time of his decease." The senate reacted favorably to his request and appointed commissioners to determine what part of the estate he should inherit. More ominously, they also instructed the attorney general to investigate the state's right to the estate via escheat. Under the Escheat Act of 1787, an escheator was appointed in every district, and he was required to notify the Court of

Common Pleas of any estate where there was no legitimate heir. They were to "act on their knowledge or belief, or the information of another. . . ." The committee that reviewed Scouler's petition issued its report in December 1810. They agreed that his claims were "well founded," and they appointed a committee composed of Francis Peyre, Thomas Gourdin, and Charles Sinkler to investigate the matter and determine what portion of the estate Scouler should inherit. They also instructed the attorney general to investigate the estate to determine if it should be escheated.[43]

In March 1821 Francis Kinloch filed a bill with the Equity Court asking to liquidate the Cleveland estate. He was serving as its executor, appointed in January 1818 to replace Thomas Palmer, Jr. after the 1817 ruling of the Constitutional Court. Kinloch claimed that the estate was "very impoverished," that "the Negroes being destitute of clothing and the little crops which they had made on the plantation having been consumed by fire." He had sold bank shares that had made it possible for him "to clothe the Negroes and to furnish supplies for the plantations use but either from the severity of the cold weather, inclemency of the season, no crop has been made for the last three years. . . ." His siblings, Cleland Kinloch and Mary Cleland Huger, whose claim was equal to his, supported his petition. In March 1821 advertisements appeared in the press for the sale of the estate; it included her three plantations, a "Prime Gang" of thirty-three slaves, 400 bushels of corn and peas, a horse cart, and twenty-six head of cattle. That sale apparently broke apart the slave community that had survived since the previous century. It appears that Catherine challenged this sale and that she and Kinloch reached an agreement. In March 1822 she filed a petition with the same court claiming to be a "nearer relation" than the Kinlochs, but agreeing to release her claim in return for one third of the net proceeds of the estate. The Court found that "there are no claimants of the Estate" except Catherine and the Kinlochs, and they ordered that the estate be sold and one third of the proceeds turned over to Catherine. Once Catherine's share was paid, she paid Jane Scouler, Jasper Scouler's niece and heir, one half of her monetary inheritance. In 1822 the Santee Canal Navigation Company purchased Pierce's Old Field Plantation. Francis Kinloch purchased Tucker Plantation at auction for $570 and then sold it to Mary Hillen for the same amount two months later, indicating that their long-standing agreement to work together to secure the estate continued. Raccoon Hill was not mentioned, probably because Catherine's prior claim on it was recognized.[44]

Just when it appeared that the long dispute over Elizabeth's estate might have been settled, Isaac Porcher, escheator for the district, laid claim to the estate on behalf of the Pineville Academy, a school catering to the sons of the planter elites of the area that had been designated by the legislature to receive the proceeds of any escheated estates in the parish. It was only at this stage that Porcher brought the question of Elizabeth's race out into the open, and it is worth noting that Frederick Porcher in his memoir noted that his family was one of those in the area that "asserted the prejudice of race, and would hold no intercourse" with Elizabeth. Isaac Porcher was Frederick's uncle. He claimed that when Kinloch took over as executor the estate was valued at over $13,000. Kinloch had died and it was his executor, Charles Mayrant, who was serving as executor of the Cleveland estate. Porcher complained that Mayrant and the other heirs now "pretend that the said Elizabeth Hardcastle did not die Intestate, that she was not a Mulatto or the offspring of a Negro and that said Personal Estate is not Escheated." Porcher, on the other hand, "charges the truth to be that the said Elizabeth was a Negro, Mulatto or Mustizo according to the true intent and meaning of the several acts of the Legislature of the State . . . relative to Slaves and Free Persons of Color and that at her death she left no legitimate kindred entitled to the distribution of her Estate and that the same has Escheated. . . ."[45]

Porcher's questions about Elizabeth's race threw the earlier settlement of her estate into confusion. If Porcher was correct, then Elizabeth would be regarded under the law as a free woman of color. Under South Carolina law, a free person of color could leave real property to his or her children, but not to other relatives, a law which threatened Catherine's inheritance. It may be that Elizabeth's decision to deed Raccoon Hill Plantation before her death was an attempt to insure against just such a threat. In addition, the South Carolina courts had refused to recognize the inheritance claims on the part of collateral heirs below nieces and nephews in cases where people died intestate. If that were upheld in this case, then neither the Kinlochs nor Mary Hillen could inherit either. In June 1822 a jury agreed with Porcher and ruled in favor of the Academy. At issue were the questions of Elizabeth's and Catherine's race and status: were Elizabeth and Catherine black and, if so, were they slaves; was Elizabeth illegitimate since the marriage of her parents could not be proved; and what was Elizabeth's exact relationship to the Kinloch family? The judge instructed the jury that only property Elizabeth conveyed during her lifetime was inheritable. The jury ruled in favor of escheat. They found that "Elizabeth Hardcastle was a free woman of color and died Intestate" without "leaving any person capable of taking her Real Estate as heirs of descent." They accepted her transfer of Raccoon Hill to Catherine before her death.[46] For the first time, Elizabeth Cleveland was labeled as a free person of color.

Charles Mayrant, Mary Huger, Catherine Cleveland, and Mary Hillen all appealed this decision. They based their appeal on a number of technical issues and on their contention that Elizabeth was not illegitimate and that her relationship to the Clelands and to Catherine had been proven. The judge, Charles J. Colcock, skipped over these issues to focus on what he considered to be the most important question: *"Whether the descendent of a negro can, by the laws of this State, hold land?"* He reasoned that in all nations and throughout time, class distinctions had existed, and those classes had enjoyed different rights, and "that distinction has, by a kind of common consent of all, been applied with more right to the class of persons to which the claimant belongs than to any other." He noted that from an early period, some slaves had won their freedom, and they were allowed to remain in the country. "From this it resulted," he observed, "as a matter of inevitable necessity, that they were permitted to acquire property for their support . . . and if it be said they are not members of the body politic, it is certain they are not aliens. . . ." They had to have a place in society and, he argued, "this class of people . . . are a part of our militia, required to perform the duties pioneers and musicians—and on a late occasion, formed an efficient body in the construction of the works of defence [*sic*] for this city. They pay all the taxes which are imposed by the Legislature on property, and an additional tax besides. . . ." He referred to his own personal experience where, from his earliest childhood, he knew a free black man who owned a plantation and slaves.

He noted the difficulty in determining race and status in South Carolina. He described a recent case when a man was arrested and brought before the bar for trial when someone objected that one of the witnesses, a woman, was a mulatto. The judge refused to make a decision about her race based on her appearance, which clearly did not mark her as black, and testimony was offered that showed not only that she was a mulatto, but that the prisoner was as well, and the trial was moved to another court. The judge observed that, "Such instances are not rare—there are many such persons in the community, and many of them holding lands." They also paid taxes on that land as free people of color. By the common law of the land, he reasoned, free blacks were entitled to own property. He reviewed the laws of the state that recognized the rights and duties of free people of color. Far from being excluded from society, he found that they were afforded the "special protection and control of the law, and although the station assigned to them is a degraded one, yet they are recognized as forming a part of the body politic; and if not citizens, they are subjects." If the legislature imposed specific taxes on the property owned by free people of color, as it did in 1822 and 1823, then the legislature had decided the question and free people of color were clearly entitled to hold property. Despite all that, the Court ruled that the plaintiffs were unable to prove their relationship to Elizabeth and so the escheat was allowed to stand.[47]

That decision sent Mary Hillen back to the legislature, and she filed a petition attempting to have that decision overturned. Hillen claimed that she was "equally near as kin to the last Mrs. Hardcastle as any other relation." She pleaded that she was "stricken in years, & in straightened circumstances and asks from your liberality that bounty which you have never refused to persons in her helpless and unprotected situation." She added that her son served in the U.S. Navy during the War of 1812 and died at Tunis in March 1817, and having "devoted her richest Treasure to our common Country," she asked that her petition be granted. The executor of the estate noted that Kinloch had spent eight or ten years contesting the will, and that finally an agreement was reached which included Catherine Cleveland that allowed for the settlement of the estate, and that the estate had been liquidated. He noted that the effort to escheat the estate had come eighteen years after Elizabeth's death. He observed that many people who had inherited from the estate had spent that inheritance and were not in a position to refund it.[48] In December 1829 the legislature finally brought the matter to a close. The Santee Canal Company's title to Pierce's Old Field Plantation was upheld, as was Mary Hillen's title to Tucker Plantation. Another tract of land referred to as "Scouter's," which must refer to Scouler, was also transferred to her, and she was allotted over $2,000 from the estate, less

the value of the real estate. Raccoon Hill was not specifically mentioned, and this was probably because its transfer to Catherine by gift
during Elizabeth's lifetime was recognized.[49]

Catherine would have been about seventy years old by the time the
case was fully closed. Elizabeth's foresight had provided her niece with
the security she sought to give her and her family. The long battle over
Elizabeth's will had raised the question of Catherine's status and her relationship to her aunt. When Catherine challenged her aunt's will in
court, the lawyers prepared a set of questions to be administered to witnesses. Unfortunately, those responses, if they were ever given, have not
survived, but the questions themselves are revealing. They offer insights
into how the community evaluated race and status, and how they sought
to define the relationship that existed between Elizabeth and Catherine.
They asked whether or not the witnesses remembered "Free Katie," suggesting that this was the name by which she was commonly known.
Then they asked if Catherine had "been upon the footing of a guest or a
relation in the House of Mrs. Hardcastle? Did she ever sit at table or was
she ever addressed by or did she every address herself to Mrs. Hardcastle
in terms expressive of relationship—did she call her niece, or did Katie
call Mrs. Hardcastle Aunt?" They pressed to know "when, and where,
and how often you heard her call her so—whether she stated how she
came to be her niece—whose daughter she was—& . . . whether she was
legitimate or illegitimate. . . ."[50]

They also asked if Elizabeth "ever gave her any the least education?
Did she send her to school or treat her as she would have done a niece?"
Elizabeth was literate, as the references to her exchanging letters with
Mrs. Hillen and reading her will indicate, and she signed legal documents in her own hand. Catherine, however, signed with her mark
indicating that she had not learned to write. Certainly Elizabeth appreciated the advantages that education offered having studied in England,
and yet she did not teach Catherine herself or have her educated. There
were schools for young women in Charleston during this period, but
Catherine's color would have barred her from attending them. The question was intended to suggest that Elizabeth's failure to educate Catherine was evidence that Elizabeth did not consider her an intimate relation
or as her legitimate niece. There are hints of their close relationship
scattered in the legal documents. Harriet Palmer and others testified
that Elizabeth referred to Catherine as her niece and was eager to pro-

vide for her. Recall, too, Ann Lehre's touching recollection that Elizabeth begged her to befriend Catherine (though that request suggests that Elizabeth's dearest friends had not already befriended her niece). As she lay dying, she also asked that Catherine take her two horses "and take care of them for her sake." At one point the Reverend Connor testified that he was "the only white person in the house," but noted Catherine's presence there with him and at Elizabeth's bedside. He also observed that there were "a number of Negroes" in the sickroom who were "much distressed," and Thomas Palmer ordered them out of the room, but Catherine stayed behind with Connor and Palmer. He also testified that Elizabeth often left her keys "in the hands of the Negroes, particularly Lucy and Catherine." The people surrounding Elizabeth may not have considered Catherine a white person, but they did recognize her privileged position with her aunt, one nurtured in a relationship that had endured over seventy years. The overriding evidence of Elizabeth's devotion to Catherine was her careful and considered attempts to protect her niece's freedom and her property. As the court stated in its 1809 ruling, "The principal object of her Solicitude, and of her Bounty, appears to have been her Niece, Catherine Clieland, . . . her nearest Relation."[51]

Catherine had lost the closest thing to a mother she had ever known, but she had her own large and growing family to occupy her. She had eight children: Rebecca, Joseph, Isaac, John, Catherine, James, Paul, and Phillis. All of her children used her surname, and there is no mention of a husband for Catherine in any of the surviving documents. Did she choose a partner from among the small number of freedmen living in St. John's or St. Stephen's parish, from the enslaved community, or from the white men? There is no hint in the record, though the fact that she did not marry might suggest that her partner or partners were more likely either enslaved or white since she could have easily wed a fellow free person of color. Rebecca had three children of her own in 1808 and, as with her mother, there is no evidence that she ever married. Family tradition held that the father of her children was Native American, and there were small numbers of Native Americans still living in the area, so that story could be true. Joseph and Isaac were also adults by then. The remaining five children were younger, born between about 1790 and 1805. When Catherine appeared in the census, as she did in 1830 at Raccoon Hill, she was listed as the head of her household.

Elizabeth had expressed reservations about the reliability of Catherine's eldest sons, Joseph and Isaac, and they disappeared from the historical record relatively early.[52]

Catherine may not have been literate, but she shared some of her aunt's business acumen, and she worked to provide for her family as Elizabeth had for her. When Elizabeth's estate was finally settled in 1822, Catherine received one-third of the proceeds of the sale of Pierce's Old Field and Tucker plantations, and she used those funds to purchase a house in Charleston on Maiden Lane. At that time she also gave her son John Cleveland her power of attorney. By this time her family was divided between Charleston and Raccoon Hill. John was a carpenter in the city, a common occupation for skilled free men of color, and her son Paul was a successful businessman there who, in 1850, owned eight slaves. In 1829 she sold a portion of her land, but she continued to reside at Raccoon Hill with her son James, who was listed as a farmer in the 1850 census, along with his family—which included his wife Susan and seven children, among them a young granddaughter who carried her grandmother's name, Kate.

The 1820s were turbulent times for free blacks in South Carolina. In 1820 the state prohibited manumission except by an act of the legislature, acting out of concern about the "great and rapid increase of free negroes and mulattoes in this state." Following Denmark Vesey's failed conspiracy in 1822, even harsher laws were enacted. The free black population in the state had soared from 4,554 to 6,826 from 1810 to 1820, a rate of 50 percent. Free blacks who left the state could not return, every free black *male* over the age of fifteen was required to have a white guardian who lived in their district and who could attest to their good character. Failure to comply with these laws resulted in re-enslavement. They also prohibited free blacks from moving into the state, and by these means hoped to create a free black population that was stable or shrinking, one known to them and acculturated to the state's racial mores. The plan succeeded in slowing the growth rate of the free black population, which increased by just 45 percent over the next forty years. Free blacks adopted a strategy of accommodating themselves to the new realities, accepting the boundaries set by whites, and distancing themselves from slaves often to the point of owning slaves themselves. As time passed, the laws were not rigidly enforced, and many masters allowed slaves to live as free without legal papers, but they risked re-enslavement. As we have seen, Elizabeth provided Catherine with legal documents verifying her free status, and her sons also had such papers.[53] Elizabeth had intended to leave Catherine slaves in her will, but during the long legal battle the slaves were sold by the administrators and there is no evidence that Catherine became a slave owner herself. Her ownership of a plantation did allow her to distance herself from whites to an extent that many free blacks could not.

Catherine's situation was both similar and dissimilar from that of other free blacks in the state. She was unmarried and the head of a large household. About one-third of the free black households in South Carolina were headed by single women, and about three-fourths of those women had children. All of her children were classified as mulatto, but whether that came from her own mixed-race heritage or because the father of the children was white is impossible to know. Free households headed by women with mulatto children were rare—only four such cases existed in 1860. Catherine's ownership of a plantation put her in a privileged position, and like her aunt who did not remarry after her first husband's death, she may have remained unmarried in order to keep control over her property. Free blacks who owned their own land were the most independent from whites, but only one in ten free people of color owned their farms. A tiny number of free blacks owned as much land as she did; in 1860, 94 percent of the free black population owned no land or only a small plot. Free blacks were often at the mercy of whites in the market, over wages and prices, in negotiating contracts, and as laborers. That problem was especially acute for free women who were usually found in the lowest occupational levels; indeed, three out of every four free women of color was a laborer. Most of them were servants, but others were farm workers. Male artisans, like Catherine's sons in Charleston, had more control over their labor, but they had to compete with white artisans which imposed its own burdens. About a third of free men of color were skilled artisans. Most free blacks were poor—one third reported no wealth at all—and Catherine's ability to provide for her family and to enable her sons to join the ranks of the artisans and landowners is a very significant accomplishment. In general, free mulattoes were better off than free blacks. Rural parishes were closely knit communities, and Catherine's roots there were deep. She was part of a "dense network of human relations," and she was clearly judged favorably by her neighbors. Free blacks understood the importance of these relationships, cultivated them, and benefitted from them.[54]

Catherine often visited her sons in Charleston, as she did in 1836 when she took the opportunity to draw up her will. She noted that the house on Maiden Lane had been destroyed by fire. The "Great and Calamitous Fire," as the newspaper described it, began about 12:30 on a Friday night in June 1835 and raged for nine hours before it could be stopped. It destroyed 300–400 houses, businesses, and churches, including almost every house on Maiden Lane where blacks and whites lived alongside one another in wooden houses and tenements. The newspaper report noted among the houses lost was a "two-story Wooden Dwelling occupied by Capt. Kelly, owned by James Cleveland, a colored man." She noted in her will that she had received $727 from the city for the building and lot, and that she had invested $605 of that amount in shares of the state bank. She left those shares to her son John. The rest of her estate was divided equally among six of her children; Joseph and Isaac were not mentioned in the will which probably indicates they had predeceased her or left the state. Her sons' ownership of slaves and property would have put them in the ranks of the free black elite. Her daughter Rebecca, known as Beck, died in 1849, of old age. Rebecca's daughter Martha, also known by the African name Mindah, died in that same year of consumption. Catherine lived on until January 1859, by which time she would have been about 100 years of age. She was buried in the family cemetery at Raccoon Hill.[55]

Catherine's descendants continued to live there well into the twentieth century. One of her great-great-great-grandsons, Joseph Lefft, remembered growing up there in the big, two-story plantation house hearing stories about Catherine. The family lived on the plantation until the land was acquired by the Santee-Cooper Electric Power Company in 1939 to construct Lake Moultrie. A survey drawn at that time showed "Katy Cleveland's Burial Grounds," and by that time Catherine lay there surrounded by over 150 of her descendants. The family was allowed to continue using the cemetery after the purchase, and her memory survives among her descendants even today.[56]

Elizabeth and Catherine Cleveland may have been the two most exceptional African women to step off a slave ship in colonial Charleston. They are profoundly atypical, and in that sense their lives might seem to have little to tell us about the larger worlds they inhabited. A consideration of their lives requires that we refocus our lens and broaden our conception of the British colonial world and of the Atlantic World. While we have long known that the histories of West Africa and South Carolina were linked by the slave trade, the Clevelands' decision to move to the Lowcountry demonstrates that there were other connections between those worlds that have not been fully appreciated. They represented a different Atlantic World, one occupied and traveled by African Creoles, to use Ira Berlin's formulation, or "Atlantic cosmopolitans" to use James Sidbury's and Jorge Cañizares-Esguerra's terminology. Sidbury and Cañizares-Esguerra chide scholars for refusing to recognize how frequently Britons intermarried with other races in West Africa and the Americas.[57] Certainly Elizabeth embodied an Atlantic cosmopolitanism—not only in her mixed-race ancestry, but in her English education and in her ability to pass smoothly into the Lowcountry planter gentry. That elite, mixed-race slave traders on the West Coast of Africa believed that they could educate their children in England, travel across the Atlantic to the slaveholding South, buy land and plantations, be secure in those investments, and be able to build lives free of the constraints of race, suggests that members of the early modern Atlantic community had notions of that world that historians have not fully grasped. What is most astonishing is that they were correct in those assumptions. There is another example of African-based slave traders coming to South Carolina from Sierra Leone and investing in land and slaves, which is added evidence of a shared network of information across and around the Atlantic World. In 1772 an African creole slave trader from Gambia, a woman named Penda Lawrence, accompanied Captain Stephen Deux to Charleston. He secured a certificate of freedom for her which read in part: "Lawrence is a free Black Woman and heretofore a Considerable trader in the River Gambia . . . [who] hath voluntarily come to be and Remain for sometime in this province. . . ."[58]

Elizabeth's success defied not only expectations of race, but also of gender. Elizabeth did not arrive in the Lowcountry as anyone's dependent, but rather as a woman prepared to engage in what would normally be considered the male dominion. She came prepared to invest money, to select and purchase plantations and slaves, to buy, sell, and negotiate on equal terms with men. Many other women in the Lowcountry engaged in similar pursuits, but almost always as daughters, wives, or widows. When she married, she retained legal control of her property, and once widowed, she chose not to remarry but rather to engage in long-term and open relationships with her partners, again openly defying convention. South Carolina followed English common law and differentiated between single or widowed, and married women. While single and widowed women had property rights similar to those of men, a married woman's legal identity merged with her husband's. This *feme covert* status meant that married women could not own or convey property, but married women, with the permission of their husbands—which Elizabeth clearly had—could claim *feme sole* status which gave them rights to invest money and to hold and convey property. Elizabeth was not alone in her determination to maintain control over her property; South Carolina women were more likely to have premarital agreements protecting their property rights than those in any other North American British mainland colony.[59]

It has become commonplace for scholars to argue that race was socially and culturally constructed, but Elizabeth's and Catherine's lives provide opportunities to explore the making of whiteness in the colonial and early national South at the ground level. As the only colony on mainland North America with a black majority, one might expect the South Carolinians to be especially vigilant guardians of race. Curiously, only Virginia and North Carolina among the southern colonies attempted to legally define whiteness and blackness during the colonial period. Both colonies traced ancestry back three generations, and the North Carolinians sometimes went back yet another generation. Any person with a black parent, grandparent, great-grandparent or even a great-great-grandparent was legally defined as black. That effort became even more determined in the aftermath of the American Revolution, and in 1785 Virginia passed a more stringent law proclaiming that anyone with one African ancestor in the previous two generations was legally black. Obviously, in these colonies and states Elizabeth would have been legally black. Most states of the Upper South followed Virginia's lead, but South Carolina and Georgia stood apart, and neither in the colonial period nor the early national period did either make any attempt to legislate whiteness or blackness. Ira Berlin suggested that perhaps their reluctance grew out of considerable racial intermixture there and the fear that "any attempt to define who was white and who was black would push too many persons of both colors to the wrong side of the color line and create racial chaos."[60]

The creation of race and racism had many unforeseen consequences, and interracial sex was one of them. Intended to separate individuals, race also created taboos that fostered sexual longing across the color line, and created hierarchies of power that fostered sexual coercion. Interracial sex was common in South Carolina and more openly discussed there than almost anywhere else in North America, an openness that gave South Carolina more in common with Caribbean colonies in that regard. Interracial sex led to interracial children, and those children posed a challenge to the system of race and the effort to link race and slavery. South Carolinians, like slaveholders everywhere, had no reservations about enslaving their own children, but what if those children appeared white? Since slavery was conflated with race, the enslavement of people who appeared to be white threatened that system, and in rare cases white men wanted to give freedom to their mixed-race children. Manumission grew out of this rather messy reality and provided a legal means of freeing slaves, including those of mixed-race if their owners so desired.[61] A door was opened for some mixed-race individuals to pass as free. In some cases, light-skinned slaves escaped to freedom and passed as white in their new homes. In other cases, the community colluded in that passing. The cases of Elizabeth and Catherine show how complex this became in practice.

Phenotype was obviously crucial in both of their cases. Elizabeth was the daughter of a mixed-race mother and an English father, and she was recognized as white. Catherine, the daughter of a mixed-race father and an African mother, was considered a free woman of color. It is important to stress here that the phenotype of children born to mixed-race couples can vary across the spectrum and does not necessarily whiten, but contemporary evidence indicates that Catherine was dark skinned. In Latin America it was said that "money whitens," and there financial success allowed even darker-skinned free people to enter the white community, but there were limits in the American South that denied Catherine that status, despite the wealth and social position enjoyed by her aunt. Her very presence in Elizabeth's household and her acknowledged relationship to her must have been a difficulty for Elizabeth in her efforts to enter the ranks of the gentry. It is also clear from the records that Catherine was relegated to the free black community, but whether or not Elizabeth participated in that categorization of her niece is less clear. She certainly acknowledged their relationship and provided well for her niece and protected her freedom.

There can be little doubt that the first crucial elements in Elizabeth's success in entering the ranks of the gentry were her wealth and connections. She came to the Lowcountry with substantial resources that she was ready to invest. Those investments in plantations and slaves immediately helped identify her as white, and created a reason for white members of the community to endorse her whiteness with an eye to financial gain. Was there a tacit agreement between Elizabeth and the Palmers, for instance, that they might expect to gain by endorsing and protecting her whiteness? Elizabeth was clearly aware that their attentions to her resulted at least in part from an interest in her estate.

Another factor in her ability to join the ranks of the gentry was her connection to the elite Cleland family. It is possible to imagine that the arrival in Charleston on a slave ship from Africa of two female mixed-race relatives might not have been cause for celebration, but those relatives acknowledged that relationship and helped Elizabeth integrate into the Lowcountry elite. They even exaggerated that relationship and claimed to be more closely related to her than they actually were. They facilitated her purchase of plantations in their neighborhood and, perhaps even more importantly, helped her perform whiteness. That ability to perform whiteness was essential to Elizabeth's success. Frederick Porcher's critical assessment of Elizabeth's position in her community offers insight into this process at work.

Here, Elizabeth's education in England comes into play. Even Porcher acknowledged that she was "said to be quite an accomplished woman, and these accomplishments were acquired at an English school." A look at Samuel Johnson's famous dictionary can clarify what was meant by "accomplished" in the eighteenth century. One definition of accomplish was "to adorn or furnish mind or body," and the related meaning of accomplishment was "embellishment, elegance, ornament of mind or body." The South Carolina gentry prized the advantages offered by an English education. Before and after the Revolution, more South Carolinians went to England to be educated than from any other North American colony or state. While it was common for members of the

Lowcountry elite to educate their sons in England, that was not true of their daughters. As privileged citizens of the wealthiest colony in British North America with close commercial, social, and cultural ties to the metropole, these South Carolinians eagerly adopted British manners and sought British educations where they "were schooled in the importance of dress, objects, and possessions for confirming one's place in society." Elizabeth's dress and deportment, her fashionable furnishings, and her many accomplishments which, as Porcher noted, she acquired at an English school gave her a distinct social advantage and indicate that she, too, had learned the importance of those things for the performance of whiteness.[62]

Porcher offered some insights into just what all this meant in day-to-day lives. Along with her landholdings, her personal property, and her accomplishments, Elizabeth's status was further cemented by her marriage to William Hardcastle, an Englishman and a respected physician whose race was beyond question. Porcher commented on her marriage and noted that she "continued to live in St. Stephen's parish as his widow," an indication of the importance of that status to her standing in the community. It may be that she chose not to marry Jasper Scouler during their twenty-five-year relationship because his status was lower than Hardcastle's had been, and her social capital as a rich and respected widow was higher than it would have been had she married an artisan and army deserter. Archibald Kenedy, for example, said of Scouler, "when ever he got work, he done it, sometimes he could not get work. . . ." Maurice H. Cooper observed that he "was an Indigent man when he first came to Mrs. Hardcastle." Cooper also noted that he was ill in the last years of his life, and "must have been an expense to Mrs. Hardcastle," which probably accounts for the sale of his slaves by the sheriff. Esther Boineau, who knew Scouler for many years, described him as "generally an invariable liar." Whatever Elizabeth's personal feelings toward Scouler may have been, she retained control of her property, maintained her higher status, and avoided lowering her status by marrying him.[63]

Another measure of whiteness was Elizabeth's social position in her community, and as Porcher described it, that position "was a curious and anomalous one" because the community itself was divided between those who accepted her as white and those who "asserted the prejudice of race." Elizabeth cannot precisely be described as "passing" for white. African Americans who passed generally left the area where they were known, moved to a place where they were unknown, changed their names, adopted new identities, and hid their pasts. Elizabeth did not hide her past—she was known to be African, and Catherine's presence was a constant reminder of the family's mixed-race origins. She attended the local Anglican and later Episcopal church that catered to the gentry. She served as a witness on legal documents, something reserved for white citizens. The first marker of social acceptance that Porcher mentioned was that some people "would hold no intercourse with her . . . others on the other hand visited her and were visited by her." None of the houses she lived in survive, but they probably were built in the style typical of Lowcountry plantation homes: a two-story wooden (occasionally brick) building with a single-story porch or "piazza" across the front and sometimes across the rear of the structure which provided a shady spot to sit during much of the year. Planters in the parishes "showed a strong commitment to the parish society," and created networks nurtured in part through a lively and exclusive social life characterized by entertaining at home. Elizabeth's English education served her well in a colony where the elite members were committed to the values of the English gentry, a commitment reflected in their tastes in food, clothing, and architecture.[64]

If tea was the social preserve of women, dinners were rites of hospitality that brought both sexes together. Dinner parties were popular among the Lowcountry planter elite and served to strengthen the ties that bound this closely knit aristocracy together. Porcher reported that he had "heard Mr. DuBose say that he had eaten many a good dinner in her house, in company with the Peyre family." Porcher understood that sitting down to dine with someone in their home was a mark of social equality, and the DuBose and Peyre (or Perry) families were among the most prominent in the community. During the Reconstruction era, whites complained that Republicans were not content to give blacks political equality, but also intended to enforce social equality by compelling whites and blacks to "mingle with each other in the private parlour or at the private dinner table." That members of the male planter elite like DuBose recalled the dinners in her home so approvingly years after the events indicates that Elizabeth succeeded in these rites of hospitality. Again, the inventory of her estate shows that she was well prepared for these occasions. Her home was furnished with a mahogany table and chairs, and the table would have been set with her Queen's Ware plates or her other set of china and her silver utensils, including a silver waiter. Soup, perhaps the turtle soup Charlestonians loved, was served with a silver ladle, and salt from her pair of silver cellars. Her two liquor cabinets, two decanters, and many wine glasses indicate that liquor flowed freely. After dinner they played games on her card tables, and coffee was available to be served from silver pots.[65]

It was probably in these social settings that the gap between Elizabeth and Catherine was most in evidence. Since contemporaries classified Catherine as one of the "Negroes," it is very unlikely that she would have been present at the tea table or the dining table. Her dark complexion and her lack of Elizabeth's accomplishments marked her lower social status and would have barred her from these gatherings. Elizabeth probably kept her out of sight on such occasions—one hopes that she was not compelled to serve her aunt and her white guests. Catherine's removal to Raccoon Hill may have been intended, at least in part, to put social distance between the two women.

What can the life narratives of these two women tell us about the larger Atlantic World? Their experiences, though exceptional in many ways, point to what Markus Vink, a scholar of the Indian Ocean, called the "porousness, permeability, connectedness, flexibility, and openness of spatial and temporal boundaries and borders." Elizabeth's circumnavigation of the Atlantic, from Africa, to England, back to Africa, and to the Americas, and Catherine's more limited but still daunting trip from Africa to South Carolina, challenge our understanding of Africans' place in the Atlantic World, their understanding of it, and their ability to move through it and to exploit its opportunities. Their cases illustrate how class and gender as well as race operated to shape Africans' experience of the Atlantic World. As members of an elite Anglo-African slave-trading and slave-owning dynasty, Elizabeth and Catherine traveled the Atlantic not as slaves, but as mistresses. While the vast majority of Africans who arrived in Charleston came as slaves, the Clevelands came with the financial resources and cultural capital to join the slaveholding planter elite. Elizabeth's ability to join the ranks of the gentry demonstrates an unexpected permeability to the constructs of race and class in colonial South Carolina, but Catherine's inability to do so demonstrates the limits of that flexibility. And in the end, even Elizabeth was declared legally black by the state of South Carolina, a reminder that the modern nation-state "has been one of the most important agents of identification and categorization," with the power to create and impose the racial categories that judges and other bureaucrats then attached to individuals.[66]

2

Finding a Transatlantic Middle Ground between Black and White

IN 1770 JOHN HOLMAN, a prominent, English-born slave trader on the Rio Pongo, located in modern Guinea, contemplated a move to the Lowcountry of South Carolina. He wrote to his friend and fellow slave trader Henry Laurens in Charleston about the prospects for investing in rice plantations in the area. Laurens wrote an encouraging response: "Five hundred pounds Sterling will secure you a Snug and improveable little Estate and twenty working hands, Men and Wives for the field, a Woman or two about the House will be a good Number for improving such an Estate to advantage under your own Eye." He urged Holman to pay a visit and look the place over before making his decision since "in such Cases men are a good deal governed by their own Fancies." He suggested that Holman also visit the Georgia Lowcountry where lands could be purchased more cheaply and where Laurens himself had invested. It took Holman some time to act on that suggestion, but in 1787 he traveled to South Carolina and was so impressed with what he saw that he arranged to purchase a much more considerable property than the snug little estate that Laurens had proposed. Instead, Holman invested in a large tract called Blessing Plantation on the Cooper River for which he paid £2,500 sterling. As a major slave trader on the West Coast of Africa, he had no need to purchase slaves in South Carolina; he intended to bring enslaved Africans with him. To be sure that such a move would be allowed, "he went in conjunction with his friend the Honorable Henry Laurens to the Custom House and informed

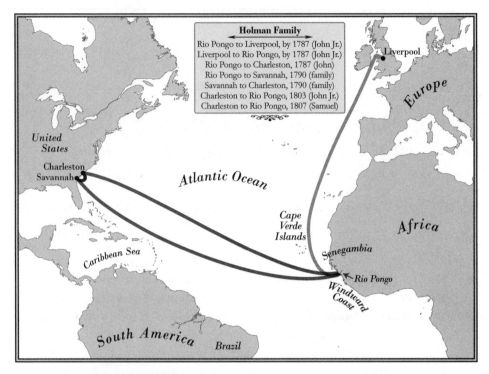

Map 4. Holman Family

the Collector Mr. George Abbot[t] Hall of his intentions to come with his slaves to settle in South Carolina," and Hall informed him that "he might freely bring his slaves with him."[1]

In 1789 Holman, along with his family, left the West Coast of Africa on board a slaver called the *Eliza* with Captain John Olderman, bound for Charleston, carrying fifty enslaved Africans owned by Holman who intended to take up residence with them on the Blessing Plantation. Much to his dismay, when he arrived in Charleston in April 1789 he discovered that the state legislature's ban on slave imports prevented that move. He learned that he would be fined one hundred pounds for each slave brought into the state under a law passed on March 28, 1787 "which prohibits the importation of all Negroes" and which took effect "in his absence." That fine was so steep that "he was liable to be reduced to beggary." He was forced to disembark in Savannah, Georgia, instead, and from there he searched for some solution to his predicament. He appealed to his old friend and business partner Henry Laurens for assistance, and Laurens scrambled to help. He wrote friends in Savannah like Joseph Clay, urging him to assist Holman in his "unfortunate situation," and he described him as "a very worthy honest Man from the Coast of Africa." Laurens added, "Your friendship in this case will particularly oblige me." More importantly, he used his political connections in South Carolina to support Holman's petition to the South Carolina Senate for an exemption to the importation law. In that document, Holman wrote that he was "obliged to seek a temporary residence in Georgia where for several months he has been subject to the inconveniences of wanting a home, friends, money and credit, all of which he could have commanded in South Carolina." He pleaded that the Senate consider "his peculiar and very hard case" and allow him "to come with his slaves and settle in Carolina." Hall certified that Holman had indeed sought his approval to bring his slaves into the state, and Laurens also officially endorsed Holman's claims, an endorsement that carried great weight. Laurens had a long career in the state's politics; he was first elected to the Commons House of Assembly in 1757 and reelected continually down to the Revolution. Though basically conservative, he embraced the Patriot cause and became a leader of the revolutionary movement in South Carolina. He represented his state in the Continental Congress, and in 1777 he was elected president of that body, succeeding John Hancock. Captured by the British en route to Holland on a diplomatic mission, Laurens was imprisoned in the Tower of London from 1780–1781. After his release, he was one of the commissioners that negotiated the Treaty of Paris ending the Revolution and recognizing the independence of the United States, after which he withdrew from public life.[2] Laurens left the slave trade in 1767 ostensibly on humanitarian grounds, though his critics saw that as blatant hypocrisy since he continued to facilitate the trade. In 1776 he was the owner of 767 slaves. Thanks to Laurens's support, in February 1791 the South Carolina Senate approved Holman's petition and allowed him to "come with his negro slaves and settle in this state." The petition mentioned only Holman and his slaves and not his family, but he brought with him his wife Elizabeth, his sons John, Jr. and Samuel, and his daughters Esther, Elizabeth, and Margaret. It may be that his wife and children were counted among those fifty slaves he brought with him from the Rio Pongo for Elizabeth was African and their children were Anglo-Africans.[3]

This Anglo-African family was an exceptional one for South Carolina, but not for the Rio Pongo where these sorts of "commercial marriages" had a long history. The Rio Pongo was the collective name given to seven rivers that drain a twenty-five-mile stretch of the coastline in what is today the Republic of Guinea. Dense mangrove swamps and numerous rivers and creeks kept the region isolated, and in the absence of large-scale political organizations, villages were the basic political unit. Each village had a chief who might remain independent if the village was large and powerful enough, but in most cases each village was under the protection of a local paramount chief. The low, wet land was ideal for rice farming. Among some of the coastal groups like the Baga, paramount chiefs paid symbolic deference to a king whose power was actually quite limited. The Baga were the first settlers in the coastal region and claimed the right to the land. Susu traders had come later from the interior and either conquered the Baga or settled among them. The transatlantic slave trade emerged there in the sixteenth century with the arrival of Portuguese traders from the Cape Verdes and Bissau, and expanded greatly in the early eighteenth century with the founding of a Muslim state by the Fula known as the Almamate located in Futa Jallon further into the interior. The Fula's wars of expansion gave them a steady supply of prisoners; those who refused to convert to Islam were enslaved and provided captives for trade to the coast. They traded slaves to the Susu and Baga in exchange for salt for their cattle and the firearms and gunpowder their warfare demanded.[4]

The *lançados*, the Portuguese traders in the Rio Pongo region, often operated on their own rather than as licensed agents of the Portuguese government since private traders and even low-ranking government agents found that West African rulers would give them private concessions that allowed them to trade as independent operators instead. In some cases, these men were perceived as having defected to the Africans or at least working in close cooperation with them. Drawing on traditional practices involving the presence of useful strangers in their midst, African community leaders protected the lançados and their property, and cooperated with them to promote trade and good relations. They allowed the lançados to rent land for their homes and commercial buildings, but that was limited to the use, not the ownership, of land. Again following traditional practices, the resident strangers were allowed access to local women, usually relatives or dependents of the local rulers.

Lançados married into their host societies, following local marriage rites, a practice that facilitated trade. Local women provided these men with the necessities of life, nursed them during illness, and served as interpreters of language and practice as well as commercial partners. The lançados were widespread along that section of the coast by the early sixteenth century, and by the end of the century some of them had risen to hold important positions within their communities. Their African wives and mixed-race children took advantage of their role as cultural mediators to further their own ambitions as traders and cultural intermediaries.[5]

In some societies along the Senegambian coast, particularly those with patrilineal or bilateral descent systems, the lançados and their Luso-African descendants were not fully integrated into society—they could not get land to cultivate, they were excluded from participation in religious and secret societies, and were not viable marriage partners to anyone except their fellow Luso-Africans. The situation was far different along the Rio Pongo and other matrilineal societies south of the Gambia River where lançados not only married into local societies, but were more fully integrated into them. Their children were a part of their mother's family and the larger society, shared in the rites of passage, and joined the powerful Simo or Poro societies that governed those communities. Luso-African children might follow their father's footsteps as traders and cultural brokers or they might choose to integrate into their mother's society instead. Wives and children could inherit property and often parlayed that into powerful trading establishments on their own right. Andre Alvares de Almada, writing late in the sixteenth century, described a Luso-African community on the Rio Pongo established by Bento and Jordão Correira from São Tomé that contained some five hundred relatives, friends, and retainers who ruled over three thousand Africans. The Portuguese and Luso-Africans traded in gold, rice, dyes, ivory, cloth, and, of course, slaves, a commerce oriented toward the Atlantic rather than the old salt trade that moved from the coast to the interior. Their ability to win the confidence of European captains and acquire goods on credit from them afforded a major advantage over their African competitors and made them important middlemen between the European captains and the long-distance traders from the interior who supplied those trade goods, including slaves.[6]

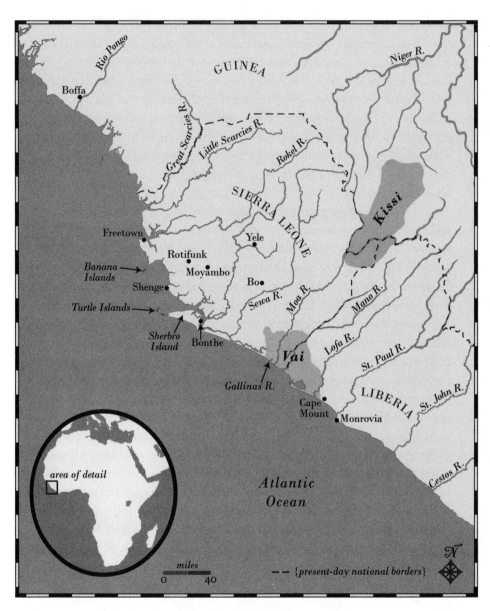

Map 5. Senegambia, Sierra Leone, and the Windward Coast

The Portuguese and their Luso-African descendants soon faced competition from other Europeans in the Rio Pongo region. Portugal's military and naval power weakened under Spanish rule (1580–1640), and Portuguese merchants could not compete with their European rivals who brought a better variety of trade goods at cheaper prices. Portugal went into an economic decline from which it never fully recovered while the Dutch, French, and English traders, backed by state-sponsored trade companies, moved into the Senegambia region. From the 1720s to the 1750s the English and French expanded their trade there, and their growing presence coincided with the creation of the Fula Almamate in Futa Jallon. During the second half of the eighteenth century, the almamate subjugated the Susu along the Rio Pongo and compelled them to allow Fula caravans to trade directly with the Luso-African and European traders. The French and English established forts and factories at places like Gorée and Bunce Island, but the Rio Pongo continued to attract renegades, often former captains or sailors on slave ships, who operated outside those establishments. Like the Portuguese before them, they found a ready welcome from local chiefs who granted them land and rights to trade over a specified area then generally cemented those relationships through marriage. Their success in trade allowed them to gain large numbers of *grumetes*, as their slaves and well-armed skilled workers were known, and thereby grow in power and influence. During the second half of the eighteenth century, the Rio Pongo became a major market and drew increasing numbers of merchants and traders from Britain and America.[7]

By the second half of the eighteenth century, the Rio Pongo and Rio Nunez regions became the primary markets for slaves from the Fula Almamate, and British and American traders dominated those markets. Holman was among that cadre of traders who settled in the Rio Pongo basin in the mid-eighteenth century. In his 1791 petition he reported that he had "resided for upwards of twenty-five years on the Coast of Africa where he was engaged in commercial transactions the exports of which chiefly entered in South Carolina." Holman's early life is obscure. He was from a London trading family; he had four brothers, all merchants, who invested in his African enterprise. He probably arrived on the coast in a merchant ship or perhaps, like his associate John Ormond, as a cabin boy on a slaver who jumped ship. When he arrived on the Rio Pongo he settled along the Dembia River, one of the many rivers that fed into the Pongo, and he married a local woman named Elizabeth whose name suggests that she may have been of Anglo-African origins. More and more British and American traders were moving into the Rio Pongo, but many of its residents still claimed an Afro-Portuguese ancestry. John Mathews, who visited the Rio Pongo in the 1780s, noted the presence of European and Luso-African traders there, and called it "one of the principal rivers for trade in this part of Africa." The Luso-African traders continued to profess Catholicism and were visited once or twice a year by a priest from Bissau, but he thought they were only nominally Christian, and "In every other respect they follow the customs and ceremonies of their pagan countrymen; but generally exceed them in treachery and revenge." He also described the Fula caravans: "the black merchants who bring slaves and ivory down to this river, and the adjoining one of Dembia, bring also large herds of cattle, goats, and sheep, which form an article of traffic with the neighbouring countries."[8]

Holman's factory would have followed the plan common to such trade complexes in the area. Typically, the trader's home was the largest building, often two stories with storerooms adjacent or on the first floor and living quarters above surrounded by wide verandas. There might be other residential quarters for employees and for wives and concubines. A large barracoon, an enclosed barracks, housed slaves awaiting sale, and a wharf provided anchorage for slave ships. The largest compounds were walled and some were even defended by cannons. Some major traders kept large numbers of slaves to produce rice during the rainy season which was traded to the slave ships in huge quantities, and then they sold the slaves during the dry season once the rice was harvested. Holman's rice production was extensive. Daniel McNeill, captain of slave ships from Boston, once purchased 6,720 pounds of rice from him. The business was a complicated one and success depended on maintaining good relations with the European and American ship captains, with the local chiefs, and with the Fula traders from the interior. Holman's trade networks extended up and down the African coast and across the Atlantic World. For example, Holman cooperated with other traders in his neighborhood like John Ormond, with other European and Euro-African traders on that part of the coast including the Clevelands on the Banana Islands, with Hodgson and Company of Liverpool and their agent Thomas Powell on the Iles de Los, and with slave traders like Daniel McNeill of Boston and Henry Laurens in Charleston, South Carolina. Holman and Ormond made their part of the Rio Pongo a major slave-trading destination. By the 1780s about 4,000 slaves left the Southern Rivers annually, and Holman's business was fully integrated into the larger Atlantic economy.[9]

In his petition to the South Carolina legislature, Holman boasted of his extensive trade to South Carolina. His close relationship with Henry Laurens facilitated that trade. Laurens was renowned even by his critics as "a man well versed in the traffic of the world," and his association with Holman added to that worldwide vision and reach. In 1770, for example, Laurens wrote Holman to thank him for a keg with four dozen "Lafers," referring to laugher pigeons, the small variety identified by their trill and then regarded as great delicacies in Charleston. Laurens noted that Holman's gift "enabled me to make half a dozen acceptable presents to the Ladies in my Neighborhood, who are very fond of those Things for their dining Tables." He added, "I thank you for them and shall not forget the Debt. Your kindness has made me a beggar." Holman sent Laurens other African luxury goods like leopard skins, and Laurens asked for other exotic goods such as "half a dozen, or for a single one of the small African Deer's feet. I am not clear if there is not a Creature on the Coast of that Specie still more diminutive than the Antelope. If there is, it is that I mean & to have a Leg and Foot with the hoof on. A single one will put it in my power to bestow a great Gift upon a great Man among our Indians" (probably Little Carpenter, a Cherokee chief). The luxury goods and curiosities were intended to establish reciprocal relationships that facilitated the real business at hand—the slave trade.[10]

Despite Laurens's claim to have abandoned the slave trade in 1767, he sent a different message to slave traders like Holman. In 1770 Laurens encouraged Holman to send slaves to Charleston consigned to him for sale, and he assured Holman that "you may depend upon it that I shall either sell them myself, or put them into such hands as will do you the most Service in the Sale & the most perfect Justice in every Respect." He instructed Holman to "send none but young ones, I don't mean Children. When a small parcel of old or ordinary Slaves come to hand, it is exceedingly difficult to dispose of them at any Rate." When Laurens was in London he had Holman consign his slaves to John Lewis Gervais in Charleston. In September 1772, for instance, Gervais sold forty slaves from Holman for £45 sterling each, and Laurens promised

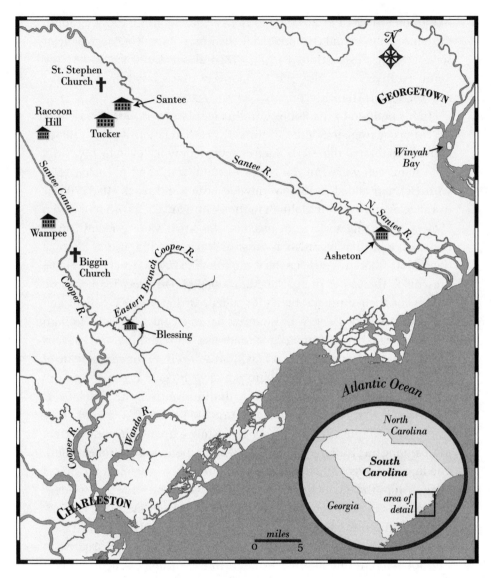

Map 6. Holman Lowcountry Plantations

to use his influence with Holman to have him invest those funds with Gervais & Chollet who were in need of capital. Laurens's efforts to help Holman settle with his slaves in South Carolina was the result of a long, carefully nurtured, and mutually beneficial relationship that stretched back several decades.[11]

The extent of Holman's trade connections, the credit extended to him, and the size of his investments are all markers of his financial success. One further indication of his wealth was his ability to send his son, John Holman, Jr., to Liverpool for his education. Like the Clevelands and the other traders in the Sherbro, the European and Euro-African traders on the Rio Pongo including Ormond, William Skelton, and Louis Gomez, educated at least some of their children in Britain. Holman and Elizabeth had five children: two sons, John, Jr. and Samuel, and three daughters, Esther, Elizabeth, and Margaret. He had other children by his lesser wives, including sons John Cameron, Richard, and William (Billy). While apparently only John, Jr. received the benefit of an English education, all his sons worked in his business with him, and William managed a factory his father opened in the Bashia region on the Fatala River. Later in the 1790s William managed the factory built by John Ormond after his death.[12] Given his wealth and his position of influence on the Rio Pongo, it is unclear what motivated him to move his family to South Carolina, but events in Africa may explain his decision.

Holman first expressed his interest in investing in a South Carolina plantation to Laurens in 1770 and made his move in 1789. The concentration of slaves on the coast in the enormous holdings of men like Holman had created a tinderbox that erupted into violence in the mid-eighteenth century when the entire coastal region saw large-scale slave rebellions. Unlike household slaves who were born on the coast and had certain customary protections—they were considered a part of their owners' extended family, often took their name, and might be hired out but would not normally be sold into the Atlantic slave trade—the thousands of slaves working the African rice fields, recently sold to the coast from the interior and awaiting sale, had no such protections. As John Mathews reported, they were "held in no higher estimation than any other animal that contributes to its cultivation." It is not surprising that they rose up in violent rebellion. In some cases they attacked slave vessels, in others they set up fortified maroon villages and attracted followers from across the region, and in others they collectively fled into the interior. A major 1783 uprising in Moria, located just south of the Rio Pongo, broke out when some masters and their armed retainers set out on a military expedition against Sumbuya, a neighboring state. The long conflict between Moria and Sumbuya fed the ongoing rebellions in which the rebels played one side against the other. Such uprisings continued over the next thirteen years. In 1791 John Ormond's slaves took advantage of his absence due to illness and rose up: they sacked his warehouses and destroyed goods valued at £30,000 sterling. In another massive uprising in 1795, slaves beheaded many of their masters and set the rice fields ablaze. These rebellions were large scale and successful enough to pose a serious threat to the political and economic stability of the entire region.[13]

In addition, in 1789 a Moslem holy man from the interior declared himself a Mahdi, a messianic redeemer who, according to prophecy, was destined to make the entire world Moslem and lead a jihad. With 15,000 followers, he invaded Moria, already weakened by war and a succession crisis. Local rulers and elders prostrated themselves before the Mahdi and massive numbers of slaves ran away and joined his army. Among his targets were the British traders in the coastal region. He required his followers to wear yellow garments, and even some of the European traders did so to try to save themselves. The traders on the Rio Pongo felt the threat. Francois-René Granger, the captain of the *Stanislas*, a French slave ship, was on the coast at the time and made a hasty escape. His letter describing the events there circulated widely in the Atlantic press. He wrote, when "the prophet . . . having been informed that a very rich and powerful English resident named *Orman* [John Ormond] lived at the head of the river Pongo or Rio Pongo for more than thirty years past; he dispatched 400 armed men with an order to send him the following trifling presents:—100 black slaves—100 women ditto—100 negro boys—100 blackgirls—100 Arabian horses 100 dogs—100 cats—100 of all the different kinds of European merchandise specified in the treaty; saying that he being sent of God, nothing should be refused him." The captain wryly commented, "I know not whether or not Ormon [*sic*] will grant the modest request of the prophet . . . ; but I hardly believe he would be disposed to make the same presents even to Mahomet himself." Apparently, Ormond was forced to pay tribute. As the second richest trader on the Rio Pongo, Holman must have felt similarly threatened, and he may well have seen a South Carolina plantation as a safe haven for his family and a safe investment to protect some of his capital.[14]

Holman had no intention of abandoning his successful business in West Africa, nor did he plan to remove his entire family permanently to South Carolina. Holman brought his wife Elizabeth and their five children to South Carolina, but he left behind his children by other African women and put those sons in charge of his African operations. He set up a cross-Atlantic commercial family business, unusual and perhaps exceptional in the Anglo-American Atlantic, but more common in the Luso-Atlantic commercial community. There are many examples from Ouidah, for example, of Portuguese and white Brazilian traders who settled there, married local women, and fathered Luso-African families who then engaged in transatlantic trade between Ouidah and Brazil and moved between both places. Those connections became even more common in the nineteenth-century slave trade from Lagos to Brazil. Such connections might well have matured between South Carolina and Senegambia had the Atlantic slave trade continued in the United States after 1808. There were a number of Charleston-based slave traders who established factories on the Rio Pongo and Rio Nunez, who maintained dual residences there and in South Carolina, and who were forced either to give up the trade or move to Spanish Florida or Cuba after the 1808 ban. They were men like John Fraser, Zebulon Miller, Stiles Lightbourn, and Paul Faber, all of whom lived and traded between the Rio Pongo-Rio Nunez and Charleston. Fraser, a native of Scotland, operated two factories on the Rio Pongo, one known as "Charleston" and the other as "South Carolina." He married an African woman named Phenda, the widow of another trader, and had several mixed-race children. He educated his son James in Charleston and sent at least one of his daughters to Liverpool where she was in the care of Thomas Powell, a merchant who also had residences in Charleston and on the Iles de Los. In 1809 he brought 370 Africans to work on his East Florida rice and cotton plantations, an enterprise that he might well have established in South Carolina before the 1808 ban. When Fraser moved to Charleston in 1807 and then to Spanish Florida after the 1808 ban, he left Phenda to manage his factory on the Rio Pongo. When he died in 1813 he willed his extensive estate to his African wife and their children. Similarly, Zebulon Miller, a slave ship captain and trader, operated a factory at Bangalan and lived in Charleston.[15]

When Holman brought his African family and his African slaves to the Blessing Plantation in St. Thomas and St. Dennis Parish in the South Carolina Lowcountry, he set up a community that in microcosm resembled the factories on the Rio Pongo. The swampy, sub-tropical environment of the Lowcountry shaped by the slow, sluggish rivers like the Cooper River on which Blessing Plantation was built would not have been entirely unfamiliar, and there, as on the Rio Pongo, rice was the chief agricultural crop. Many plantation homes in the Lowcountry were two-story structures, often of wood, with a long veranda across the front, dominating a village of storage and outbuildings and rows of slave cabins. A wharf on the Cooper would have enabled travel and trade by water which, in the Lowcountry as in the Rio Pongo, was more convenient than travel by land. The very slaves that Holman brought with him had probably worked planting rice on his African estate. Those enslaved Africans would have set about creating their own community on Blessing—perhaps some were already part of a family unit, others would have chosen partners from their fellows on Blessing or with other slaves from neighboring plantations. The presence of a number of infants and children among them indicate that they had already formed several families. While the percentage of Africans in the South Carolina population had fallen steadily since the colonial period, still almost a quarter of the state's enslaved population were native Africans (compared to only 2 percent in Virginia), and given the re-Africanization of that population with the surge in imports from 1803–1808 in anticipation of the ban going into effect, many of those Africans would have come from the Senegambia region.[16]

Indeed, life may have changed less for the enslaved Africans than for the Holman family. On the Rio Pongo, the Holmans enjoyed a privileged status as members of a regional elite. There, their mixed-race heritage offered them many advantages, but in the South Carolina Lowcountry the situation was different. Elizabeth Cleveland, arriving thirty years before the Holmans, was able to join the white planter elite. Her wealth, her British education, her important family connections to members of the Lowcountry planter elite, and perhaps a lighter phenotype and a more flexible or porous racial categorization made that possible for her, but it was not possible for the Holman family, though there is no evidence that they even attempted to join the ranks of the white planters. What they did instead was to ally themselves with wealthy mixed-race families in a strategy that would have shaped their choices on the Rio Pongo.

John Holman had managed to move his family to the safety of South Carolina and set up his household on a large plantation well staffed with his enslaved Africans, but he did not enjoy that life for long before his death in July 1792. The will he wrote shortly before his death offers additional insights into the family's situation. His considerable estate was valued at £3,451 and included fifty-seven slaves. He left one-half of the estate to his eldest son, John Jr., one-eighth to his son Samuel, and the remaining three-eighths in a special trust for his daughters Esther, Elizabeth, and Margaret. The special trust was administered by Henry Laurens, Jr., the son of his old friend Henry Laurens whose own health was failing and who was in no condition to administer a trust. What is perhaps most revealing about the will is his manumission of his "Woman Slave Elizabeth, the Mother of the Said John and Samuel Holman," and his charge to his sons to "use her with Tenderness and Affection." He also declared not only his children in South Carolina to be free, but also John Cameron, Richard, and William Holman, the sons he left behind in Africa. Unfortunately, there is no way of knowing what status Elizabeth had in the Holman household—did she live openly as his wife, the mother of his children, and mistress of the house and plantation, or was her status that of a slave whose intimate relationship with Holman was kept hidden? Given her status as Holman's wife on the African coast, it seems most likely that she acted out that same role in South Carolina. While such an arrangement would not have been tolerated by the white planter elite, it would have been acceptable among the community of free people of color the Holmans joined. Holman was eager to protect his mixed-race family from any threat of enslavement and to protect their extensive property. The special legislation allowing him to enter the state with his slaves could have been interpreted to apply to his Anglo-African family as well.[17]

The selection of marriage partners was as strategic a decision in South Carolina as in Senegambia, and Holman's three daughters married into the same extended family of free people of color whose background was like their own. As a result of Revolutionary ideology and an economic downturn following the American Revolution, the number of free people of color in the region grew dramatically through manumission and self-purchase from 32,357 in 1790 to 61,241 in 1800 and 108,265

by 1810. Growth slowed thereafter with the cotton revolution and an
upsurge in the value of slaves. The vast majority of those manumitted
lived in the Upper South, 98,000 in that region compared to 14,000 in
the Lower South in 1810. In the Lower South the population was lighter-
skinned, more urban, and composed of more women and mixed-race
children. By 1800 there were more free blacks in Charleston than in
Boston. The numbers of free black slave owners was small; across the entire state there were only forty-five in 1800 but 230 by 1830. The overwhelming majority of the free people of color, including those who owned
slaves, lived in Charleston, not in the rural areas like the Holmans.[18]

All the Holman daughters married into the mixed-race Collins
family. Robert Collins, a white planter who owned a plantation in the
same parish as John Holman, was likewise the father of a mixed-race
family who inherited his considerable estate. When he died in 1799,
he left his 545-acre plantation to Susanna, the African-American mother
of his children, and to their five daughters and three sons, all of whom
were legally regarded as free people of color. Since dividing the plantation
among so many children would have left it unviable, they shared
the plantation as tenants in common and used the slaves they owned
to work the land together. One of his sons, Elias, married Elizabeth
Holman, and another son, Robert, married Margaret Holman. James
Anderson, nephew to Robert Collins, Sr., married Esther Holman. Each
of Holman's daughters inherited nine slaves, and those workers helped
their husbands either work the Collins plantation or build estates of
their own as a part of the same extended family.[19]

Clearly, the Holmans allied themselves with mixed-race, free black
families in South Carolina. Additional evidence of their identification
with the Lowcountry's mixed-race elite can be found in Samuel Holman's membership in the Brown Fellowship Society. Organized in
1790 by "five brown men," all natives of Charleston, the Society quickly
became the most prestigious organization for free people of color in the
city. Membership was limited to a carefully selected cohort of fifty who
paid an initiation fee of $50 per person and monthly dues. The Society
functioned as a charitable insurance society. The fees and dues allowed
the Society to pay $1.25 per week to members who were too ill to work
and a $60 annual stipend to widows and orphans. It provided its mem-
bers with burial in its private cemetery. In addition, they supported five
"poor colored orphans" or needy adults per year. Nothing in the written

rules barred free blacks, but in practice, the Society was open only to free people of mixed race. The exclusive Society provides evidence of a "separate mulatto identity" in the South Carolina Lowcountry that would have been familiar to the Holmans and their fellow Luso- and Anglo-African traders on the Rio Pongo. These elite free people of color saw themselves as occupying a middle ground between blacks and whites, and many of the Society's members, like the Holmans, were slaveholders.[20]

The marriages between the Holmans and the Collins-Anderson extended family merged these prominent free families of color. Elias Collins parlayed his wife's inheritance into a large estate. Using her slaves as collateral, he borrowed enough money to purchase land and slaves. He purchased a rice plantation of over 800 acres, and he dramatically increased the number of slaves he owned from sixteen in 1810 to thirty-two by 1820 and forty by 1840. In 1842 he bought a second plantation called Northampton in the same parish, this one a vast estate of over 3,500 acres. In a will he made a few years before his death in 1842, Collins left his wife the slaves she brought into the marriage along with their increase, and he left their daughter Margaret Mitchell and son Robert Michael two equal shares of the estate. Another two equal shares were to go to his infant son and daughter by an enslaved woman, a complex family arrangement similar to Elizabeth's own. He had tried to protect his enslaved concubine, Mary, and their children by selling them in 1839 to three of his friends and relations for the nominal sum of $5 with the stipulation that they be treated as free people. That wish was carried out, but the Court of Equity still saw them as slaves and refused to allow them to inherit the property he willed them.[21]

Margaret Holman's husband, Robert Collins, Jr., was also a planter, though he did not enjoy the same level of success as his brother. Still, he owned two farms, Pleasant Hill and Hickory Hill, and when Margaret died in 1842 she transferred ownership of her eight slaves to her husband who promptly sold them for a nominal fee to their children, Sarah, Robert, Martha, and Charlotte. Esther Holman and her husband, James Anderson, also planted rice on a 541-acre plantation called Bulls Head. She appears in the 1820 census as the head of a household with eleven slaves. The Anglo-African Holman sisters and their free black husbands prospered and were far more successful than most free people of color in South Carolina. Their descendants also prospered and were among the state's wealthiest free people of color. Their ownership of slaves placed them among the most economically successful farmers of that group, and unlike some freed people whose slaves were family members, their slaves were workers. The exact number of freed people who owned slaves in the state is unclear, but there were probably only 50–100 outside Charleston, and the ownership of more than two or three slaves was limited to the wealthiest freed people.[22] While no direct evidence survives from the Holman sisters, the lives they built in South Carolina appear to have been stable and successful. Each married members of the same free black family, put down roots in their adopted home, reared families, and lived in prosperous circumstances, as did their children and grandchildren.

John Holman's Anglo-African sons John, Jr. and Samuel struggled after their father's death, and a dispute over Holman's estate pitted the sisters against their brothers. In 1803 the Holman sisters and their husbands brought suit against their brothers for mismanagement of their father's estate. They alleged that some slaves had continued working on the Holman plantation where they had made "considerable Crops" and "large sums of Money," and that others had been hired out, but the brothers and Henry Laurens, Jr., the other executor, had refused to divide those profits with the sisters or account for the estate. They argued that Holman had left few debts and that an £850 bond owed to the estate by the merchant and slave trader John Lewis Gervais should have been sufficient to cover any debts. John Holman responded that one reason for the delay in settling the estate was that some of his own property had been included in his father's estate inventory, and that he being "an African born, & totally ignorant of the Laws & usages of this State, & not knowing for what purposes an Inventory & valuation of the property was making, he took no concern therein."[23]

Financial disagreements, in part related to the ongoing efforts of John and Samuel to engage in the slave trade, brought the brothers and sisters into further conflict with one another. In 1798 John moved to the Georgetown district where he rented a rice plantation on the Santee River from George Parker, a move that put him in Elizabeth Cleveland's neighborhood, though there is no indication that the two ever met. After renting for several years, he agreed to purchase the plantation from Parker, using his slaves as collateral with the first payment due in August 1804. In 1803 John planned to return to the Rio Pongo; he appointed

Parker to act as his attorney in his absence. He may have already been back to Africa since there are records indicating that he was sending his children, born to him and his "mulatto" wife Sally, from the Rio Pongo to a missionary school in Freetown, Sierra Leone. It is unclear from the sparse records whether Sally, who was African American, was from South Carolina or Sierra Leone, but the two had at least four children: Margaret, Betsy, Elizabeth, and John III (known as Samuel). In keeping with tradition on the Rio Pongo, he sent their son John III to Liverpool to be educated. He established a factory on the Fatala along with his half-brother William, and by 1813 they had also expanded their operations to the Bangalan basin. Zachary Macaulay, the anti-slavery activist and governor of Sierra Leone from 1794–1799, visited William Holman, whom he described as a mulatto, and wrote:

> We found Holman very frank and ingenuous, and Slave-trader as he is, I could not help respecting him. I talked much with him on the enormity of the trade. He said he knew it well, and was unhappy in it, but what could he do? He and his family would starve. I had no success in trying to convince him of his obligation to quit it. He would quit it, however, from inclination and a feeling of its inhumanity, if he could do without it. I . . . urged the possibility of an abolition. He began to talk seriously of preparing against that event, and I promised him cotton and coffee seeds.

Traders like Holman did not only trade in slaves. The Fula caravans brought slaves along with other valuable trade goods from the interior. Theodore Canot, a trader on the Rio Pongo in the 1820s, described the goods a 700-person caravan brought down. It included 3,500 hides, nineteen large ivory tusks and 600 pounds of small ivory and gold, fifteen tons of rice, thirty-six bullocks, and 900 pounds of beeswax. He estimated those goods to be valued at $7,185 while the forty slaves were worth $1,600. William owned his own schooner manned by an African crew that enabled him to move trade goods and slaves along the coast. It is unclear if the Holman brothers operated separate factories or were partners in the same factory, but given the tense and sometimes violent encounters between the traders on the Rio Pongo, they needed one another. Adam Afzelius, who visited the river in 1795–1796, noted "how badly the traders treat one another in this river" and described beatings and other violent encounters among them. Like his brother, William Holman also married a mixed-race wife. On his visit to the Holman factory, Afzelius met Holman's wife and described her as a "Malatter [*sic*] a fine woman with a like child."[24]

John intended to use his South Carolina connections to invest in the booming slave trade underway in Charleston after South Carolina reopened the international slave trade in 1803. Between 1803 and 1808, when the U.S. government closed the African slave trade, Charleston merchants sponsored over sixty voyages, and John and Samuel Holman hoped to capitalize on that trade. Since he and his half-brother would supply the slaves at the Rio Pongo, and his brother Samuel would line up investors for voyages from South Carolina, they could take profits from both ends of the voyage and expect a hefty return. When Afzelius was in the Rio Pongo area he found a brisk trade with over sixty ships having arrived since the last rainy season, and "most of them Americans." John Holman's daughters made strategic marriages with the sons of other mixed-race trading families: Betsy Holman married a member of the Lawrence family and Margaret wed Jellorum Harrison, both members of prominent, well-established, and politically powerful families that extended the family's reach into the Dembia and Nunez Rivers.[25]

While John reestablished himself on the Rio Pongo, Samuel worked with investors in South Carolina in order to send slave ships to his brother's factory there. Even though he was a free person of color, Samuel had no trouble finding investors among Charleston's white slave trading community. In October 1805, for example, Samuel entered into a partnership with Moses Myers and John Taylor to fit out a ship from Georgetown, South Carolina, the state's second busiest port, for an African voyage. In the fall of 1805, he entered into a partnership with Charleston slave trader Frederick Tavel for a "joint venture to the coast of Africa." Tavel advanced the necessary funds, and John used his South Carolina slaves as collateral to cover his $12,000 share of the investment. In 1807 Samuel embarked for Africa leaving his factor, Anthony Chanet, to supervise the estate. After his departure, John Holman's creditor, George Parker, seized all the slaves on the estate for outstanding debts, an illegal seizure that resulted in "a great contest among the creditors of the Holmans." The result was a decade-long legal battle during which John lost much of his property, including his plantation and the majority of the slaves. Samuel was able to regain the property that Parker had illegally taken from him, but that required a long legal battle. John also brought suit against Samuel in 1808 and in 1811, but the court found that both of the brothers "appear to have acted at different times in an inconsistent and contradictory manner" and noted that it "would be cautious in lending an ear to the applications of either of them."[26]

Just as the U.S. abolition of the African slave trade disrupted the commercial activities of the Charleston merchants engaged in that business, the British abolition of 1807 had a similar impact on the traders on the Rio Pongo. The Holmans' transatlantic slave trading operation was undermined on both sides of the Atlantic. Authorities in the British colony of Sierra Leone and the British naval cruisers, which had begun patrolling the coast in 1808 only to be increased in 1811, put pressure on the traders on the Rio Pongo. In 1787 the British established their "Province of Freedom" in Sierra Leone, and that colony grew rapidly after the introduction of the Black Loyalists in 1792 and the resettlement of Liberated Africans rescued from captured slavers after 1808. Zachary Macaulay believed that if the Sierra Leone experiment was to succeed he had to establish commercial ties along the coast. The English-speaking traders on the Rio Pongo, less than one hundred miles away, were an obvious choice. He also believed that it was necessary to convince the slave traders to abandon the slave trade and adopt commercial agriculture and legitimate trade instead. He built goodwill by offering schooling in Freetown to the children of traders and African elites, and he offered them free coffee plants and cotton seed. William Cleveland, John Cleveland's son who became head of that family's business after James Cleveland's death in 1791, was one of the traders on the Sherbro who embraced his mission as did Lightbourn, William Lawrence, Paul Faber, and other important traders on the Rio Pongo, all of whom received coffee plants and stated their intentions to abandon the slave trade. Missionaries from the Edinburgh Missionary Society first arrived on the Rio Pongo in 1798, and they were followed by a larger contingent of missionaries sent there by the Church Missionary Society between 1808 and 1817. The traders recognized the advantages of missionary schools and closer trade ties with Sierra Leone so long as the missionaries did not openly challenge the slave trade. Their presence and their efforts to discredit the slave trade resulted in conflicts and trade wars between the traders and landowners who supported the missionaries and the die-hard slave traders who opposed them. The Holmans no longer appear as major slave traders during these years, which may indicate that they cast their lot with the missionaries and legitimate trade. Margaret

Holman's marriage to Jellorum Harrison, a leading missionary, may indicate such an alliance given the long history of strategic marriages in the family. Perhaps William Holman was sincere when he told Macaulay that he would quit the trade from feelings of humanity if he could find another way to make a living.[27]

While the Holman brothers may have shut down their slave trading business voluntarily, it is also possible that their factories were destroyed in the conflicts between the river traders and the British which disrupted the slave trade in this period. In 1814 Sierra Leone Governor Charles William Maxwell, eager to root out the slave trade at the Rio Pongo, sent three vessels and 150 troops up the river as far as Bangalan; they destroyed factories, captured several merchants, and transported them, their goods, and their chattels to Freetown. Maxwell's raids on the Rio Pongo traders followed the passage of the Slave Felony Act of 1811 which authorized the prosecution of British slave traders wherever they operated and of foreign slave traders who operated on British soil. Their goods were sold and their slaves were freed and apprenticed in Sierra Leone. The British launched a similar raid in 1820 after the HMS *Snapper* sailed up the Rio Pongo and her crewmen boarded a slaver. While they were examining the ship's papers, Africans from the shore attacked them, killing seven British sailors. Some sailors escaped overland back to Sierra Leone, but others were captured. A squadron from Sierra Leone attacked the factory, burned it, and recaptured the crewmen. Officials in Sierra Leone informed their superiors in 1823 that the "chief traders" on the Rio Pongo have "altogether abandoned the trade with a determination not to return to it under any circumstances," and were instead engaged in legitimate trade "as planters and general merchants." The Holmans may have been among the chief traders who became planters and merchants, but many of the slave traders did not actually abandon that traffic despite their pledges to do so. John Ormond and Stiles Lightbourn had not given up the trade for plantation agriculture, though Faber had begun a coffee plantation. While the slave trade declined briefly, it reemerged after 1827, and the Rio Pongo remained an important source for the illegal slave trade for decades thereafter.[28]

Samuel followed his brother back to the Rio Pongo in 1819, but their breach did not heal and the family disputes left the Holman siblings estranged. John recorded his will in Charleston in 1822 when he was still trading on the Rio Pongo. He appointed his fellow trader Stiles Lightbourn as his executor. It was a natural choice since Lightbourn was from Charleston and had married Elizabeth Bailey Gomez (known as Queen Niara Bely), the mixed-race daughter of a prominent slave trader on the Rio Pongo. His son, Lightbourn, Jr., was schooled in Charleston, and Lightbourn, a ship captain, moved back and forth between the Rio Pongo and Charleston, leaving his capable wife to manage operations on the Rio Pongo. John left his brother Samuel and his sisters the sum of one shilling to share between them, a bequest clearly intended to send a final message. He left his entire estate to his "Well beloved wife Sally and Well beloved Nephew Samuel Holman." He also recorded that "my Wife Sally is and has been Liberated and made free from me and my heirs forever and that no person or persons have or can have any claim on her." He also asked his nephew to care for her "as his own Mother." He died a few months after the will was recorded. Samuel's fate is unknown.[29]

John Holman's ambitious scheme to create a transatlantic, commercial slave trading and plantation enterprise administered by members of his Anglo-African family carried the Holmans on a remarkable circuit of the Atlantic World. Using the same marriage strategies he would have adopted on the Rio Pongo, his daughters made advantageous marriages to members of an extended, free mixed-race family in South Carolina, and the wealth they brought into those unions helped their husbands prosper and ensured their descendants a place among the very richest free people of color in the state. His Anglo-African sons were not so fortunate, and though they attempted to extend that transatlantic slave trading business, through bad luck, bad timing, and mismanagement they squandered the fortune their father left them in South Carolina, a loss that drove them back to the Rio Pongo, where they resumed the family slave trading business, but left them permanently estranged from one another and from their sisters.

While Elizabeth Cleveland, with a background very similar to that of the Holmans, had used her advantages of wealth, kinship, and education to join the ranks of the Lowcountry's white planter elite, the Holmans either made or were forced to make different choices. Racial attitudes had hardened between Elizabeth's arrival in the 1760s and the Holmans' arrival thirty years later. The Holmans' Anglo-African heritage was a major advantage on the Rio Pongo, but less so in South Carolina where their status as free blacks placed legal and cultural limits on what they could accomplish. Still, the presence of a number of white slave traders working between Charleston and the Rio Pongo, most of them with mixed-race families of their own, provided them with advantageous trading partners. They used their connections on both sides of the Atlantic to lay the foundations of a transatlantic slave trading enterprise, but that grand scheme foundered after the United States and Britain closed the Atlantic trade in 1808. Had that not happened, it is conceivable that the Holmans and their network of elite mixed-race traders moving back and forth across the North Atlantic could have cemented a close-knit, transatlantic slave trading network like that between Lagos, Luanda, and Benguela in West Africa and Salvador and Rio de Janeiro, Brazil in the South Atlantic.

When it became clear that the United States would close the African slave trade in 1808, South Carolina reopened it and the Holmans were among the traders who joined in that final rush of legal importations. Since many of those newly enslaved Africans were children, the African presence continued in the South for many more decades, though the rapid growth of the native-born slave population left those Africans in an ever-decreasing minority. For that reason, scholars have paid more attention to the African presence in the South before 1808 than after that date. In addition, the illegal slave trade brought in more Africans after 1808, particularly through Spanish Florida and Texas before those states joined the Union in 1845–1846. Historians have not fully explored this illegal traffic, but estimates suggest that as many as 50,000 Africans were smuggled into the U.S. between 1808 and 1860.[30] The following chapters will explore the lives of some of those Africans in the antebellum South.

3

―――――――

From Manservant to Abolitionist
and Physician

IN JANUARY 1837 the New England Anti-Slavery Society held its fifth annual meeting in the loft of the stable attached to the Marlboro Hotel in Boston. Some people in the audience were concerned about the structure's stability, but William Lloyd Garrison assured them that "the floor was well propped; and he felt gratified with the conscious-ness that Abolition today, as on every day, stands upon a *stable* founda-tion." The audience applauded his witticism. The body heard a number of fiery speeches from white abolitionists, and then a former slave took the podium. Identified only as "Mr. Johnson," he announced to the group that "he could tell us something about slavery. He *knew* what it was." His remarkable narrative of freedom was transcribed in an effort to capture his dialect, and two versions of the speech were published, one in the proceedings of the society and one in Garrison's anti-slavery newspaper, the *Liberator*. The day after Johnson's speech, white aboli-tionist Joshua Coffin, a founding member of the New England and American anti-slavery societies, conducted a follow-up interview. Each of these versions has slight but important variations. For a day and a half the overwhelmingly white crowd gathered in the stable attic had listened to well-meaning northern white speakers, but once Johnson rose, they heard a less polished but far more direct and first-hand ac-count of the institution they so despised. He said, "I was born in Af-rica, several hundred miles up the Gambia River. Fine country dat, but we are called heathen in dis Christian—no, I don't know what to call

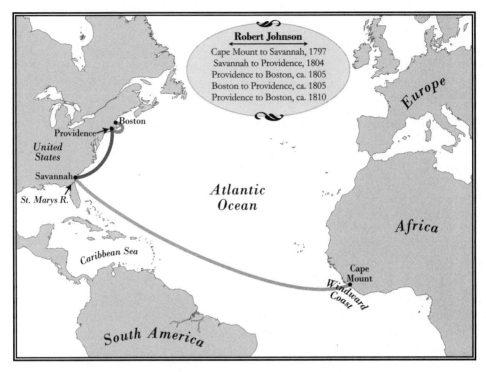

Map 7. Robert Johnson

it—in dis—*enlightened heathen country."* That jest brought laughter
from the crowd who had already heard a great deal about the contra-
dictions between southern slavery and Christianity.[1] In Coffin's interview he reported that he was a member of the Kissi ethnic group.
The Kissi live in an area where Sierra Leone, Liberia, and Gambia
meet, and they made up a sizeable proportion of enslaved Africans
sent across the Atlantic from the Windward Coast and Sierra Leone
in the late eighteenth and early nineteenth centuries (see Map 5 in
Chapter 2). They lived primarily in villages and minor settlements,
and their society was politically fragmented, organized around lin-
eages and families.[2]

He described a close-knit community where people shared what
they had and took care of one another's needs, a description that stood
in stark contrast to the negative descriptions of African barbarity so
common in pro-slavery discourse. "The villagers in that country are very
kind," he noted. He said,

> When you go into house, first question is, have you had anything to
> eat? Bring water—you wash—and en eat much as you want, and all
> you got do is tank em for it—not one sip [cent] you pay. If you are sick,
> nurse you, and make you well; not one sip you pay. If you want clothing,
> one woman put in two knots warp, one puts in two knots filling, and so
> on; den men weave it, and you cut out just garment you like; not one
> sip you pay.

By this time he had his audience's attention and sympathy, and they
applauded his description of his idyllic home. Johnson was doing more
than simply recounting the history of his homeland. He held up an al-
ternative West African communal social system based on reciprocal exchange that was radically different from the capitalist system in which
American slavery was so deeply embedded.[3]

He was ripped from that community by kidnappers from the Vai nation, and he gave the group a graphic description of his capture by slavers from the coast. The Vai lived along the coast of modern-day Liberia
and Sierra Leone; major slave-trading centers like Gallinas and Cape
Mount were in their territory. Their geographical location and linguistic ties to widespread Mande-speaking groups who also engaged in
the Atlantic trade enabled them to become major slave traders. When he
was nine years old, he went out with his aunt to gather figs which grew
wild in the area. He described how he had "to crawl amongst the bushes"
to gather the fruit, "when all at once I feel something pull my leg. I look
round, and could see no aunt, nothing but man of my own color; and I
never seed my aunt since." He recalled a long march of six weeks from
his inland home to the coast.[4] This sort of opportunistic kidnapping of
children was widespread because they were easy to capture, unable to
resist, and could be sold quickly. Francis Spilsbury, who visited Sierra
Leone early in the nineteenth century, reported that kidnapping was
common on the coast. He learned that "a man will lay in wait until he
can seize a boy or girl who is prime, that is four feet four inches high,
thus he hurries down to a factor or ship, and sells," an apt description of
Johnson's capture. His kidnapping is evidence of the increasing number
of children caught up in the slave trade in the late eighteenth and early
nineteenth centuries. The percentage of children in voyages from Sierra
Leone, for example, rose from about 15 percent at the beginning of the
eighteenth century to 25 percent by the end of the century, and those
numbers continued to climb until the second quarter of the nineteenth

century when over 40 percent of the slaves exported from that area were children, and the numbers were even higher for the Gallinas and Sherbro regions. Historian Benjamin Lawrance, in his study of the children on board the *Amistad,* has drawn attention to the critical role children played in the slave trade of the late eighteenth and nineteenth centuries. Johnson's case is one more identifiable example of childhood kidnapping and enslavement that closely mirrors those of the children on board the *Amistad.*[5]

Johnson was sold in Cape Mount, located on the Windward coast in modern Liberia. That is where he saw his first white man. Africans from that region were highly sought after in the Lowcountry, and slave dealers often identified slaves for sale from Cape Mount to attract more buyers and higher prices. Johnson identified that first white man as Captain Edward Boss of Newport, Rhode Island. Boss made two slave voyages from the Windward Coast to Georgia, as captain of the *James* in 1795 and the *Angenoria (a) Agenoria* in 1797. The *James* left Cape Mount with 110 captives and arrived in Savannah with 98 survivors and the *Angenoria (a) Agenoria* left Cape Mount with 125 slaves and arrived in Savannah with 110 captives. Coffin reported that Johnson said he was brought to Savannah by Captain Robert Watts in a ship called the *Hunter,* but there is no record of Captain Watts or any slave ship by that name. Coffin must have misunderstood Johnson; Robert Watts was a slave dealer who advertised slaves for sale in Savannah brought on the *James* from Cape Mount in September 1796, and he also advertised slaves for sale from Cape Mount on the slaver *Angenoria,* Edward Boss, master, in August 1797. Johnson was almost certainly on the *Angenoria.* Watts was the city's busiest slave seller; he sold twenty-nine cargoes totaling almost 2,500 slaves between 1795 and 1799. Once in Savannah, Johnson remembered his difficulties in finding palatable food. Like many African captives, he preferred food more familiar to him than the steady diet of cornmeal he received which he "could not eat." He subsisted on a little rice (the staple food for the Kissi and the primary crop for the South Carolina and Georgia Lowcountry) and hominy, but also managed to escape from his holding pen to "go out every day to plunder" for food. His habit of running away prevented him from being sold as quickly as the other captives; an exasperated Boss spent two days searching for him before he sold him at auction. Johnson recalled that Boss told him "you musn't go away today," and gave him all the rice he wanted. Johnson pointed to a table in the room and told his audience that Boss "set me on a table like dat." He described the auction where "Capt. Boss talk to people, dey look at me, and feel of me. By and by man wid mallet begin to talk and swing mallet; dey talk once in while, he jabber, jabber, jabber, I no understand; den he fetch his mallet down, and all stop."[6]

Johnson's purchaser was Oliver Bowen, whom he regarded as "more father than master," a relationship encouraged by Johnson's youth. Commodore Oliver Bowen, a native of Providence, Rhode Island, whose family had a long history of involvement in the African slave trade, won his title in the Revolutionary War as a naval commander and was granted 1,500 acres of land in Georgia in 1784. He relocated there and continued to engage in the slave trade. In 1790, for example, he was captain of the slave ship *Providence,* a Rhode Island ship that left West Africa with 87 slaves and arrived in Cuba with 78 survivors. Curiously, by 1790 he was a member of the Providence Society for Abolishing the Slave Trade. For Johnson, torn from his family and enslaved as a child, Bowen played the role of patron. The boy was not sent into the Lowcountry's deadly rice swamps, but served as Bowen's personal servant. He reported that Bowen "always said he should set me free before he died. But he died soon. . . ." His master fought a duel with a Mr. Dennis in Augusta; he was wounded in the hip and died two months later. The *Liberator* article noted that Bowen left Johnson to his brother Jabez Bowen in his will, but in his interview with Coffin, Johnson claimed that Bowen freed him and another slave named Eliphalet in his will, but Jabez unlawfully violated that will, sold Eliphalet, and kept him as his personal slave. Bowen's death, then, was a serious blow to Johnson who had lost his patron and his freedom. For most slaves, the death of a master posed a serious threat, and it could lead to being moved or sold, and though Bowen's sudden death drastically altered Johnson's life, he remained a body servant in the Bowen family and was not sold away as Eliphalet was. Body servants like Johnson might enjoy special privileges that field hands would never see, but life at their master's beck and call had its own special hardships. They were always on call, masters could be irritable, harsh, or abusive, and servants could be scapegoats for any of their master's frustrations. Johnson did not lodge any charges of mistreatment at his new master, but he clearly did not hold him in high regard as he had Oliver Bowen. Jabez Bowen, a Republican, was appointed a Superior Court judge on Georgia's Eastern Circuit in 1804.

Johnson traveled with him around his circuit, and he once accompanied his master to a dinner party at John Houston McIntosh's plantation home on the St. Mary's River, the border between Georgia and Florida.[7]

He began his description of that dinner party in the same light-hearted vein that had captured his audience's attention, but the story took a dark turn. He told them that the host of the dinner party

> had a wife as black as dat hat. A young colored woman, *as likely for her color* [meaning as beautiful for her color] as any woman in dis assembly (a laugh), waited on table. She happened to spill a little gravy on the gown of her mistress. The gentleman took his carving knife, dragged her out to wood pile, and cut her head off; den wash his hands, come in finish his dinner like nothing had happened!

He recounted other terrible punishments of slaves that had caused severe injury and death, but none as horrific as the gruesome murder of a girl over such a trivial event.[8]

Johnson's story was so gripping and yet so lacking in specifics that Joshua Coffin interviewed him the following day in order to get more details of the murder, and even though the event occurred three decades before, Johnson provided much more detail. He recalled the surnames of all the guests at the dinner. He identified the host only as "McIntosh," and given the date and location, the most likely person is John Houston McIntosh who resided in St. Mary's. John Houston McIntosh was the son of Lachland McIntosh, a native of Scotland, a prominent leader during the Revolution, and a planter. Following in his father's footsteps, he was also a wealthy planter who served in Georgia's state constitutional convention in 1798. In 1791 he married Eliza Bayard of a prominent New York family when he was nineteen and she was twenty-three. He was especially active in southern Georgia along the St. Mary's River, and in 1803 he took an oath of allegiance to Spain so that he could acquire plantations in the booming St. Mary's and St. John's rivers area of Florida where he made a fortune producing timber and Sea Island cotton with slave labor. Even though he took an oath of allegiance to Spain and held considerable property there, he continued to reside mostly in Georgia. That area was very much a frontier, where racial lines were more porous and where planters like Zephaniah Kingsley, who had been a slave trader operating on the African coast, Francis Richard, and many others openly took African wives and concubines and often freed them and their biracial children. Perhaps nowhere else on the eastern seaboard of the United States could McIntosh have entertained a group of gentlemen with his African mistress sitting at the table, and that probably would not have happened had white women been present.[9]

The other guests at the dinner party were prominent Georgians and visitors: two were identified only by their surnames, Bulloch and Flournoy, one, Judge Mitchell, also by his title, and one, Christopher Olney, by his full name. William Bellinger Bulloch was born in Savannah in 1777 to a prominent family; he studied law and opened his practice in Savannah in 1797. He was appointed United States district attorney in 1804. Thomas Flournoy was born in North Carolina, moved to Augusta, Georgia, shortly after the turn of the nineteenth century, and opened a law office in 1807. David B. Mitchell of Savannah was appointed a federal district attorney by Thomas Jefferson in 1801 after serving as mayor, superior court judge, and state senator. There were two Christopher Olneys in Providence, father and son, and both died in 1809. Given the father's age, the son would be the more likely visitor to Georgia. He owned a cotton textile factory in Rhode Island, one of the largest in the state, a business that could well explain his visit to an area that produced Sea Island cotton. His textile mill also produced the "Negro cloth" used as clothing for southern slaves, and he could have been visiting the Lowcountry's large plantations in search of buyers for that fabric. The Bowens certainly knew the Olneys in Providence, and both Jabez Bowen, Sr. and the elder Olney served as Grand Masters of the St. John's Freemason's Lodge there.[10]

Johnson gave Coffin a more graphic description of the fatal meal. He recalled that Bulloch

> called to Delia, a slave about 17 years of age, to hand him the gravy. She did so, and in doing it, accidentally split some of it on the gown of the female at the table. On seeing this, McIntosh rose in great wrath, seized the carving-knife with one hand and Delia with the other, dragged her to the wood pile, and cut her throat!! She died instantly. Some of the guests, with myself, rushed to the door and witnessed the transaction. Mr. McIntosh dropped the knife, and called for a bowl of water to wash his hands. Mr. Olney, not being used to 'their ways,' immediately called for his horse and rode off and was told the next day that he had better return to the North, than find fault with their customs.[11]

Clearly, the gruesome image was burned into the mind of the young man who would have been about the same age as Delia.

The leniency of the southern legal system cannot alone explain the brutal murder. Masters did not simply murder slaves because they could. Certainly more was at work here than the accidental spilling of a bit of gravy, but what? The evidence does not provide an answer to this important question, but several possibilities suggest themselves. It would seem most likely that the case grew out of simmering tensions within the complicated McIntosh household. Was Delia a rebellious slave, difficult to control and given to insults to her superiors in the household? Did she reserve those insults for McIntosh's African mistress? That McIntosh's rage resulted from an incident involving the two women suggests some ongoing tensions between them or with him. Did McIntosh's African mistress fear that his attentions might wander to the beautiful Delia? Did she goad her lover into murdering her rival? Did Delia encourage her master's attentions, or did she resist her master's advances with fatal consequences? Historian Eugene Genovese observed that jealousies and frustrations within the plantation household "could reach terrible proportions" within "the close conditions of life in the Big House. . . ." In the same vein, Elizabeth Fox-Genovese described the complex relationships and sexual tensions that defined life in the Big House. Slave women's resistance, she observed, was more "likely to be individual rather than collective," and Delia may well have been showing a form of that resistance. In such cases, a tense and dangerous contest of wills could provoke brutal violence. A master's sexual exploitation of enslaved women could lead to all sorts of jealousies and acts of violence from masters and mistresses alike. As Fox-Genovese noted, "mistresses and slaves lived in tense bonds of conflict-ridden intimacy that frequently exploded into violence on one side or the other." The power of the master had to be absolute, and southern courts never agreed on its limits.[12]

A less likely scenario is that Delia's murder grew out of the dinner party itself. Did McIntosh stage his vicious attack on Delia to somehow impress the men around his table? Such an attack would seem to violate the paternalistic ideal for southern slaveholders and its code of honor that frowned on such brutality directed at women. While masters could inflict brutal punishments on any slave, those punishments were expected to be applied with some consideration for the gravity of the offense. It is difficult to imagine what message McIntosh could have intended to send other than murderous rage or perhaps a cold-blooded willingness to shed the blood of innocents. His call for a bowl of water to wash her blood off his hands before resuming dinner certainly added a theatrical touch. Only Olney, the northern visitor, was disturbed enough by what he saw to flee the grisly scene, and if Johnson is correct, he also talked about what he saw in an indiscreet and censorious way. He was invited to leave the state as a result.

Was Johnson the only witness who could not erase that terrible crime from his memory? It apparently haunted his master as well. On Monday morning, April 23, 1804, Bowen prepared to open the Grand Jury of Chatham County, Georgia, in Savannah. According to custom, the County Sheriff met the judge at his home, drew his sword, and ceremonially escorted him to the courthouse where Bowen delivered an explosive charge to the jurors. There were no requirements for what form these charges might take, and it was not unusual for a judge to discuss topics of general interest to the community. No doubt the jurors expected another boring monologue from the bench, but Judge Bowen had a surprise in store. He began his speech by observing that "the period has at length arrived when the citizens of Georgia shall hear from the Bench sentiments which ought long since to have emanated from our Legislature." He warned that the state was in dire peril, and that the Legislature, which was charged with guarding the safety of the state, had ignored that threat. He asked if the "wealthy and the powerful" had "silenced the cries of oppression and the voice of truth"? No doubt that opening had captured the jurors' attention, and they must have leaned forward in their seats to hear the source of the dangers the judge identified. "Hear then, my fellow citizens," the judge proclaimed, "listen to what experience and wisdom suggest as the only means of rescuing you from the abyss that yawns beneath your feet and now, even now, opens its destructive and capacious jaws to ensnare you."[13]

The source of that danger? Slavery. Bowen appealed to jurists like Blackstone and Coke and to the laws of Nature and God in a ringing indictment of the institution. He denounced his fellow Georgians as "impious wretches" and called on them to cease their "calumnies on that God whose decrees are just and immutable and who will confound your misinterpretations of his ordinances! How then does slavery exist," he asked, "not from the fiat of heaven but from the municipal institution of base, degenerate man!" He held up examples from history, including the specter of the recent Haitian Revolution, and warned his stunned listeners, "What then have we eventually to expect? What but blood, massacre, and devastation!" The only defense, he suggested, was a gradual plan of emancipation that would free female slaves at the age of ten and males at the age of twenty-one. Masters would be required to educate their slaves, teach them Christianity, provide for them, and their punishment would be limited to twenty lashes unless a magistrate on the scene approved a harsher punishment. His call that the jurors "let these observations . . . occupy your attention" was quite unnecessary; as they sat in stunned silence they could think of little else. He tried to assure them of his love for the state and the purity of his intentions:

> I possess as great a stake in this country as the most wealthy, for my little all is here, and no man's heart beats higher with a love of country than mine. But although I love my country much, very much, I adore the principles of liberty, of justice and of humanity, and I will no longer acknowledge this my country, when these sound principles are prostrated by such accursed avarice, such infamous conduct—but I will seek in other climes for that tranquility and repose which is here every moment liable to be interrupted, the instant I am convinced there is not virtue enough in Georgia to listen to and pursue the paths I have pointed out to you. . . . I despise from my soul the threats of the haughty and the vindictive . . . and have dared to avow sentiments which . . . can alone secure my country from all the horrors of civil warfare.[14]

Newspapers reported that he "went so far as to say, that if the legislature did not do it, he would head them himself, and assist in cutting the throats of the white inhabitants," a sentiment that does not mesh with the tenor of the rest of the judge's remarks, but echoes Delia's brutal slaying. He also ordered that his remarks be published in the local newspaper.[15] His comments were described as "bolts out of a clear blue sky," "a cyclone on an April day," and "a rattlesnake in a feather bed."[16] Or as Johnson described it, in a clever play on Bowen's warnings, "they had an 'insurrection' in court."[17]

The Grand Jury returned on Wednesday to answer the judge's volatile charge. They denounced his remarks as "injudicial, insulting to our government, and repugnant to the general interests of our country; but disseminating principles that may tend to involve the community in the horrors of domestic insurrection." They recommended that the charge not be published and instead called for it to be forwarded to the Clerk of the Superior Court, to the Governor, and to the Legislature.

Outraged by what he called a "gross and direct insult on this court," Bowen ordered the County Sheriff to escort the jurors to the gaol for contempt. As they filed out, the crowd in the courtroom began to shout, *"no, no—they shall not go,"* which caused Bowen to pull a brace of pistols from his pocket and exclaim, *"Where is the damn'd rascal who dares say NO? shew him to me, and I'll blow his brains out!"* The Grand Jury proceeded to the gaol and the members of the local bar left the courtroom behind them and met to consider the dangerous situation. They resolved to host an "entertainment" for the Grand Jurors at the gaol that evening and to dine with them there as a show of support. They sent word to the city's newspaper editors not to print the judge's remarks, which they denounced as dangerous. They applauded the jury's conduct and agreed that they would boycott the court as well. They declared that they viewed with "utmost abhorrence, the prostitution of judicial dignity in Judge Bowen's drawing and presenting a pistol against a multitude of the citizens, and using the most profane and indecent language while on the bench, and during the sitting of the court."[18]

Their meeting was followed by a general meeting of the citizens of Savannah. They, too, expressed their support for the Grand Jurors' strong stand and called on the editors of the city's newspapers not to print the judge's remarks. They set up a subscription to support the jurors during their confinement, and called on the Legislature to investigate Bowen's conduct. They also agreed to confer with the members of the bar on how best to proceed. They ordered that their resolutions be published in the newspapers and as a broadside. A warrant was issued for Bowen's arrest on charges of attempting "to incite domestic rebellion." He tried to escape and pointed a loaded pistol at the County Sheriff, but was arrested and jailed. Only a military escort prevented him from being "torn to pieces" by the outraged citizens of Savannah.[19]

The next morning the lawyers representing the jurors appealed for a writ of habeas corpus from the Inferior Court which was promptly granted. That writ, which praised the "patriotism, firmness, and dignity" of the jurors was issued by James Bulloch, the clerk of the court and son of William Bellinger Bulloch, one of the guests at McIntosh's dinner party. Upon their release the jurors thanked the citizens of Savannah and the members of the bar for their support, and they added that Bowen should never have been appointed to the bench to begin with, and only got the job because the salary was so meager that no one of ential head of that family.³ Europeans held him in high esteem; Nicholas Owen, an English trader who lived in Sherbro along with his brother in the 1750s, described Tucker:

> He has been in England, Spain and Portugall and is master of the English tongue; he has 6 or 7 wives and a numerous ofspring of suns and daughters; his strength consists of his own slaves and their children, who has built a town about him and serves as his gremetos (gramattoes or servants) upon all occasions. This man bears the charactar of a fair trader among the Europeans, but to the contrary among the blacks. His riches sets him above the Kings and his numerous people above being surprised by war; almost all the blacks ows him money . . . so he is esteem'd and feared by all who has the misfortune to be in his power. He's a fat man and fair spoken, and lives after the manner of the English, having his house well furnish'd with English goods and his table tolarably well furnish'd with the country produce. He dresses gayley and commonly makes use of silver at his table, haveing a good side board of plate.⁴

In the late 1730s William Cleveland was employed as a sailor on a ship that wrecked near the Banana Islands in what is today Sierra Leone. King Skinner Corker, the son of Thomas Corker and Senhora Doll, employed Cleveland as a clerk. William was the younger son of Captain William Cleveland (a Scotsman who spelled his surname as Cleland before his move to England) of the Royal Navy who had traveled to that part of Africa on his naval expeditions. Cleveland was good at his job and won the confidence of his employer who married him to his only child, Kate. He learned the business well enough that he struck out on his own. He returned to England and raised enough capital to launch his own ships.⁵ William and Kate had two children, a son John, born about 1740, and a daughter Elizabeth, born probably the following year. William had apparently adopted the local custom of having more than one wife, for he had another son whom he also recognized, James, by a woman belonging to the Kissi nation.⁶

Like many Englishmen who resided on the West Coast of Africa, Cleveland sent all of his children to England to be educated. It was most common for Englishmen on the African coast to send their sons to England—their educations there were usually a prerequisite to their employment in the Royal African Company's factories—but it was not unheard of for daughters to be sent as well. Elizabeth probably attended one of the boarding schools in Liverpool operated by women. For these

real legal ability would accept the position.[20] He spent two weeks in jail
before his father, Jabez Bowen, Sr., arrived in Savannah to pay his
$8,000 bail. Future president John Quincy Adams thought "it to the
credit of the Georgia people that they suffered him to get away with a
whole skin." Adams wrote, "For although there is nothing more strong
as to principle in the charge, than Mr. Jefferson himself has published
in his *Notes on Virginia,* yet Bowen went one step further. He drew the
inference from the theory, and then the madness of the doctrine appeared in full view." A few weeks later in May 1804 the Georgia Legislature impeached Bowen on charges ranging from destroying court
documents, to inciting rebellion, to threatening citizens with a pistol
from the bench. The case made headlines all across the country, and in
his native Rhode Island his remarks were "so highly approved" that an
edition "on fine paper" was printed for distribution.[21]

Bowen left Georgia never to return. Johnson's life was altered radically by the move. He left Georgia for Rhode Island, home to Bowen,
but completely unfamiliar to Johnson who left a region with a black
majority for one where African Americans made up a small minority of
the population. He had no choice but to accompany Bowen to Rhode
Island, but he yearned for freedom. His relocation to free territory
opened up new possibilities for him to gain his liberty. Georgia was far
removed from free territory, but not Rhode Island, which was free, yet
its gradual abolition law meant that slavery continued there. Taking
advantage of the close proximity of free territory, Johnson ran away
to Boston, the largest city within striking distance and one where he
could blend in with the African American community; however, he
was soon arrested and returned to Bowen in Rhode Island. The attempt
was not a total failure, though, since he and Bowen entered into "an
obligation" in August 1805 that stipulated that he would be freed if he
served Bowen for three more years. Bowen suffered from mental problems, and it is impossible to know if his illness caused him to lash out at
his servant, but living with him could not have been easy. Johnson
recalled that Bowen became deranged a few years after his return to
Rhode Island, and was hospitalized for those issues first in Uxbridge,
Massachusetts, under the care of Dr. Samuel Willard who operated a
hospital for the insane in an old schoolhouse there for over twenty
years. In addition, a smaller building functioned as "a kind of water-cure
establishment, where the unruly ones used to suffer the wet pains and

penalties of their misconduct." In some cases, patients were confined in a box drilled with holes, their heads protruding from the box which was then lowered into the water. According to Johnson, Bowen recovered sufficiently to return to Providence, and it was probably during this time that he was able to uphold his agreement with Robert. Bowen manumitted him in August 1808. Bowen relapsed, probably after Willard's death in 1811. He was determined to be insane and placed under guardianship in 1815 when he was already receiving treatment elsewhere. After his relapse, Bowen was treated in Philadelphia where he was "an outrageous madman at times, with frequent intervals of perfect reason." The description of him as an outrageous madman suggests that during those times he would have been a difficult master. He died there in 1816 at the age of forty-three after "a rapid decline."[22]

Do Bowen's mental problems explain his outbursts to the Grand Jury? Did Delia's savage murder prey on a disturbed mind? There was no question about Bowen's sanity before his return to Rhode Island, and as inflammatory as his charge to the Grand Jury was, it was learned and reasoned. The fact that he brandished pistols in the courtroom might signal emotional distress or a reasonable defensive response to the mob mentality that gripped the community in the wake of his remarks. Bowen's call for a gradual plan of abolition was hardly radical or even unusual, outside of South Carolina, at least. Such plans had little chance of success, but they were widely discussed in the Upper South and promoted by gradual abolition societies until Virginia's 1832 rejection of such a plan in the wake of Nat Turner's rebellion and the South's embrace of slavery as a positive good closed those doors.[23]

Johnson is harder to trace in the historical record than his more famous former master, but when Bowen took Johnson to Providence, he became part of a small but thriving African American community. In 1810 there were 865 blacks in the city, 8.6 percent of the population, and Robert Johnson appears in the 1810 federal census living in a household with other free people of color. He does not appear in any later census or in other records from Providence, and he probably moved to Boston after that date.[24] That would explain his appearance at the anti-slavery meeting there in 1837.

Robert Johnson appears in an 1839 meeting of Boston's African American community in support of *The Liberator*, as Garrison and his anti-slavery newspaper were under assault from several directions in the 1830s and 1840s. Many abolitionists were outraged by Garrison's attacks on the clergy for their reluctance to embrace radical abolitionism, and for his embrace of a radical form of Christian pacifism, others by his attacks on political institutions and his declaration that voting was sinful, and still others by his support for equality of men and women in the movement. These increasingly hostile disagreements led to major schisms in the anti-slavery movement and a drastic decline in the number of subscribers to *The Liberator*. In that context, the overwhelming support Boston's African American community expressed for Garrison and his newspaper was especially significant. At their meeting, they resolved that "we retain unshaken confidence in the integrity and abolitionism of Wm. Lloyd Garrison," and they called his newspaper "the beacon fire of Liberty." Moreover, they appointed a committee to solicit subscriptions and donations to support the newspaper in its hour of need, a committee that Johnson joined. In his address before the New England Anti-Slavery Society, Johnson pointed to Garrison and said, "Dat man is de Moses raised up for our deliverance," a proclamation followed by "tremendous applause." His ringing endorsement of Garrison in his speech echoed the sentiments of this committee and offered additional evidence of his radical abolitionist views. Indeed, it may be that Johnson's given name was not used in the reports of his speech because he was so well known among the abolitionist community that it was unnecessary.[25]

Robert Johnson was also an officer in the African Baptist Church, usually referred to as the Belknap Street Church, a center of anti-slavery political activity and the site of important events like August 1 Day or West India Day which celebrated the British abolition of slavery in its colonies on that day in 1834. The church was built entirely by black labor and dedicated in 1806, and it was a part of a wider movement across the United States of the creation of "African" churches and fraternal and charitable organizations. Historians have seen these institutions, and their use of the term "African" in their titles, as evidence of an emerging African corporate identity. Johnson's position as an officer in that church is important evidence of his conversion to Christianity and his own identification with an "African" identity that was more inclusive than his ethnic identity as a Kissi native. A school for black children operated in its basement, and a bequest from Abiel Smith, a white merchant, led to the city integrating that school into the public school system, making it the first public school for blacks in the country. Belknap Street was the center of the black community in Boston, and Johnson's position in that church is evidence of his stature within the community. The black population of Boston stood at about 2,000 during the 1830s, substantially larger than Providence's community, but the conditions for African Americans in Boston were not much different from those in the town Johnson left behind. The vast majority of blacks held menial jobs, and they were segregated into the crowded streets on the north side of Beacon Hill around Belknap Street, a neighborhood referred to derisively as "Nigger Hill." Discrimination and segregation did not result in passivity, however, and may have actually encouraged the activism, community solidarity, and mutual aid that characterized African American life there. Along with a Methodist and a Baptist church, the community had strong leadership, social and reform societies, a Masonic Lodge, and a public school as well as several private ones. The strength of that community may have been the magnet that drew Johnson there, as it resonated with his memories of his close-knit African village.[26]

Along with his service to the Belknap Church, Johnson was also a member of a committee appointed to consider "the deplorable state of the Smith School" in 1848. The school was named after wealthy Boston merchant Abiel Smith who, at his death in 1815, left a $5,000 legacy to fund a free school for blacks. The funds were first used to supplement a school that had long operated in the basement of the African Meeting House. Eventually, the city used the bequest to build the Abiel Smith School next to the meeting house which opened in 1835. By the 1840s blacks complained about poor conditions at the school and alleged that its principal was an abusive racist. They bemoaned the fact that, unlike white children who attended neighborhood schools, all black students in the city were forced to attend the segregated school regardless of where they lived. Rather than call for the school's improvement, some blacks boycotted the school and community meetings continued to push for change. They were encouraged by successful black boycotts in Salem and Nantucket that resulted in integrated schools. At the 1848 meeting, the "Colored Citizens" resolved that "we all belong to one common family, having one common cause, it is our belief that *separate schools* for the education of children are injurious in their effects upon society, and ought to be abolished." They argued that education was the right of every citizen of the state, and proclaimed, "We know our rights, and knowing them, dare maintain them." The black community continued to meet and promote their cause, and though an 1849 lawsuit failed to integrate the city's schools, the state finally did so in 1855.[27]

Johnson and his compatriots joined some of the most important political debates around issues of slavery and freedom. In April 1850 the Belknap Street Church was the setting for an "Anti-Webster Meeting of the Colored Citizens of Boston and Vicinity" where the assembly, with Johnson as President, condemned Daniel Webster who had made an important speech in Congress in support of the Fugitive Slave Act, as part of the Compromise of 1850, and of African colonization, a cause he had endorsed as an initial contributor, if halfheartedly. One of the most controversial speeches ever made in Congress, his endorsement of the Act set off a firestorm in Massachusetts and outraged the African American community in Boston. The assembly, made up "in part of those who have drunk deep the dregs of slavery" like Johnson himself, warned that they and their children were put at risk by the bill, which they denounced in the strongest possible terms. Webster had also supported allocating millions of dollars in support of colonization, which the group condemned as "a scheme of infinite wickedness," and they resolved their "united and unalterable opposition to the scheme of African colonization, as also to every other plan for perpetuating the God-defying system of American slavery." Garrison arrived late, but got an enthusiastic welcome, and he added his voice to the denunciation of Webster and the Fugitive Slave bill.[28]

After the passage of the Fugitive Slave Act in September 1850, African Americans in Boston held another meeting, even more spirited than the previous one. They were especially aroused because over forty of their number fled Boston within three days of President Millard Fillmore's signing it into law, and the news of arrests of blacks in New York City had reached them in Boston, "borne on the wings of the wind," like all news touching slavery and freedom. Garrison was there again, and he was "hailed with enthusiastic demonstrations." This time he read the bill and "electrified the audience with his bold denunciation of the law and its supporters, and by his earnest appeal to all lovers of liberty, now to test their principles, at whatever cost." Johnson and others addressed the audience and urged them "to do all and to dare all, in imitation of Patrick Henry's immortal sentiment, *Liberty or Death!*" Johnson was appointed to a committee to prepare for the next meeting to be held the following week at Belknap Church. At that October 11 meeting the group approved a long list of resolutions against the Fugitive Slave Act, drawing on constitutional law, Biblical and Christian precepts, and the Revolutionary principles of equality. Johnson joined a long roster of speakers, including Garrison, in denouncing the bill. Johnson declared that people in the hall were not just speakers, but men of action, many of them "men of over-alls—men of the wharf—who could do heavy work in the hour of difficulty." He also addressed the women, who in their capacity as washer-women and domestics often visited the hotels and boarding houses, and could be "on the lookout for the Southern slave-catcher or the Northern accessory." His words to the "wise women" were greeted with "lively demonstrations."[29] Throughout these meetings, the free blacks of Boston emphasized their common cause with their brothers and sisters enslaved in the South. The assembly resolved "that the ties of interest and consanguinity between the Northern nominally free colored man and the pining slave on Southern plantations are inseparable; in the appropriate language of Daniel Webster, when alluding to the two great sections of country, 'There will be no Alleghanies between us.'" As a former slave himself, Johnson provided a direct link between the slave South and free North, and he did not forget those slaves in the South who remained under slavery's yoke. At an 1837 abolition meeting, for example, he spoke in support of a resolution proposed by the Reverend Charles Fitch that read, "That while we look well to the dangers which threaten ourselves, . . . we ought to keep full in mind the wrongs and sufferings of the slave."[30]

In 1850 Johnson was one of eight men who organized a lecture by noted British abolitionist George Thompson at the Belknap Street Church. This was Thomson's second visit to the United States, and it happened to coincide with the agitation over the Fugitive Slave Act. Thompson, a radical member of Parliament, an advocate for the rights of blacks and a close friend of Garrison's for twenty years, was scheduled to speak at Faneuil Hall, but loud cheers for Daniel Webster, Jenny Lind, and the Union from a hostile mob interrupted that plan, and the city's "colored citizens" opened the Belknap Church for him instead. Frederick Douglass and Sojourner Truth shared the platform with him, and Truth wrote that he treated her "as if I had been the highest lady in the land . . . and never seemed to know that I was poor and a black woman."[31] In

this way, Johnson and his fellow black abolitionists connected themselves to the international abolition campaign, and perhaps more importantly, they claimed their ownership of notions of civil rights and
citizenship. All of the events supported by the black community in
Boston, those related to education reform, abolition, and political pro-
test, and growing out of independent institutions like churches, arose
from their commonality and connectedness. This sort of relational connectedness or what Charles Tilly refers to as "netness," a set of persons
who comprise both a category and a network, is crucial in enabling
collective action.[32]

Johnson's narrative offers another important clue to his life. He
described the difficulty he sometimes faced in being paid for medical
prescriptions "on account of not being a licensed physician." Robert
Johnson is listed in an 1835 city directory as a physician on Southac
Street in the West End, one of the few black physicians serving the
community. He offered no clues about how he became a physician, but
his interest in medicine may have begun when he nursed Jabez Bowen
during his illness. He was almost certainly self-taught, for there were
very few opportunities even for free blacks to study medicine apart
from the occasional apprenticeship during the antebellum era. That
lack of educational opportunity may be one reason Johnson worked so
diligently to promote integrated schools for free blacks in Boston. An
1855 city census shows him to be living in a neighborhood with other
free people of color, and his household included Hercules Johnson,
aged seventeen, almost certainly his son. His eventful life came to an
end in Roxbury, Massachusetts, on April 15, 1861, days after the start
of the great war that would finally destroy the institution of slavery he
struggled against for so long. In his death records, Africa was given as
his place of birth, he was listed as an 89-year-old physician, and he was
survived by his wife, who unfortunately goes unmentioned in other
records.[33]

Robert Johnson's remarkable journey from enslavement to freedom
highlights the shifting identities embodied in one man's long life, and
the importance of the fault lines separating slavery from freedom in
helping to shape those identities. His movements around the Atlantic
World call attention to what Frederick Cooper termed the *"politics* of
difference."[34] Johnson and his allies in Boston challenged the meaning
of race, remade it as they shifted away from an *African* to a *Colored* iden-

tity, and laid claim to civil rights and citizenship that had long been denied them. The shifting Atlantic and continental fault lines between slavery and freedom gave Johnson and other black abolitionists more room to maneuver and, joined by white abolitionists, they were able to articulate a radical vision of freedom and equality. He could not have launched that challenge from Savannah, nor could he and his allies have articulated their collective behavior south of the Mason-Dixon Line. By defining blacks as citizens on the one hand, but denying them the full rights of citizenship on the other, the state of Massachusetts helped foster an "oppositional consciousness" among the state's black citizens, and the struggle for the full rights of citizenship provided the framework for their mobilization.[35]

The wealth of verifiable detail in the narrative lends credence to the most disturbing part of Johnson's narrative, the vicious murder of Delia. Johnson's carefully and cleverly constructed narrative told his own story, but highlighted Delia's murder as well. Johnson knew that if her story were ever to be told, he would have to tell it. His speech contained few specifics about her death, but in a subsequent interview, he was able to give many more details. Those details do not fully authenticate his narrative of events, but they do lend credence to it. It is fitting that we join Johnson's quest not to allow Delia's death to go un-mourned and unrecorded, the very outcome that McIntosh counted on when he slit her throat over two centuries ago. Johnson's laser-like focus on the brutality of slavery emphasized slavery's power to "decivilize" and "brutalize" the enslaver more than the slave, and he contrasted that brutal system with communal life in his African homeland.[36]

The most important question remains, however, can the story be true? In relating the story, abolitionist Joshua Coffin issued a challenge that echoes down to the present, "let the investigation be made, and the truth, whatever it is, be made known." Such an investigation is almost impossible to conduct given the passage of time. My research has not revealed any outside collaboration of the event, but almost all the other details in Johnson's narrative can be verified. One important question must be asked—*could* the story be true? Could a master murder a slave and face no punishment? Could a murder carried out in front of a group of prominent men leave no archival trace? Overwhelming evidence from across the South demonstrates that masters were almost never tried for the murder of a slave, and even when they were tried, historians

Eugene Genovese and Elizabeth Fox-Genovese noted that "in Georgia . . . masters who were found guilty got off with modest fines more appropriate to misdemeanors." It took a long time for southern courts to even acknowledge that it was possible for a master to murder his slave since they could not imagine that a person would willingly destroy his own property. Under South Carolina law, the murder of a slave was a misdemeanor until 1821. Georgia's law was somewhat more advanced; under its constitution of 1798, "Any person who shall maliciously dismember or deprive a slave of life shall suffer such punishment as would be inflicted in the case the like offense had been committed on a free white person, and on the like proof except in case of insurrection by such slave, and unless such death should happen by accident in giving such slave moderate correction." But regardless of the law, masters in Georgia were not prosecuted any more frequently than those elsewhere in the South. Genovese admitted that "masters and overseers undoubtedly murdered more slaves than we shall ever know." Writing later in the antebellum era, Georgia Supreme Court judge Eugenius Nesbit summed up the legal conundrum; if the law "protects the life of a slave, why not his liberty? And if it protects his liberty, then it breaks down, at once, the *status* of the slave."[37]

The status of the master was another crucial factor in whether or not a master who murdered a slave would face prosecution. Most of the men gathered around McIntosh's table were among the state's planter elite. They held positions of power and influence. Indeed, they made and enforced the state's laws. McIntosh was safe in his knowledge that his friends and guests would never prosecute him for the murder of a slave. Scholars have found only a handful of such cases from across the antebellum South; almost all of those ended in acquittals or, in rare cases, in verdicts of manslaughter—and, tellingly, only one case of a master executed for murdering his slave has come to light. Legal scholar Ariela Gross made the crucial point that southern courts celebrated the paternalistic planter ideal, and she concluded that "the only cruelty that led to liability, as a rule, was that committed by others than masters or hirers."[38]

The men gathered around McIntosh's table had the influence and connections to silence the murder of a slave. Of course there is no trace of Delia's murder in the southern historical record and archival-based memory—men around that dinner table were the makers and enforcers of the law with the power to write out of the public record a crime carried out in an isolated area and inflicted on an enslaved girl. When Johnson found a way to inscribe Delia's story into history—into a record outside the control of southern slaveholders—he performed his own act of resistance and rebellion against the silence of the archives. When he gave fuller details to Coffin he did so with the expectation that those details would be recorded. Southern white elites had firm ideas about who should be allowed to speak and who should not, about whose voice mattered in the legal and public spheres and whose did not. Slaves who made their escape to free territory found a voice that had long been denied them and one that enslaved blacks could not possess.

In his speech before the New England Anti-Slavery Society, Johnson declared, "I will contend for liberty as long as I live." Johnson's work stands as an example of the sort of achievements native Africans could attain, his rich life defined by activism on behalf of enslaved blacks in the South and free blacks in the North. As one of the few black physicians practicing in Boston, he provided medical care that might not otherwise have been available to his community. His civil rights activism is part of a self-understanding far different than what he knew as a child of the Kissi nation or even as a slave in Georgia. He adopted a radical abolition position, one that included distributing David Walker's fiery *Appeal to the Coloured Citizens of the World* to his friends and acquaintances and which led him to endorse violence in the fight against the Fugitive Slave Act as well as pledge to wear a sword and behead anyone who threatened his compatriot William Lloyd Garrison. Some free blacks in the South saw the Colonization movement as a means of escape from a racist and oppressive society, and a few native Africans managed to return to Africa through its offices, but Johnson joined the majority of free blacks in the North who denounced that effort and demanded freedom and equality in the United States instead. Johnson continued to identify himself as a native of Africa, as he did in his speech before the New England Anti-Slavery Society, but his rejection of a return to his homeland and his emphasis on the kinship between free blacks in the North and slaves in the South, rather than on a kinship with Africa, was part of a wider movement among black activists after the 1820s. Blacks increasingly moved away from identifying themselves as Africans, which had been illustrated by the use of *African* in the name of the churches, benevolent societies, fraternal societies, and schools, and toward a use of the term *Colored* instead, a self-understanding that formed the basis of a connectedness that supported collective action, as evidenced by the use of the term to describe the meetings of the "Colored Citizens" of Boston that Johnson helped lead. When black activists self-identified as *Colored Citizens* or *Colored Americans,* they rejected the negative connotations that surrounded terms like *Negroes* and *Africans. Colored* acknowledged a racial unity, but spurned any suggestion that difference implied inferiority, and the use of this term by David Walker suggests the revolutionary implications it could contain.[39] The distance that separated the Kissi child kidnapped while gathering figs with his aunt from the radical Boston abolitionist cannot be measured in miles. His long journey, his shifting roles, his changing locales, demonstrate that his identity was not static and fixed, but rather subject to time and place, closely linked to the specific goals and contexts that shaped his life strategies. Even though he rejected colonization and showed no desire to return to Africa, his impassioned speech before the New England Anti-Slavery Society in which he celebrated the communal virtues of his African homeland demonstrates that he had not simply forgotten or rejected the values he learned there as a child, but rather wove them into his own vision of a better American society.

4

Navigating a Way to Freedom

THE PARTIES GATHERED in Judge William H. Robertson's chambers in Katonah, New York, on Wednesday morning, August 12, 1857, for a hearing that would decide the fate of a five-year-old girl named Ellen, described as a "bright-eyed, light-complexioned little girl," who was "smilingly unconscious" of her role in the proceedings. Ellen had been brought north in April 1857 by Louisa and Eugenia Kerr, wealthy sisters from Savannah, Georgia, who came to New York for an extended stay and planned to keep Ellen with them there. The hearing was prompted by Ellen's grandfather, now calling himself John Bull but better known as Dimmock Charlton, who had once been owned by the Kerr family along with his wife, their children, and grandchildren. Charlton had managed to purchase his freedom and was desperately trying to free the rest of his family. By bringing Ellen to New York, the Kerr sisters had unwittingly given him a chance to fight for his granddaughter's freedom. Charlton followed the Kerr sisters to New York City and took his story to the press where he was praised as a "venerable and intelligent native African" whose "face is an honest one," and whose "integrity and reliability are so well vouched for that it would be found difficult to doubt or discredit his story."[1]

When the Kerr sisters learned of Charlton's quest through those newspaper stories, they fled to the home of a friend, David A. Griffin, in Sing Sing, located in Westchester County about thirty miles up the Hudson River from New York City. There they hoped to hide themselves and the child, but sympathetic residents informed Charlton of their whereabouts. Charlton was indeed fortunate that the sisters chose Westchester

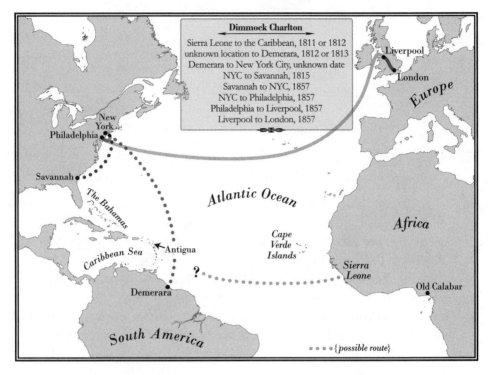

Map 8. Dimmock Charlton

County as their hiding place, because his case came to the attention of the county's most prominent abolitionist and lawyer, John Jay, who had a reputation for taking on fugitive slave cases pro bono—and for winning them. Jay was the namesake and grandson of the Founding Father whose family estate was located outside Bedford in Westchester County. Like many of the Founders, the first John Jay was a slaveholder though, unlike many others, he freed his slaves and embraced manumission and emancipation.[2] His second son William, the younger John Jay's father, was a committed abolitionist. William spent much of his life in Westchester County where he served as a county judge from 1818 to 1842 when the efforts of anti-abolitionist Democrats in the county forced him off the bench. He embraced a wide range of reform movements, and he was an early supporter of the American Anti-Slavery Society. In a generous eulogy delivered at Jay's funeral, Frederick Douglass proclaimed that "his mightiest works were wrought for us." Jay left Douglass $1,000 to assist runaway slaves.[3]

John inherited his father's anti-slavery views. As an undergraduate at Columbia College, he was a founder of the Young Man's Abolition Society in 1834. That same year he helped protect the property of prominent abolitionists like Arthur Tappan from mobs in anti-abolition riots in the city. He became a successful corporate attorney in New York City. He also launched very public campaigns against the Episcopal Church's conservative position on slavery and in support of the African American St. Philip's Episcopal Church request for admission to the Diocesan Convention. He had already successfully represented several fugitive slaves in high-profile cases, at no cost to the African Americans involved, and Charlton was very fortunate that fate had led the Kerrs to Jay's home turf.[4]

Jay and Judge Robertson were from very different backgrounds—Robertson's was humble compared to Jay's—but they were politically allied. Westchester County usually leaned Democratic, but both Jay and Robertson were Whigs who moved quickly into the new Republican Party. Judge Robertson was born in Westchester County in 1823 and educated in the newly established public school and at Bedford Academy. He taught school for three years, and then he trained for the law with Judge Robert S. Hart of Bedford. He began his political career in 1845 when he was elected superintendent of public schools. He was elected county judge in 1855, when he joined the Republican Party, and served in that capacity for twelve years. Like many Republicans, he had been a member of the Whig Party and a supporter of Henry Clay. He was regarded as "one of the shrewdest and ablest of the Republican politicians in the State of New York." He was a skilled campaigner known to visit the local bars and work the beer pumps himself while singing "We'll set them up again, boys, what'll yer have? Speak often and fast." His earthy campaigning style was said to "hypnotize" even the Democratic voters, though it would not have appealed to the patrician Jay.[5] There is no evidence that Robertson showed an interest in the abolition cause despite his political leanings.

The politics of abolition divided Westchester County, probably one reason that Robertson avoided it. The tentacles of the Cotton Kingdom extended even to this county which was home to both a manufacturer of cotton gins and of cotton gin saws. The county's newspapers were also divided over the issue and violence sometimes erupted, especially around presidential campaigns. William Jay was president of the

Westchester County Anti-Slavery Society when it took the controversial step of calling on its members to support candidates who favored the cause. As a result, a riot broke out in a meeting of the Anti-Slavery Society in Bedford courthouse a few months later. A mob attacked the courthouse, and William Jay had to dismiss the meeting and flee before he was carried "home upon a rail." Commenting on a letter from William Jay criticizing Daniel Webster's position on slavery, the *Hudson River Chronicle*, hostile to abolition, alleged that its proponents were "more friendly to the abolition of Slavery than they are to their own Country—and were they left to choose between the extension of slavery, and the dissolution of the Union—they would prefer the latter." John Thomas Scharf, a nineteenth-century historian of the county's history, wrote that while the county's residents were opposed to the extension of slavery, support for abolition was weak until the passage of the Fugitive Slave Act which pushed more people into the anti-slavery camp.[6]

These sharp differences over issues of slavery and abolition in the county heightened interest in Ellen's case. Hers was not, strictly speaking, a fugitive slave case, though the agitation over that law helps explain the extensive newspaper coverage of the case and this must have worked to Jay's advantage. Jay was able to get a writ of *habeas corpus* from Judge Robertson to prohibit the women from taking the child from the area before the case could be settled. The Kerr sisters launched a fund-raising campaign for the $350 their brother demanded for the child in order to purchase her freedom, and they claimed only to have the child's best interest at heart, but that effort quickly backfired with the public when the press reported that Charlton had paid Kerr to free his entire family but had been cheated by his master.

The Kerr sisters were not native Southerners; the family immigrated to Savannah from Ireland in the 1830s and, like many immigrants to the region, quickly adapted to its mores. Sisters Eugenia and Louisa Kerr had joined Savannah's Hibernian Society by 1839. In 1840 they purchased a desirable lot for $800 from Michael Dillon, a fellow Hibernian Society member, and built a matching pair of elegant townhouses. Unlike townhouse rows where the entrance to each house is situated on the same side, this pair employed reflecting plans to create a large outdoor living area in between them. Ellen and her family would have lived in the servants' quarters in the rear.[7]

In the hearing, Louisa Kerr testified that her brother, James Kerr of Savannah, had owned Ellen's entire large family, but he had sold Ellen's mother and then her grandmother "neglected" her. She described a relationship that was in part maternal and in part purely economic, a relationship grounded partly in emotions and partly in the chattel principle. The girl was valued at $400, Louisa explained, because *"her light complexion increased her value,"* an unwitting reminder to northerners that light-complexioned enslaved girls fetched a high price from predatory slave owners. She claimed that neither she nor her sister wanted to return Ellen to slavery, but added that neither they nor their brother could afford to lose the value of the child. She observed that her brother had discounted Ellen's price from $400 to $350, but could go no lower. The Kerr women planned to live in New York for several years with only occasional visits to Savannah, and they thought Ellen would be better cared for with them. Louisa also said that she was "very reluctant to have the child taken" from her since "I am attached to her, and wish to keep her with me," she explained. And she added that she had "already commenced to educate her." Historian Deborah Gray White found that "sometimes genuine affection flowed between white mistresses and slave children," and the childless Kerr sisters may well have genuinely cared for Ellen and her welfare, though they still kept their eyes on the bottom line. It was also not unusual for mistresses to educate their favored slaves. Their relationship with Ellen was so close in part because the Kerrs had sold Ellen's mother despite Ellen's youth, and their criticism of Ellen's grandmother and grandfather as caretakers was not unusual among slaveholding women.[8]

Jay argued persuasively that "no doubt could be reasonably entertained in regard to the law of the case, and the rights of the child." The only legal basis to keep the child enslaved, he argued, would be to claim that she was brought to New York in transit without any intention to remain there, but Louisa's testimony made it clear that their stay was to be a protracted, open-ended one. He acknowledged that the Kerrs might be ignorant of the laws of the state, but that did not provide any defense. Louisa knew that the trial was going badly for her, and she became "greatly affected." After hearing Jay's arguments, she had "no doubt" that Ellen was free according to New York law, but she did not want the child to be turned over to her grandfather, "whom she very heartily denounced." Judge Robertson agreed with Jay's views of the case, and ruled that Ellen was free, but Louisa's impassioned attack on Charlton's character gave him pause. David Griffin, acting on Louisa's behalf, requested that she be appointed Ellen's guardian. Robertson refused to release Ellen into her grandfather's custody "without further inquiry," but he was equally reluctant to return her to the Kerrs. He placed her in care of the constable, Zeno Hoyt, until he determined what would be in the child's best interest. Louisa and Griffin "lingered awhile," attempting to persuade Robertson to change his mind, but he was resolute. Louisa and Ellen had an emotional parting—the child was too young to celebrate her freedom and only understood that she was being separated from "an all sufficient friend."[9]

The parties reassembled in Robertson's chambers on Monday, August 17, to hear his final ruling on Ellen's custody. Louisa tried every avenue to win custody. She promised that she would execute a deed of manumission, though she had to admit that the legality of such a document would be questionable since she was not the sole owner of Ellen. She also offered to get guarantees from prominent friends in New York City for Ellen's safety, but these appeals fell on deaf ears. Jay argued that the County Court had no authority to appoint a guardian, Robertson agreed, and Ellen was placed in her grandfather's custody. Charlton was not in a position to provide for her, and his intention was "to place her in a family where she will be kindly, judiciously and carefully brought up." It was a cruel irony that Charlton succeeded in winning his granddaughter's freedom, but that did nothing to reunite his family and, in fact, only further divided them. Her case demonstrates that not only the African slave trade separated children from their parents; even successfully winning freedom suits could have that tragic outcome for once enslaved families. The abolitionists who had championed Charlton's cause expected that he would turn the child over to one of their number, but he had been cheated out of his freedom too many times to take the risk of having Ellen remain in the Unites States. They were not happy with his decision to send her to a Canadian family instead, but Charlton was fearful that she would somehow be reclaimed by the Kerrs and removed her from any threat of re-enslavement.[10]

Charlton's future was uncertain. He had struggled to gain freedom for himself and his granddaughter, but he was destitute and the rest of his family remained enslaved in Savannah. He had no desire to return to Savannah and appealed to the British consul, claiming to be a British citizen based on his service on a British warship during the War of 1812. Charlton's detractors raised questions about the claims he made in his remarkable narrative, and it is difficult to verify many aspects of his story. Joseph S. Fay, a New Yorker engaged in the shipping business in Savannah, wrote a letter to the editor after reading the initial article about Charlton's quest to reclaim Ellen. Fay claimed that he had known Charlton for over twenty years, but he only heard Charlton claim British citizenship in the last two years, something he regarded as "highly suspicious."[11]

In order to assess Charlton's claim, it is necessary to return to his enslavement in West Africa and his experience on board the slave ship that carried him across the Atlantic. He reported that he was born around 1799 among the "Kissee" people along a large river or, in his words, "away up on the fresh water." His name was Tallen and, when he was twelve years old, he and six other boys were captured in a slave raid by the "Mandingos" who spent four weeks marching him and others of his ethnic group from the interior to the coast to be sold. This part of the narrative meshes with the history of the slave trade in this period. Like Robert Johnson, he was a member of the Kissi ethnic group, a further indication of their numbers among enslaved Africans shipped from the Senegambia. While Johnson was simply grabbed in what Benjamin Lawrance refers to as an "opportunistic abduction," Tallen was taken in a targeted raid aimed at taking children, a more highly organized form of enslavement. "Mandingo" was the name Europeans gave to the Mandinka whose trading communities lay on both sides of the Gambia River and who were important players in the slave trade in the Senegambia by 1800. Some of those Mandinka traders worked as agents of the slave traders on the coast. The name "Tallen" does not appear on any list of names of enslaved Africans from the Sierra Leone region. The closest match would be the name "Tali" which could have easily been understood as "Tallen." Indeed, northern abolitionists who heard him recount the story of his early life observed that he spoke "broken English" and that "it may be easy for him to mispronounce or the hearer to misapprehend the name by which he calls his people," or, one assumes, the name he called himself. He did not give the name of the place where he was enslaved, if he ever knew it, but the history of the slave trade in the early nineteenth century strongly suggests that he was sold into the Atlantic slave trade on the coast of Sierra Leone. When the British outlawed the Atlantic slave trade in 1808, the trade shifted away from areas like the Gold Coast which had predominated in the previous century toward more isolated areas where the British were unable to control it. The illegal slave trade expanded in two areas in Sierra Leone, the Rio Pongo and the Gallinas / Sherbro Island region, where shallow creeks and rivers allowed the African slave traders to hide their barracoons from the British patrols. Evidence demonstrates that Kissi-speaking peoples composed the largest proportion (over 20 percent) of slaves sent to the Caribbean from the Rio Pongo in the early nineteenth century, and about half of that number was sent from the Gallinas / Sherbro Island region which was more distant from the Kissi homeland. It is most likely, then, that Tallen/Charlton would have shipped out on board a ship from the Rio Pongo and it is less likely, though entirely possible, that he could have been on a ship departing from the Gallinas / Sherbro River area. It is even possible that he could have been sold into slavery by Elizabeth Cleveland's relatives on the Banana Islands or by the Holmans on the Rio Pongo (see Map 5 in Chapter 2).[12]

Charlton did not give the name of the slave ship that carried him across the Atlantic, but he did identify it as a Spanish ship. That information meshes well with the history of the trade for this period. The Spanish predominated in the slave trade at its beginning and at its end, but largely fell out of the business during the century and a half when the trade was at its peak. It was only after the British and Americans outlawed the trade in 1808 that the Spanish reentered the slave trading business in a major way, and that trade was based primarily out of Cuba. Between 1811 and 1820, Spanish ships left Africa with an estimated 124,236 enslaved Africans, numbers second only to the Portuguese. The majority of those slaves came from Senegambia (29,166), but the numbers from Sierra Leone were a close second (22,624).[13]

The Spanish slaver left the West African coast and headed out across the Atlantic, and Tallen and the other captives suffered terribly; he recalled "many of them dying for want of fresh air and exercise during the three weeks they were stowed away in her suffocating 'between decks.'" The ship would have been far out into the Atlantic when it was captured and seized three weeks later "by an English war-brig." The British relied on the belligerent right of search to stop and seize ships belonging to hostile powers during the Napoleonic Wars, and once a ship was captured it was taken to a prize court for trial. He did not identify the British ship, or give the location where the trial was conducted or where the ship was condemned and he and the other captives were freed. If we survey only Spanish slave ships which left Sierra Leone in 1811 or 1812 and were captured by the British navy then tried in Caribbean courts, the list of possibilities narrows considerably. The most likely candidates would be the *San Jose y Animas,* which was tried in the Vice-Admiralty Court in Antigua, or the *S. Isabel,* tried in the same court in the Bahamas. The *San Jose y Animas* left Sierra Leone with 239 enslaved Africans on board and 211 remained alive when the ship was captured. The *Sancta Isabel* left Sierra Leone with 265 slaves and 238 survived the Middle Passage. The ship had been at sea for thirty-eight days, close to Tallen's estimate, made many years after the event, that he spent three weeks at sea. That information is not available for the *San Jose y Animas.*[14]

Why consider only ships condemned and tried in the Caribbean ports when many more were seized and tried in Sierra Leone? That decision is guided by Tallen's claim he had "been christened 'John Bull' on board the British vessel," and that he "was sent to the British brig *Peacock,* to serve as cabin-boy." Enslaved Africans who were freed from captured slavers in Sierra Leone were resettled there. So many liberated Africans came from the Kissi people that they had their own town there, and had Tallen been freed after trial in Sierra Leone, he would have likely settled there. Liberated Africans who were freed in Antigua or the Bahamas could be apprenticed to planters or business owners on those islands, some were taken to Sierra Leone, and others joined the West India Regiment or enlisted in the British Navy which was particularly desperate for sailors during this period. Records from Antigua and the Bahamas reveal that about one quarter of the Africans liberated there enlisted in the British Navy. There is no record, however, of any of those Africans joining the crew of the *Peacock,* but the records are incomplete. It is also possible that Tallen, now known as John Bull, could have been transferred onto the *Peacock* at a later date.[15]

Adding to the mystery of how John Bull came on board the *Peacock,* Thomas Threthowen, a crewman from the warship who was interviewed in the 1850s when Dimmock Charlton was trying to substantiate his story, reported that the African came on board the ship at Demerara.

Contemporary reports from crewmen also noted that three men "and one boy" boarded at Demerara.[16] If that version of the story is accurate, then Bull must have somehow made his way to Demerara and either he voluntarily joined the ship's crew or could have been coerced. As historian Denver Brunsman observed, the British impressed sailors in large numbers all around the world, but press gangs "did most of their work—and damage—in the Atlantic." British law prohibited the impressment of foreigners, but the British did not recognize Africans as foreign citizens, and they were sometimes compelled to serve on board British vessels. Many Africans also served voluntarily on British ships—enslaved Africans often escaped to British ships—and some estimates place the percentage of blacks in British crews as high as 25 percent, though exact numbers are hard to come by, and those numbers probably declined after the eighteenth century.[17]

However he came on board, he was just in time to witness the *Peacock*'s dramatic duel with the U.S.S. *Hornet*. The H.M.S. *Peacock*, an 18-gun brig-sloop, was launched in 1806 and by 1812 was under the command of William Peake, a member of a prominent naval family. She was assigned to the Jamaica station in 1812. In his magisterial history of the United States Navy's exploits during the War of 1812, future president Theodore Roosevelt looked back on "that period of our history during which our navy stood at the highest pitch of its fame." With six frigates and a handful of smaller craft, the tiny U.S. Navy seemed poorly prepared to take on the British Navy, the world's largest. One of many disadvantages the U.S. Navy faced in this David versus Goliath contest was that because of the worldwide reach of the British Empire, British ships could find safe harbors virtually anywhere, but U.S. ships had no safe harbors outside of the United States. Nonetheless, U.S. ships set out on far-flung cruises in search of British prizes and targets. According to Roosevelt, these cruises were "something *sui generis* in modern warfare." "It was an unprecedented thing," he wrote, "for a small frigate to cruise a year and a half in enemy's waters, and to supply herself during that time, purely from captured vessels, with everything— cordage, sails, guns, anchors, provisions and medicines, and even money to pay the officers and men!" One of these cruisers was the U.S.S. *Hornet* which set out in October 1812 for South America and the Caribbean. One of the most celebrated American victories over the ships of the

British navy during the War of 1812 was the U.S.S. *Hornet*'s engagement with the H.M.S. *Peacock*.[18]

Sailing around the northern coast of South America in February 1813, the *Hornet* captured a British brig, the *Resolution*, with $23,000 in specie, and on February 24 the ship reached Demerara. A Dutch colony, Demerara had been captured by the British in 1781 who returned it to the Dutch in 1801 but quickly recaptured it a year later. By 1807 the British had acquired Demerara, Berbice, and Trinidad along with other territory in the Caribbean, all ripe for development, giving the British control of over ⅔ of sugar supplies.[19] Off the mouth of the Demerara River, Captain Lawrence spied a British vessel, the brig *Peacock*, commanded by Captain Peake. At 4:20 P.M. the *Peacock* hoisted her colors, the two ships maneuvered for battle, and at 5:25 they exchanged their first broadsides at the short distance of half a pistol shot. The *Peacock* suffered serious damage while the *Hornet*'s hull was unscathed. Thomas Threthowen, a sailor on the *Peacock*, recalled hearing John Bull utter "several shrieks" when the main mast fell overboard. The ships reengaged quickly, and Captain Peake was killed along with four of his men under heavy fire. The *Peacock* surrendered after only fourteen minutes. Sailors from the *Hornet* quickly boarded the ship which was sinking fast. In an effort to save the ship, they threw the guns overboard and tried to plug the holes in the hull, but those efforts failed. They tried desperately to evacuate the crew, including many who were seriously wounded, but the ship went down so quickly that four of the *Hornet*'s crewmen and thirteen British sailors drowned when the ship went under. The *Peacock* had a crew of 130. Eighteen men died, including the captain, and thirty others were wounded. Overcrowded, short of water and supplies, the *Hornet* set sail for home and arrived in New York on March 19. There, the British captives publicly thanked the crew of the *Hornet*, "We ceased to consider ourselves prisoners," they wrote, and thanked their captors for providing them with "everything that friendship could dictate."[20]

According to Bull, a Lieutenant Harrison left him with Judge Thomas Charlton in Savannah who proposed that the boy be left with him permanently, but the lieutenant refused, saying that since he was a prisoner of war that was out of his control and that Congress would have to decide what to do with the unusual captive. He did leave the boy in the judge's care temporarily, and after two months he wrote Charlton asking for the boy's return, but the judge replied that he had died of a fever. Charlton called all his slaves together and announced that from that point forward, John Bull would be known as Dimmock Charlton.[21]

Was the judge a liar and a thief? Judge Thomas Usher Pulaski Charlton was one of Savannah's most respected citizens. Born in 1779 and trained as a lawyer, he served as judge on the Eastern Circuit of Georgia from 1807 to 1811. During the War of 1812 he served as chairman of the city's Committee of Public Safety, and he served six terms as the city's mayor before his death in 1835. While he may seem like an unlikely person to kidnap and illegally enslave someone, he was protected by his status. The *Anti-Slavery Reporter* explained that the crime had to be understood by the code of Southern slaveholders which held that John Bull "belonged to nobody—[he] was a mere waif and estray which the fortunes of war had landed upon our shores from the coast of Africa, and anybody might pick it up who would be at the trouble."[22]

It is also possible that the judge purchased Dimmock illegally. South Carolina was the last state to import slaves before the trade was outlawed in 1808. Even after the United States outlawed the trade, imports into the lower South continued, especially in the years immediately following the ban. In 1814, for example, the port collector in Darien, Georgia, wrote the Secretary of the Treasury that "African and West India negroes are almost daily illicitly introduced into Georgia, for sale or settlement, or passing through it to the territories of the United States for similar purposes." Some of those slaves could have found their way into the busy Charleston market. In some cases, the U.S. Navy seized American ships carrying slaves and brought them to Charleston for trial. When those ships were condemned, the Africans on board were placed under the authority of the city marshal who hired them out but, in fact, the liberated Africans often disappeared into the local slave population. There were similar reports from Savannah. Whether Judge Charlton acquired Dimmock from a Lieutenant Harrison or acquired him by other illegal means, he would have had a motive to dispose of him quickly.[23]

Charlton wasted no time in selling Dimmock; the very next day he sent him to the shop of John P. Setze, a tailor. Setze was a native of France, born in 1797, who immigrated to Charleston in 1815. After spending the day there, Dimmock told Setze that he was ready to go home, and Setze told him that he had purchased him from the judge. Dimmock found an opportunity to escape, and he ran back to Judge Charlton's house. He reached the house, ran inside, and asked the judge if he had sold him. The judge said that he had not, but just then Setze burst into the room, grabbed Dimmock, and began to drag him away. The judge pulled Setze aside and spoke to him in hushed tones. He then told Dimmock that he wanted him to go with Setze and learn the tailor's trade, but the frightened boy refused to go. The judge then told Setze to take Dimmock to Augusta where the tailor owned another shop. There would be less danger that Dimmock would run away or that the judge's theft would come to light. After thirteen months there, Setze sold Dimmock to Captain Davis Dubois.[24]

Dubois was captain of steamers running between Augusta and Savannah in the 1820s, and by the time he purchased Dimmock he was about to take charge of a new steamer, the *General Washington,* to make that familiar run. He employed Dimmock as steward. The ship was described as "elegant," one of several intended to run as packets between Georgia's two largest cities. Set apart by the "superior power of their engines, and their light draught of water," they were expected to move more quickly than stage coaches. The fact that she was to be "commanded by Captain Dubois, long advantageously known as a commander," was an additional advantage. The Savannah press noted in October 1826 that the ship would begin operations as soon as her northern-built engines had arrived. Once she was in operation, the *General Washington* made what had been a 2½ day voyage in 33 hours. After two years, Dubois sold Dimmock to Captain John Robinson of Savannah who was an agent for a steamboat company making that same run.[25]

Dimmock, by now a man in his late twenties, worked hard, learned the ways of the river, and became a supervising stevedore. The most important traffic on the Savannah River was cotton, and the river was the main artery moving the expanding cotton production of upstate Georgia to the port of Savannah. A crucial part of that traffic was the loading and unloading of the heavy bales on and off river- and ocean-going ships, a job requiring skill, strength, and stamina. The soaring volume of cotton exports from Savannah illustrate how valuable Dimmock's skills were. In 1825 almost 65,000 bags of cotton left the port, but by 1840 that number had increased to over 280,000 bags. When you consider that each of those heavy bags had to be loaded and un-loaded by human hands, then the scale of the work involved comes into focus. The city expanded along with the growth of the cotton trade; in 1810 the population was 5,195 and in 1840, 11,214, an astounding 161 percent increase compared to the 18 percent increase in Charleston's population.[26]

Since his skills were in such high demand, Dimmock convinced his master to allow him to hire out his time and, more importantly, his master agreed that he could purchase his freedom for $800. Hiring out was a common practice in southern cities, but a controversial one. Many whites in those cities were wary of the practice because of the degree of independence it gave slaves which they saw as undermining the system. Slaves who hired out their time escaped the direct supervision of their masters. They could choose their employers, negotiate wages and hours, and often find their own housing. A Savannah newspaper editor warned that the practice, "more than any other single cause," was destroying "in fact, if not in name, the relationship between master and servant." The promise of freedom was a powerful lure, and Dimmock worked hard and long to save that sum. On the day he handed Robinson the $800 in cash, his master pocketed the money, had Dimmock thrown in jail, and quickly sold him. Dimmock's loss illustrates that hiring out did not, in fact, undermine the most fundamental relationship between master and slave. Dimmock remained chattel—what belonged to him belonged to his master—and agreements like the one made between Dimmock and his master had no standing before the law and could not be legally enforced. Such cases were by no means uncommon; historian Jonathan Martin suggests that cases where masters cheated slaves out of their purchase money probably exceeded those where masters honored the agreement.[27]

James Kerr purchased Dimmock from Robinson and continued to let him hire out his time. When Dimmock told Kerr that Robinson had cheated him out of his purchase money, Kerr said that Robinson was "a damned scoundrel, but *he* would deal justly with him." Dimmock believed that he had been sold for $700, and that was the price that he and Kerr agreed upon. Once again Dimmock set to work. He paid the sum in two installments, one of $300 and four months later he paid the remaining $400. He later learned that, in fact, Kerr had only paid Robinson $450, but at least Kerr assured Dimmock that he was now a free man.

By this time Dimmock had married an enslaved woman owned by a Mr. Pratt, and the couple had two daughters. According to Dimmock, Pratt had brought an entire family from Nassau, Bahamas, including his wife, her sisters, and their parents, and illegally enslaved them. While that allegation cannot be confirmed, it is possible. Ships regularly passed between Savannah and the Bahamas, and there were documented cases of free people from Barbados and the Caribbean being kidnapped and enslaved in the United States. In 1845 the British government expressed concern about boys being kidnapped from the Bahamas and sold into slavery in Florida, indicating that such kidnappings did occur.[28]

Pratt was a good master, but eventually fell on hard times and was forced to sell his slaves. He offered to sell them at a good price to someone locally who would not send them out of Savannah. Dimmock went to Kerr and asked him to help purchase and free his family, and Kerr agreed to purchase them for $2,000. Dimmock had saved $1,500 which he gave Kerr, who then purchased Dimmock's wife and children. Only later did Dimmock learn from Pratt that Kerr had paid only $600 for them. When Dimmock confronted Kerr about the funds, Kerr laughed and assured him that he had the money in the bank for him and that his wife and children were now free. Kerr allowed Dimmock to hire out his time, which allowed him to accumulate enough money to purchase freedom for himself. Kerr urged the family to live quietly with him under his "protection," and for several years the family lived secure in their freedom.[29]

That illusion was shattered when Kerr suddenly sold Dimmock, his wife, their three daughters, and their son, each to a different master. He did not sell Dimmock's mother-in-law or his granddaughter Ellen. Kerr had never legally manumitted any of them and, once again, Dimmock had no legal recourse. He had long thought that he had a claim to British citizenship, a claim that he knew could lead to his freedom. He had kept that claim hidden for years, fearful that if he revealed it he would be sold inland to an isolated plantation or farther south where he would be unable to pursue his claim. He knew that so long as he lived in Savannah he could earn money and have some chance of pursuing his claim. The sale of his family drove him to desperation, and he appealed to the British consul in Savannah, Edmund Molyneaux, for assistance, but Molyneaux, himself a slaveholder with business interests to protect, refused to intervene on his behalf. Dimmock also outlined his claim to freedom to his new master, Mr. Hudson, who believed enough of his story to become nervous then sell him to a Mr. Davidson who sold liquor near the Savannah market. Dimmock worked for Davidson for two years. When Dimmock recounted his claim for Davidson, he, like Kerr, believed his story and feared for his investment. He sent Dimmock to be sold by a slave dealer, this time at the purchaser's risk. Benjamin Garman took that risk for the sum of $550. He allowed Dimmock to hire out his time, and Dimmock again saved enough money to purchase his freedom. Unlike the previous masters, Garman honored their agreement.[30]

A year later, Dimmock sailed for New York City on the steamer *Alabama*. He feared to remain any longer in a slave state, and he hoped to further his claims to British citizenship and to gain freedom for his family. Louisa and Eugenia Kerr unwittingly assisted Dimmock in his quest by bringing Ellen to New York City. After Ellen was freed, Dimmock continued his efforts to free his family. He traveled from New York to Philadelphia where he sought assistance from prominent abolitionists there. He paid a call on Charlotte Forten, a well-known, free black writer and activist, who recorded in her journal, "Had a visit from 'Dimmock Charlton,' an interesting old, African, whose story I read some time ago in the 'Standard'." His critics followed him, however, and hostile reports about him appeared in the New York *National Anti-Slavery Standard* where it was alleged that he was "entirely unworthy of confidence," "wanting in principle," "unwilling to work," and "collecting money in Philadelphia under various false pretenses." The newspaper charged that he had raised considerable funds which he had squandered, and that they had been asked to publicly denounce him to prevent him from fleecing others. His friends rallied around him to counter those charges, including John Jay who blamed these accusations on people who resented Charlton for sending Ellen to Canada; according to Jay, that was "the only charge they have against him." Mary L. and Susan H. Cox were among his most devoted supporters. Born into a Quaker family, the sisters operated a school in the city where they taught English and French and devoted their lives to the anti-slavery cause. They edited and published his narrative along with a number of testimonials to his good character.[31]

Eager to prove his British citizenship, Charlton traveled to Liverpool carrying a letter of introduction from John Jay to John Cropper, one of the best known abolitionists in the city. The Croppers were Quakers, and John Cropper's father had made a fortune as the owner of packets running between Britain and America. Renowned for his philanthropy, when a letter arrived addressed simply to the most generous man in Liverpool, the postal service delivered it to him. Harriet Beecher Stowe visited the city in 1853, and she was his guest at his handsome estate, Dingle Bank, where the family's tableware was adorned with the famous anti-slavery image of an African in chains and the motto "Am I Not A Man and a Brother" as a constant reminder of the plight of the enslaved.[32]

No doubt with Cropper's assistance, Charlton made his way to London where he found Threthowen in Greenwich Hospital. The London *Anti-Slavery Reporter* took up his cause, but observed that it would take much time and effort for him to establish his claim for British citizenship, time that someone of his age and in his impoverished condition did not have to spend. Charlton indicated that he would like to immigrate to Canada and expressed a desire to find employment, but for the moment he was living as "a charge on the benevolent." In an 1866 letter to L. A. Chamerovzow, secretary of the British and Foreign Anti-Slavery Society, he described himself as a fugitive needing aid. There his story ends.[33]

If we take Charlton's narrative at face value, his story was a dramatic one that began with his enslavement in West Africa, the capture of the slave ship and his liberation, service on a British warship, and his illegal enslavement in Savannah where, over and over again, unscrupulous masters cheated him out of his attempts to purchase his freedom. Like many of the Africans who traveled through the Atlantic World, Charlton's self-identification shifted multiple times. Virtually every voyage he took resulted in a change of status and name. Time and again he managed to survive and even triumph in the face of grave dangers and enormous difficulties. His experiences reveal his ability to maneuver across oceans and through a complex world of competing national rivalries. He escaped enslavement as a child only to be enslaved later in the United States, both times illegally. Even then he struggled for decades to free himself and his family, and while he was not able to gain freedom for his entire family, he did secure freedom for himself and his granddaughter.

But is his story true? While there is little doubt that he was from the Kissi nation—there was no advantage in claiming one ethnicity over another—he may or may not have been liberated by the British and placed on board the H.M.S. *Peacock.* Contemporaries were skeptical that Charlton was on the *Peacock* and suggested that he made that claim only recently in order to secure British protection. His story was published in the abolitionist press, and even some abolitionists questioned his veracity. There are enough gaps in Charlton's narrative to raise suspicions. His story of how he joined the ship's crew is frustratingly sketchy. Charlton's critic Joseph Fay rightly identified a compelling reason for Charlton to claim that he served on board the *Peacock,* the chance to gain British protection and citizenship, and Charlton himself appealed to British consul Edmund Molyneaux in Savannah who apparently was not convinced of the truth of his claims. As we have seen, British consuls went to great lengths to protect Africans and African Americans that they believed to be under British protection and illegally enslaved. The dramatic story of the battle between the *Peacock* and the *Hornet,* largely forgotten today but famous in the nineteenth century, also increased interest in his case when he left Savannah for the North. Although his account of his time on board the *Peacock* is short on specifics, there is enough information to raise another question—how would Charlton have learned the story of the *Peacock* at all? Charlton himself provided one possibility. He claimed in his narrative that several of the Spanish sailors from the ship that carried him across the Atlantic joined the *Peacock*'s crew, and that one of those men, whom he said was named Mingo, was his "fast friend" in Savannah. He reported that Mingo "was familiar with the whole story." Did he listen to his friend recount the dramatic tale of the battle between the *Hornet* and the *Peacock?* Did he commit that story to memory and use it as a clever ploy to secure his freedom? That possibility cannot be fully discounted. On the other hand, Louisa Kerr, who was no friend to Charlton, testified that *"she had long known that Dimmock claimed to be a British subject, and to have been taken a prisoner of war in the brig* Peacock, *and she believed it to be true."*

The strongest independent evidence that he was on board the *Peacock* is the testimony of Thomas Threthowen. Threthowen was a crewman on board the ship, but his testimony was taken over forty years after the event at a time when he lay ill in Greenwich Hospital. The fact that he said in his affidavit that the sea battle took place in 1812 rather than 1813 raises some concern about his memory. The surviving crew manifests, logs, and daybooks from the *Peacock* confirm that a Thomas Trithowen, fourteen years of age and a native of Kerwin, Cornwall, had volunteered for service, and was classified as a "Boy of the 3rd Class." Those records do not show John Bull or any other African on board the ship (the records give a place of birth for the crew members), nor do they show any Spaniards on board apart from Salva Amazeur Basse-tore from Tenerife. The crew included a number of foreign sailors from Germany, France, Sweden, and Norway, and four sailors from the United States. Also among the crew was Jonathan Harrison, a native of Belfast. Was this the Harrison who was somehow responsible for Charlton's en-slavement? The absence of John Bull from the ship's surviving records cannot be considered conclusive evidence that he was *not* on board. If he were on board the ship, he and the Spanish sailors he mentioned would have come on board in the Caribbean, and those records went down with the ship.

How he could have been transferred from the U S.S. *Hornet* to en-slavement in Savannah is the most suspect part of his narrative, and much hinges on that chain of events. There were questions raised about his chain of ownership in Georgia, and that would indicate that however he arrived in Savannah, he was a part of the illegal slave trade. Whether he was smuggled in by a lieutenant in the U.S. Navy or through some other means, his experience opens a window onto the illegal enslave-ment of Africans in the South after 1808. Historians have long debated just how large that illegal trade was, but Charlton's enslavement is an important reminder that the link between Africa and the U.S. South was not completely severed by the 1808 ban.

Even if Charlton fabricated important parts of his narrative, that fabrication in itself is a remarkable and successful quest on the part of an enslaved African to gain his freedom. He demonstrated a sophisti-cated understanding of the Atlantic World and an ability to maneuver through that world with the goal of gaining freedom for himself and his family. While he was not completely successful in that quest, the fact that he freed himself and his grandchild against enormous odds must not be discounted. It has been commonplace to underestimate the knowledge and capabilities of enslaved Africans. They have often been portrayed as the least knowledgeable players in the drama of Atlantic enslavement, naïve captives from the African interior who were ignorant of the vast machine they were caught up in, enslaved in a new world they neither knew nor understood. Men like Tallen / John Bull / Dimmock Charlton do not fit those stereotypes, but rather show that while enslaved Africans may have entered the Atlantic World as children with little understanding of the fate that awaited them, they were able to grasp that world in all its complexity, and to use that knowledge to navigate their way through it.

5

Unidentified Africans Seek British Protection

THE THREE AFRICAN MEN waited until darkness fell, then broke out of the enclosure and made their way to the beach where a canoe was tied up. They were not long off the slave ship that had taken them from the West African coast and, after a voyage of many weeks, during which many of the men, women, and children on board fell sick and died, they were delivered to an island where they were purchased by a white man. They were taken to his plantation where they were put to work in the sugar cane fields, closely guarded, supervised, and punished when they failed to understand the commands that were shouted at them in a language they did not comprehend. Desperate to escape, the men jumped into the canoe and paddled out to sea. They had no idea of their location or direction, but they were free.

In February 1829 the British brig *Aurora*, originally from Dublin, sailed into Mobile harbor carrying a cargo of salt. En route to that port, the ship had encountered a canoe carrying three African men far out at sea in an "exhausted condition," fifty miles from the nearest land which was the island of Montserrat. Captain Joseph Proteus knew that the men were doomed if he left them at sea, so he picked them up and brought them to Mobile, Alabama, "from motives of humanity." The Collector of Customs there, Addin Lewis, threatened to seize the ship, claiming that Proteus had violated the U.S. laws against the African slave trade by bringing the men into Mobile. Proteus argued that he had no intention of selling the men and did not consider them slaves, but the collector seized the men and put them in jail until they could reach some conclusion about their status. Complicating matters even further, the men spoke no English and indeed, as James Baker, the British consul at

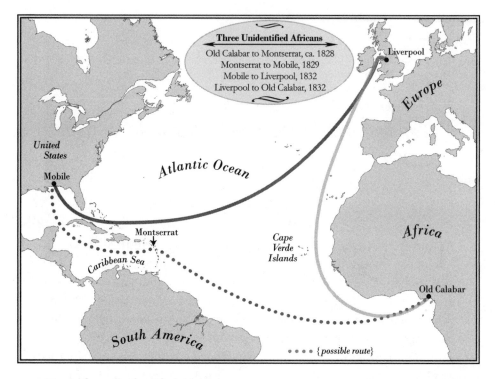

Map 9. Three Unidentified Africans

Mobile, reported, "They could not converse in any language which we understood here." From the view of the enslaved Africans, they had been picked up by another set of white men and jailed, and so, once more, they managed to escape from their captors. Since they spoke no European language, the men were clearly newly imported Africans, victims of the illegal slave trade who had escaped from one of the Caribbean islands.[1]

Again the men struck out without any idea of where they were going. They made their way out of the town and into the countryside. Here, too, were plantations, though different from the one they had escaped in the Caribbean. Without the aid of English or of any sense of geography, somehow they succeeded in eluding their captors and avoided arousing the suspicions of whites as they traveled through the countryside. Did they receive food and assistance from slaves in Alabama? It seems likely that they did, though their inability to communicate and their fear of the strange environment must have made that difficult. They ran for many miles before they were captured and jailed in Jackson, Mississippi, almost two hundred miles from Mobile.[2]

The jailor advertised them in the local newspaper, but no one stepped forward to claim them. Eventually, he advertised them for sale to pay their jail fees. James Baker perused newspapers from across the Deep South as part of his effort to keep himself up to date on any information that he might pass along to his superiors, and he saw the advertisement for the Africans and realized that they must be the escaped men from Mobile. He sent a messenger to Jackson to try to prevent their sale, but either the man arrived too late, and the men were sold before he could retrieve them, or the jailor refused to recognize that the consul had any claim on the men. In any event, they were sold and once again enslaved. Baker tried to trace them, but reported that "all research . . . was in vain until last winter, when by chance I discovered that they had again been taken up, as runaway Slaves, and were in the jail in Baton Rouge." The men had managed to escape yet again before being picked up near Baton Rouge, Louisiana, 175 miles from Jackson.[3]

This time Baker contacted the U.S. District Attorney for Louisiana and claimed that they were free men improperly taken from a British vessel, they were under British protection, and he demanded that they be returned to him in Mobile. The District Attorney consulted the U.S. Attorney General who contacted the Secretary of State. Eventually, the U.S. officials agreed with Baker and ordered the return of the Africans to Mobile. On April 6, 1832, the "three unfortunate Africans" were delivered to Baker "destitute of proper clothing." Baker bought clothes for the men, but since "it was impossible to make them comprehend the danger they were now exposed to from kidnappers had they been at large . . . it was thought most advisable for their protection to keep them in custody, instructions having been given to make them as comfortable as their situation would admit of." Once again the Africans found themselves jailed by white men, without understanding that this time they were not about to be sold into slavery. Charles Bankhead, British envoy to Washington, thanked the U.S. Secretary of State for "this humane and generous proceeding."[4]

Baker put the Africans on the first ship bound for Liverpool where they were turned over to the Collector of Customs in that port. Their arrival presented British officials with the question of their ultimate fate. Clearly, they could not simply be set at liberty in Liverpool. They

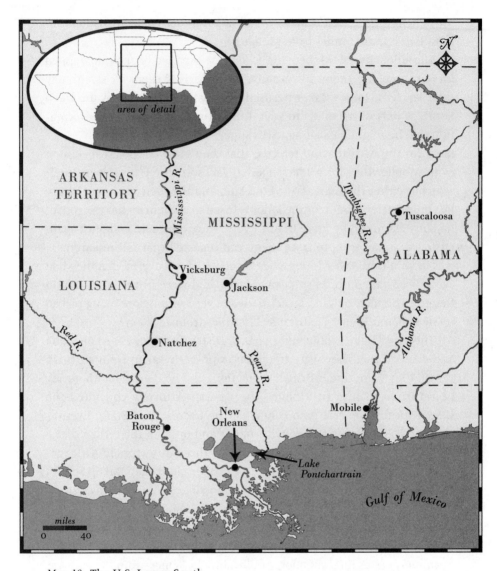

Map 10. The U.S. Lower South

could have been considered Liberated Africans, that is, Africans who were illegally enslaved and freed by the British, but instead the British officials agreed with Baker's assessment; they found that the "circumstances under which they were found at Sea do not show that they were slaves or that they fell within any of the provisions of the Slave Acts or under any restraints upon the Liberty of their Persons"—the men were simply free and should be returned to their country of origin. Apparently, the British were more successful in finding Africans who spoke their language, for they determined that the men had come from Old Calabar and should be returned to that place.[5]

Old Calabar was one of the slave-trading areas in west-central Africa most heavily impacted by the slave trade of the nineteenth century when the trade from West Africa became concentrated around the Rio Pongo-Rio Nunez and Gallinas regions of the Senegambia and in the Bights of Benin and Biafra. The Bight of Biafra supplied around 14 percent of the enslaved Africans sent to the Americas between 1800 and 1843. The creeks and lagoons that crisscrossed the Cross River delta, like those of the Rio Pongo, were ideal hiding places for slave factories, and slaves could be shipped down the Niger and Cross rivers from far inland and, in fact, from further inland than had been the case in the eighteenth century. About three-fourths of the slaves were taken in wars and raids in the Igbo-Ibibio area and sold to the coast by Aro traders. Efik traders in Old Calabar towns like Duke Town, important centers of the trade since the eighteenth century, continued to supply slaves to European traders.[6] Partly because of the British patrols, and the rapid expansion of the palm oil trade, the slave trade from Old Calabar declined dramatically after 1840. In the 1830s alone, the British liberated 17,622 captives from the Bight of Biafra while the palm oil trade increased from 3,000 tons in 1819 to 12,800 tons by 1839.[7]

Having identified the men as having been sent from Old Calabar, the Collector of Customs in Liverpool notified his superiors that he had arranged for passage for the men with Richard Lander who was preparing to leave Liverpool with three ships bound for Fernando Po, a British station near Old Calabar. Richard Lander and his brother John were preparing an expedition financed by a group of Liverpool merchants who wanted to establish a trade depot at the convergence of the Niger and Benue rivers. The son of an innkeeper in Cornwall, Richard had accompanied the Scottish explorer Hugh Clapperton to present-day

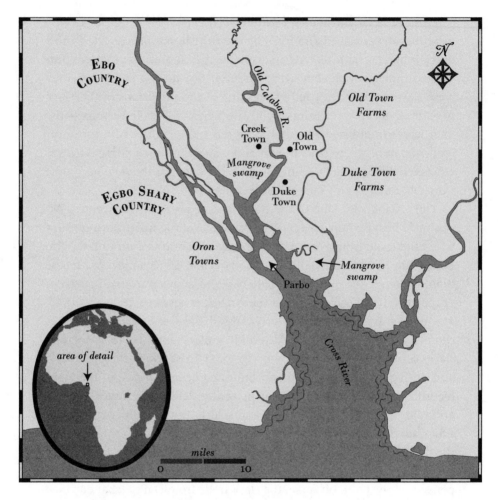

Map 11. Old Calabar

Nigeria on his 1825 expedition and returned as the only surviving European member of that team. He and his brother John led their own expedition up the Niger River in 1830 and spent about a year exploring the region. Their colorful journals of that expedition were published, and the brothers were celebrated for finding an important waterway into the African interior. Richard was awarded the Royal Geographical Society's first gold medal, a bounty of £100, and the brothers had an audience with King William IV. By 1832 they were ready to set out again. One of their three ships was made entirely of iron and was the first metal steamship to sail on the high seas.[8]

The expedition stopped at the island of Fernando Po, located in the Bight of Biafra twenty miles off the African coast, to make final preparations for the trip up the Niger. The Portuguese had been the first Europeans to claim the island in 1471, and they eventually exchanged it for the Spanish island of Trinidad. The Spanish established a settlement there in the 1760s, but abandoned it after several years. In the 1820s the British leased the island from Spain and established a base there for the use of the Africa Squadron that patrolled the coast to enforce the ban on the African slave trade. Illegal slavers took huge numbers of slaves from depots in the Bight of Biafra including the Cameroons, Bonny, and Old and New Calabar, all of which could be patrolled from the island. Given the high volume of captives from this region, the British considered abandoning Sierra Leone as the headquarters of its anti-slave trade operations on the African coast for Fernando Po which they thought offered a healthier climate and lay closer to the region where large numbers of slavers were seized. The slaves on board those captured ships often suffered and died during the long trip to Sierra Leone, and a base at Fernando Po would avoid those long, costly voyages.[9]

What became of the three Africans once the expedition arrived in Fernando Po is uncertain. It may be that the men were released there and allowed to make their own way back to their home. While the men were shipped from Old Calabar, there is no evidence of their nation of origin. They could have been Efiks from Old Calabar who were enslaved for debt or a crime or kidnapped into slavery, but it is more likely that they were brought from an inland nation and sold from Old Calabar. The worst possible outcome would have been to return the men to Old Calabar if they were from an inland nation, for they would almost certainly have been immediately re-enslaved. It is also possible that the men remained with the expedition as it made its way up the Niger and found their way home from the river. The expedition itself ended in disaster. The ships ran aground on the rivers and lay there for months while disease took a heavy toll on the crews. Richard Lander was shot during a conflict with Africans and died a short time later at Fernando Po. Only eight of the forty-seven white men who set out on the expedition survived.[10]

In many respects, these three unnamed Africans most closely fit the stereotypical descriptions of "new Negroes." They understood no English or other European languages; they had no idea of where they were, no understanding of the laws and customs of their captors. What they did understand was freedom, and they escaped captivity not once but at least three times and traveled hundreds of miles across the ocean and three southern states before being recaptured. They may have been unaware of the boundaries between slavery and freedom that defined the nineteenth-century Atlantic World, but they benefitted from those boundaries. Had those men been captured and enslaved in the eighteenth century and picked up at sea in a canoe, they would not have been set free. What is perhaps most instructive about their case aside from their determination to be free is the determination of the British to see them freed.

The threat from Addin Lewis to seize the *Aurora* may have contributed to the concern James Baker showed for the Africans, but he was relentless in his efforts to track them across the Deep South. Evidence from around the Atlantic shows that the British were tireless in their efforts to free Africans or African Americans under their protection who were enslaved. For example, William Gray, British consul at Norfolk, Virginia, from 1819 to 1845, reported the case of Pepe Redman of Williamsburg who was confined in jail there as a runaway slave but claimed British citizenship. Gray's superiors advised him that if he was "perfectly satisfied" that Redman was a British citizen, then he should demand his release and, if the authorities refused, then he should notify the U.S. and British governments. This was exactly the course that Baker followed in Mobile. In 1839 Sir William Colebrooke, Governor-in-Chief of the Leeward Islands, notified authorities in London that, based on reports from Jane McMillan, a resident of Antigua, he feared that that her son, a boy named Samuel Bryan, had been lured onto an American ship and illegally enslaved in Virginia. Lord Palmerston wrote Consul General H. L. Fox in Washington instructing him to investigate. Fox contacted William Gray who tracked Bryan down on a plantation and found him living happily as a free man. Gray wrote his mother and had the letter delivered to her in Antigua.[11]

British authorities in Cuba investigated cases of Liberated Africans from British islands who were enslaved on that island. To cite one representative example, in 1841 British officials in London pressured the Spanish government to return Wellington, a young West Indian man kidnapped from Jamaica and enslaved in Cuba, to his family in Jamaica. Wellington was born on June 18, 1815, the date of the Battle of Waterloo, and when news of that victory reached the island of Jamaica, Wellington was named in honor of the British commander. His father was George Crawford, and the boy was christened George Wellington Crawford. He disappeared from his home on August 1, 1834, the very day slavery was abolished. He was nineteen years old, described as "a strong healthy young man, about 5 feet 8 or 9 inches in height." A thorough search turned up nothing and no word was heard from him until the year following when John Alford, a black sailor working on board a Spanish vessel trading between St. Jago de Cuba and Kingston, called on John Thomas Anderson, a custom's official in Kingston, reporting that when his ship was loading its cargo at the wharf in St. Jago, Wellington came running to him, crying and begging to be returned to his family in Jamaica. He told Alford, who knew him and his entire family, that he had been kidnapped with two other boys from Montego Bay by a Captain James and a Dr. John who sold them in Cuba. Alford took Wellington to the governor of the province to seek permission to bring him back to Jamaica, which the governor refused without further documentation from the Governor of Jamaica.[12]

Anderson took down the information and reported it to the police who took depositions from Anderson and Alford. He reported the affair to the mayor, Hector Mitchell, who quickly sent the documents to the Marquis of Silgo, governor of the island, who sent them along to the authorities in Cuba. As a result, in July 1839 Spanish officials returned three Jamaican boys, two of them, Mitchell and Allen, had been kidnapped with Wellington, and the third, named Frank, at a different time, though Spanish officials claimed Wellington was one of these three. They stood by this claim even though the three boys were eight or nine when they were taken and Wellington was nineteen. Anderson reported that Wellington's mother was so distraught that her son did not return with the other boys as expected "that she became insane, and died in February" of 1840.[13]

British authorities in Jamaica took depositions from Mitchell and Frank who gave further details confirming that they had been separated from Wellington and that he had not been returned with them. Further investigations revealed the identity of his enslavers in Cuba, but Spanish authorities continued to insist that he had been returned. Letters flew between London, Madrid, Kingston, Havana, and St. Jago de Cuba over the following year and the next. British officials in Jamaica sent more and more evidence to confirm that Wellington had not been returned, and Spanish officials continued to insist that he had. John Hardy, British consul in St. Jago, summed up the problem; he complained that "the proverbial inertness of the Judge . . . the thousand facilities of evading the question as furnished by the system of judicature here, are such as to paralyze any exertions I might make. . . ." Remarkably, and despite all those roadblocks, the British remained determined to free Wellington, and in 1842 he returned to Jamaica, eight years after his kidnapping. He even identified several other free blacks from Jamaica who were enslaved in Cuba, and returned to the island to help identify them.[14]

On the other side of the Atlantic, Alexander Findlay, Governor of Sierra Leone, made similar efforts to track down Liberated Africans who were kidnapped from the colony and re-enslaved. Young boys were especially vulnerable, and Findlay was deeply shocked by the extent of the "kidnapping system," and fumed that "instead of being a free colony, slavery has been carried on in it to a very great extent." Authorities in Sierra Leone aggressively prosecuted residents of the colony who were suspected of slave trading, and they were equally aggressive in trying to recover kidnapped residents of the colony whenever possible. To cite one example, Findlay sent his men to the barracoon owned by the notorious slave dealer John Ormond on the Rio Pongo to follow up on reports that Ormond had enslaved a Liberated African from Sierra Leone. Ormond admitted that he had a Liberated African and informed them that his neighbor Theodore Canot, another notorious slave dealer, held another. They refused to surrender them unless Findlay paid $100 for each of them. Findlay refused to pay for British subjects, put the slave dealers on notice that he would hold them responsible for their welfare, and warned them that "if they were not forthcoming they would be the two dearest slaves Mr. Ormond ever had in his possession." The slave traders hastened to send the boys back to Sierra Leone.[15]

The fact that Dimmock Charlton appealed to Edmund Molyneaux, the British consul in Savannah, demonstrates that the efforts of these officials to free illegally enslaved subjects of the British crown were widely known among Africans and African Americans. Molyneaux's failure to pursue Charlton's claim is evidence that the consul was not convinced that he was entitled to British protection. In cases where the consuls believed that slaves had claims to British protection, they went to great lengths to investigate those cases and to free those slaves whenever possible. Their efforts were part of a broader effort by British officials around the Atlantic World to protect British subjects from illegal enslavement. Slaves around the Atlantic World quickly realized that the British could be powerful allies in their individual quests for freedom. The British efforts on behalf of the enslaved were not entirely altruistic, however; they were also part of a larger agenda to portray Britain as the beacon of liberty on the Atlantic political stage. British diplomatic efforts to free individuals illegally enslaved in the United States allowed Britain to keep diplomatic pressure on the U.S. government around the involvement of American citizens in the illegal slave trade and thereby added to Britain's international "moral capital." The British crusade against the Atlantic slave trade linked with the nationalist imperative to protect its citizens and subjects gave individuals a powerful claim to British protection grounded in a universal claim to human rights.[16]

6

Caught in the Illegal Slave Trade

I N AUGUST 1839, Viscount Palmerston, British Foreign Secretary, sent Henry S. Fox, British minister to the United States, a packet of documents outlining the remarkable case of a British subject named Sack N'Jaie, alleged to be held in slavery in Mobile, Alabama. Palmerston identified him as "an inhabitant of Sierra Leone . . . a person of much respectability and considerable property in that colony." In Palmerston's view, each fact of the case was "so strongly corroborated that there seems no reason to doubt its truth." He demanded that American authorities launch a "searching inquiry" into the case with a view toward setting Sack N'Jaie "at liberty forthwith."[1] The case was tied to British efforts to stop the African slave trade, a cause that Palmerston claimed was one of the "great objects always before him in life." As Foreign Secretary, he negotiated a network of treaties with European governments that gave the Royal Navy the "Right of Search," the authority to stop and board suspected slavers flying the flags of those nations, search them, and then capture suspected slavers and deliver them for trial before mixed commissions, the courts representing the various powers scattered around the Atlantic World. The Right of Search was absolutely essential for the British Navy's effort to suppress the trade. Palmerston strong-armed reluctant states like Portugal and Brazil, and more than any other politician, he put real muscle behind the international effort to abolish the African slave trade.[2] As his concern for Sack N'Jaie indicates, British diplomatic efforts extended down to the illegal enslavement of individuals under their protection.

A series of chance encounters and the superhuman efforts of Charles Smith, an African sailor, brought Sack N'Jaie's case to the attention of

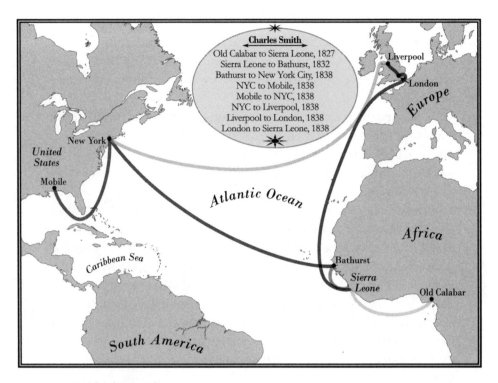

Charles Smith
Old Calabar to Sierra Leone, 1827
Sierra Leone to Bathurst, 1832
Bathurst to New York City, 1838
NYC to Mobile, 1838
Mobile to NYC, 1838
NYC to Liverpool, 1838
Liverpool to London, 1838
London to Sierra Leone, 1838

Map 12. Charles Smith

the British Foreign Office. In 1838 Charles Smith hired on as a sailor trading to Mobile. When the ship arrived there, Smith accompanied a white sailor from the ship into a public house where they found a group of people fiddling and dancing in the taproom. Smith was unaware of the codes of conduct governing race relations in that town, and unwittingly violated them by sitting down to drink with his friend when blacks were expected to drink standing outside. A group of three angry white men challenged him, demanded to know his background, and asked him to prove his freedom. Smith feared that if he produced his papers they would be taken and destroyed and he would be kidnapped into slavery, and so he explained his background to them but refused to produce documentation. The men called the constable who took Smith into custody. He spent five days in jail without a hearing, and was then handcuffed at midnight, thrown into a wagon, and hauled to a cotton plantation outside the city where he arrived about 9:00 A.M. He worked there for over two months loading cotton, sometimes in chains, until the overseer learned that he had papers proving his free status, and he was sent back to the Custom's House at Mobile where he was freed. He quickly signed on as a sailor on board a merchant ship transporting cotton to Liverpool and made his escape, eventually making his way to Sierra Leone.[3]

It was Smith's second near escape from enslavement. He did not explain why or how he was enslaved, only that he was sold into slavery from the busy depot at Old Calabar in 1827, but the slaver was captured by British cruisers. He could have been on any one of the four slave ships the British captured off Old Calabar in that year: the *Fama da Cuba*, the *Silvenhina*, the *Creola* or the *Musquito*. Their capture spared the Africans on board the horrors of the Middle Passage and enslavement in Cuba or Brazil. The *Creola*, for example, was a Brazilian ship of 85 tons, cleared for trade in Cabinda and Molembo where the slave trade was open to Portuguese and Brazilian ships. Her papers allowed her to carry 214 slaves, but "the rapacity of the inhuman master induced him to cram nearly 100 more into her . . . aggravating in a most cruel degree the horrid misery of his victims by such studied barbarity." All of those ships were sent to Sierra Leone for trial, a long journey that threatened the lives of the captives and crew. In 1821 Lieutenant Christopher Knight, commander of the HMS *Snapper* which patrolled the waters off Old Calabar, warned his superiors of "the very great distance from these rivers to that port [Freetown], which cannot fail to produce a great mortality among the slaves . . . and to be a great risk to the lives or healths of our seamen and officers who have to navigate them up, the vessels being always in the most loathsome state imaginable; and to send medical assistance is not possible. Eight weeks is by no means to be considered a long time to perform this difficult passage." Despite those dangers, the ships were taken there where they were tried and condemned by the Court of Mixed Commission at Sierra Leone, and the enslaved Africans on board were emancipated and resettled.[4]

Smith and the other freed captives were taken to Freetown which would have been a welcome sight after the stifling, inhumane conditions on board the slave ship. Framed by "a beautiful range of hills," according to Mary Church, an Englishwoman who arrived in 1833, the town had "the appearance of a large, well-built, and populous place." Church also reported that the Liberated Africans were busy building "small comfortable houses . . . all over the Town." She described the arrival of a captured slaver for trial before the Mixed Court. She wrote that the captives on board the ships were terrified, traumatized by the suffering they had endured even after the capture of their slave ship during their trip to Sierra Leone. When a ship was condemned, the captives were turned over to the Liberated African Department which had a complex of buildings near the wharves where the Africans could be fed and housed until they were resettled. Dixon Denham, Lieutenant-Governor of Sierra Leone, described the process: "the Africans are fed for several days after landing," he wrote, "and comfortably clothed & when they are a little reconciled to this new manner of treating them. Noncommissioned officers of their own Country are allowed to visit them for several days. . . ." Until their resettlement, the men were employed on public works. As soon as possible, each of the male Africans was given clothing, tools, cooking utensils, and a plot of land near a village where they could build a hut and plant crops. Others enrolled in the Royal Africa Corps. Africans from the Bight of Biafra, which included Old Calabar, made up the largest contingent of Liberated Africans in the colony and had their own political organizations and cultural practices. They were allowed two pence a day for six months until their farms became productive.[5]

In 1828 British officials created the Agricultural Society to promote the cultivation of export crops like sugar, coffee, ginger, arrowroot, and rice by the men. Women, on the other hand, remained lodged in the Liberated Africans complex until they married or were placed with a local family who agreed to support them in exchange for their labor. The Liberated Africans Department educated and cared for children until they came of age or, in some cases, they were apprenticed for a period of five to seven years during which they were to be well cared for, instructed in Christianity, brought before the General Superintendent when requested, and given ten dollars and two suits of clothing at the end of their terms. Those requirements reflected the civilizing mission that lay at the heart of the British support of the Liberated Africans. Mary Church praised the rapid progress of the Liberated Africans, each of whom within a few years was employed as "a useful artizan [artisan] in the town, or a labourer in the villages, surrounded by his family, with ample means of support, and in the practice and comforts of civilized life—The old consoling themselves for the loss of their country with the freedom of their children, and the children exulting in their freedom as their first birthright." In 1827 an estimated 12,000 Liberated Africans lived in the colony, and the number grew to over 26,000 in 1833. Before the 1830s and 1840s, the original settlers of Sierra Leone, the Black Loyalists from Nova Scotia, along with Europeans there, had dominated the colony.[6] Now a new strain of formerly enslaved Africans was integrated into the colony.

The British patrols on the West Coast of Africa needed supply bases, and in 1826 Captain Alexander Grant was authorized to establish a base on the Gambia River, 500 miles up the coast from Sierra Leone. He negotiated with the local ruler for an island near the river's mouth that he named St. Mary's Island. With a contingent of a few hundred troops, he built official buildings, garrisons, and harbor facilities at a settlement named Bathurst. In 1831 British authorities decided to send Liberated Africans from Sierra Leone to augment the struggling colony of Bathurst. They believed that "the superior fertility of the soil and other local advantages authorizes the expectation that the most beneficial consequences will be derived from that measure." They planned to send "a considerable body of Africans," supplying them with a parcel of land, clothing, farming equipment, and subsistence for the first six months. Only volunteers would be sent there; Alexander Findlay, commander of the Gambia settlement, reminded British officials that the Liberated Africans were British subjects and could not be forced to relocate to the Gambia against their will. He noted that if they were coerced they would be convinced that they were enslaved again. Liberated Africans from Sierra Leone arrived there throughout 1832, and Charles Smith was probably among them since he said that he was sent there shortly after his arrival in Sierra Leone. Authorities in Bathurst complained that the supplies sent with the new settlers was "totally inadequate" for their support. They also suggested that bringing Liberated Africans directly to the Gambia would decrease mortality. Despite the problems, British officials considered the settlement of Bathurst to be "of great importance."[7]

From 1831 to 1833 the British sent 655 men, 103 women, 70 boys, and 10 girls to the Gambia.[8] The conditions were worse at the Gambia settlement than those in Sierra Leone. The island was little more than a sandy desert. Most of the new emigrants eked out a living as subsistence farmers in one of the eleven villages scattered around St. Mary's

Island, the most fortunate ones worked in trades in Bathurst, and others lived in even worse conditions on a newer settlement on McCarthy's Island up the Gambia River. Peter Leonard, a surgeon on a British naval vessel, visited Bathurst in 1832, and described it as Smith would have known it. St. Mary's Island was sandy and completely flat, but he described Bathurst as having a "lively pleasant appearance." The houses built by Europeans, he said, "are very airy, and of tasteful construction" and whitewashed. The Liberated Africans' houses, he reported, "are generally circular, and formed of wicker work, with circular roofs, thatched and pitched, so that they closely resemble bee-hives on a large scale. They are enclosed in numbers together, within a hedge eight or ten feet high, of the same basket work material of which their walls are composed." An 1842 report noted that "almost every liberated African in Bathurst, so soon as he becomes his own master, either follows the trade of a carpenter or mason, or goes on board some ship as a sailor." That report concluded that of all the places chosen for the resettlement of the Liberated Africans, "the settlement of the Gambia was the most unfitted, and the consequence has been that in no place where they have been located has their situation been more unfortunate." Almost 3,000 Liberated Africans had been sent to the Gambia, and nearly half of them soon died there.[9]

It was a career as a sailor that attracted Smith, and for him it was a means of escape from the isolated and impoverished settlement on that sandy island in the muddy Gambia. In 1837 he sailed with Peter Hatfield on a schooner trading between Sierra Leone and Bathurst. Hatfield was himself a citizen of the Atlantic World. Peter and his brother David Hatfield were white Loyalists from Westchester, New York, who immigrated to St. John's, New Brunswick, after the British defeat in the American Revolutionary War. They became merchants and owned "considerable valuable property in St. John and . . . several vessels." Their trading network followed the Black Loyalists from Canada to Sierra Leone, and Peter Hatfield relocated to Sierra Leone to conduct business there. Hatfield reported that Smith sailed with him from Sierra Leone to the Gambia in December 1837 where he was discharged. Hatfield sent the ship *William and Robert,* loaded with lumber, from Bathurst to New York City in January 1838, and Smith signed up for that voyage. That vessel arrived in New York in April after a voyage of fifty days. Smith reported that he was hired as a seaman at a rate of twelve dollars a month with an understanding that passage back to Sierra Leone would be found for him. After about three weeks, the *William and Robert* planned to sail to St. John's, and Smith applied for and obtained a discharge.[10]

Smith spent about two months in New York City before joining the crew of another ship, and the records offer two different versions of his story. In one version, Smith said that he joined the crew of an American barque bound for Mobile. In another version, Smith said that he joined the crew of an American vessel headed for St. John's, New Brunswick. After three weeks in St. John's, the ship sailed to Mobile. As the cotton revolution took hold in Alabama and northeast Mississippi, Mobile became a booming cotton port, second only to New Orleans in the volume of its exports of the fleecy white staple. In the 1850s a visitor captured the city's total dependence on cotton: "people live in cotton houses and ride in cotton carriages. They buy cotton, sell cotton, think cotton, eat cotton, drink cotton, and dream cotton. . . . It has made Mobile, and all its citizens." Located at the head of Mobile Bay, the town spread for about a mile along the water, its streets lined with businesses, churches, and fine residences. The grand bay was shallow and the city's wharves could not accommodate large, ocean-going vessels which lay at anchorages further down the bay, and smaller boats ferried goods and travelers back and forth from the town to the upper and lower anchorages. The large numbers of sailors and the cheap boarding houses and grog shops that catered to them gave the place a rowdy reputation. British visitor James Buchanan described the fights and riots that broke out almost every night, and the high crime and murder rates which he attributed to the "dissipated, idle, gambling, reckless and murdering class." He found them congregating at the bars, particularly the "grog shops of the common order," located "at almost every corner of almost every street."[11]

Smith's trip to Mobile proved to be an eventful one. He had spent some time in New York City, but he would not have fully appreciated how different racial mores were in the Deep South. It was here that Smith unwittingly violated the racial code by sitting down to drink with his white friend which resulted in his being challenged by angry white men to prove his freedom. As recounted earlier, Smith's refusal to produce his papers brought him the fate he feared most: ahe spent five days in jail without a hearing, and then was handcuffed, thrown into a wagon, and hauled to a cotton plantation.[12]

On that cotton plantation outside Mobile, Smith was employed loading cotton, and since he was considered a flight risk, he was chained and bore the scars from those restraints on his wrists for the rest of his life. Once he began to mingle with the other slaves on the plantation on his first day, Smith encountered someone he actually knew, a man named Booray who had also been one of the Liberated Africans sent to the Gambia. Smith did not record how Booray, who had escaped the slave trade once, now found himself enslaved in Mobile, but there were many cases of Liberated Africans at the Gambia being kidnapped and sold again into the illegal slave trade. Booray told him that another resident of Sierra Leone, a man named Sack N'Jaie, was also enslaved on the same plantation. Smith had been acquainted with Sack N'Jaie in Sierra Leone, and he was shocked to see him a short distance away. He was being held in a small shed in miserable conditions, his legs in stocks and his hands in chains because he had tried to escape. The overseer prevented the two men from talking that day, but Smith occasionally managed to find time to talk with Sack N'Jaie without the overseer's knowledge.[13]

Over time, Smith pieced together Sack N'Jaie's story. Like Smith, Sack N'Jaie was a sailor who for several years had worked on and then owned small craft sailing along the West African coast from Sierra Leone to the Gambia. H. W. Macaulay, British Commissioner to the Mixed Court at Sierra Leone, described him as "one of the most honest and trustworthy men of his class that I ever met with. He is a tall, powerful man, unusually black, and remarkably handsome and well-formed." He wed in 1836, and he and his wife had a daughter who had been christened in St. George's Church in Freetown. He had recently purchased two houses there valued at £200. He was also an experienced pilot and sailor who had commanded a vessel belonging to the Valentine brothers, Rene and Durand, French traders with connections in Gorée and Senegal who settled on the Rio Nunez in 1836, and he had made several voyages to England as a sailor on merchant ships. In July 1837 Sack N'Jaie was hired by a Mr. D'Erneville, either Antoine or Pierre, who, like the Valentines, was one of two French brothers who traded on the Rio Nunez, and they probably knew him through the Valentines. The Valentines and D'Ernevilles were middlemen working for colonial companies based in Bordeaux and Marseille and trading predominantly in wax, hides, coffee, and peanuts; they engaged in legitimate commerce

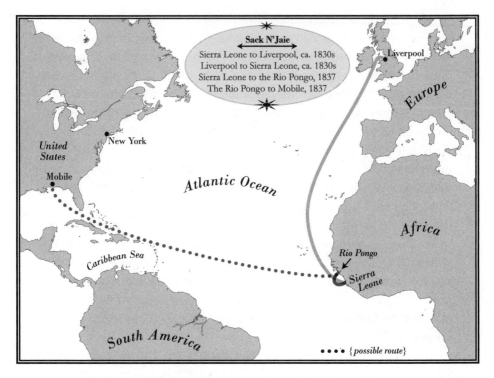

Map 13. Sack N'Jaie

rather than in the illegal slave trade which was also widespread on the Rio Nunez. Industry and a growing urban population in Europe increased demand for various types of oil and grease. The British concentrated on palm oil, which focused their attentions on the Niger Delta, while the French opted for peanut oil which lured them to the Senegambia. One or both of the brothers purchased a slave ship that had been captured and condemned at a prize auction held by the Mixed Court in Sierra Leone, and hired Sack N'Jaie to travel from Freetown to the River Nunez to pick up the gold needed to pay for the vessel, a commission that indicated the level of trust Sack N'Jaie enjoyed in Freetown and with merchants all along the coast.[14]

Sack N'Jaie's boat was under repair at the Iles de Los, so he went to Pierre Saye to ask for the loan of his sloop, a single-masted sailboat, in order to carry out this commission. He and Saye were old friends, and both of them were born at Gorée. Saye was happy to lend his 4½-ton sloop to his friend, who took six men with him: a sailor and cook from

Senegal, a sailor and carpenter from Gorée, and two of his own apprentices, young brothers from the Sherbro, With his crew of six, Sack N'Jaie set out for the Rio Nunez, about 150 miles north of Sierra Leone. Unfortunately for the crew, the period from June through July was tornado season, and those violent squalls could hit with such force that "ships are frequently driven from their anchors and compelled to put to sea to avoid being dashed to pieces." The storms came up so suddenly that, as one contemporary reported, "it is next to impossible to shorten sail before the blast strikes a vessel." Even though Sack N'Jaie and the other sailors on board were experienced sailors, they could not save the ship when a tornado struck.[15]

The ship simply disappeared, and everyone assumed that it and the entire crew were lost in the storm. As Macaulay wrote, "None, but those who knew [his] wife, can form an idea of the deep distress which the poor woman has suffered on account of her husband's loss; nor could she ever mention him without tears, for many months after his disappearance had led everyone to conclude that he was drowned at sea." In fact, Sack N'Jaie was the only one of the seven crewmen who survived the tornado. The ship was completely destroyed, and he was tossed up on a desert island near the notorious slave-trading barracoons off the Rio Pongo. He was recused by a Portuguese salt ship from St. Jago, an island in the Cape Verdes. The Portuguese were a major provider of salt which was mined on the "Salt Islands" in the Cape Verdes which were also a resort of illegal slave ships en route from the Americas to West Africa. Portugal was the second largest provider of salt to the United States in this period.[16]

Smith did not discover how Sack N'Jaie was transported from that salt ship to a cotton plantation outside Mobile. He only told Smith that he was picked up by the Portuguese, that after the first day he and other captives were prohibited from speaking to one another, and that after he was disembarked at Mobile, the ship with other illegal slaves on board sailed to Charleston. This sort of small-scale smuggling of an individual or small numbers of slaves into Mobile was not unusual.[17] Since the Atlantic slave trade was illegal, it is unlikely that a Portuguese ship sailed into Mobile harbor and offered a slave for sale. It is more likely that he was sold to an illegal slaver from Mobile, Charleston or New Orleans that had stopped in the Cape Verdes, as these vessels often did. He might also have been brought into Cuba and sold to a planter from Mobile from there. Mobile's reputation as a dangerous destination for free black sailors circulated around the Atlantic World. In January 1857 Liverpool police responded to a distress call from an American ship called the *James L. Bogart*. The police found "a regular battle going on on the deck," and the officers fired shots at the crewmen who "were nearly all black or coloured men." They had joined the ship's crew believing it to be bound for New York City, but "on learning that the vessel was bound for Mobile they refused to go, that being a slave state where they would all be re-tained in slavery. . . ." After black sailors were arrested and in some cases enslaved in southern ports, a London newspaper warned that "this shipping of free-coloured men to the Southern States of the Union is nothing more nor less than the revival of the slave trade on a small scale."[18] The presence of Booray and Sack N'Jaie on a southern planta-tion in 1838 is a reminder that the African presence in the South con-tinued throughout the antebellum era and that the importation of slaves from Africa never completely stopped so long as slavery continued.

Smith had been afraid to produce his protection papers in that Mo-bile bar, but after two months on the plantation, he decided he had to take that risk. One morning the principal overseer on the plantation came to muster the slaves and issue them clothing. Smith presented that overseer with his papers and, fortunately for him, that overseer had him carried immediately to the Custom's House in Mobile where the authorities examined his papers and set him free with the caveat that he leave the city as quickly as possible. He went directly to the docks where he saw two ships flying British flags. He went to the first one, and in another of the remarkable coincidences in his experience, he found Captain Freebody in a London barque. Freebody was based at Cape Coast Castle near Sierra Leone, and Smith had known him there. He was bound for the northern United States, and Smith was eager to leave the country behind, so he went to the second ship which he iden-tified as the *Sarah Nixon* from Sunderland, a port in the northeast of England noted especially for the export of coal. This ship was carrying cotton from the South to the bustling cotton mills of Liverpool. He signed on to that vessel as a steward. The ship sailed to New York and from there to Liverpool. Once he arrived in Liverpool, he walked to London where he signed on as a crewman on board the *Lord Wellington*, bound for Sierra Leone.[19]

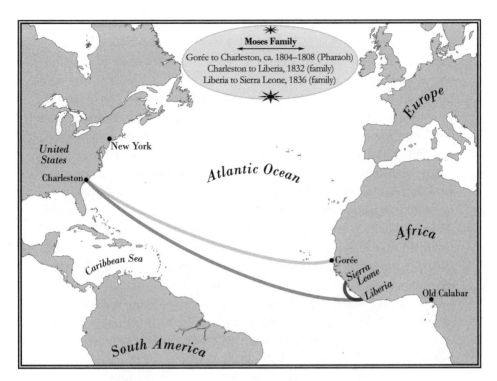

Map 14. Moses Family

Smith's intention was to notify Sack N'Jaie's family that he was alive, lying in chains on a plantation in Alabama, in hopes that they, with the assistance of British authorities, could rescue him. Upon his arrival in Freetown, he went directly to the home of Sack N'Jaie's father, Pharaoh Moses, and told him the entire story. When he had heard Smith's story, Moses appealed to British authorities in Freetown. He went to Thomas Cole, Colonial Secretary there, and gave him a deposition of his son's story and what he had learned from Smith. He closed by saying, "This information has caused a hope in my breast that my son may be restored to me." Moses's sorrow at the loss of his son was compounded by the fact that he had been separated from him many years before.[20]

The Sack N'Jaie family's saga is a story of the tumultuous vicissitudes of an African family caught up in the Atlantic World. Pharaoh Moses was a native of Gorée whose name was Pharaoh Sack N'Jaie.

Located between the Senegal and Gambia Rivers about two miles off the coast of Dakar, Senegal, the long island of Gorée lay south of the Cape Verdes, and the Portuguese arrived first, attracted by its good harbor and supplies of fresh water. It was a prize that bounced from one European power to the next before the French took it in 1677, and it was an important source for slaves in the seventeenth century, but much less important in the eighteenth century. Gorée's small population was mostly Christian, with some French officials, soldiers, and merchants and a larger mixed-race or *metis* population born of *marriages a la mode du pays* between French men and Senegalese women known as *signares*. The *signares* often acted as cultural intermediaries and many traded on behalf of their French husbands who were legally barred from commerce. Some of their children were educated in France. The *signares* inherited their husbands' property and became major owners of property and traders in their own right. The European and *metis* traders worked through petty traders who traveled along the coast and the rivers. The percentage of the *habitants*, the free people of Gorée, who owned slaves was very high. In 1767, for example, there were 326 free residents and 718 slaves with most residents owning several slaves, an unusually high rate of slave ownership. Like many West Africans, the people of Gorée recognized different categories of slaves; household slaves were integrated into the family over generations and were not subject to sale, but trade slaves, who often worked in the fields, could be sold at any time.[21]

Pharaoh Moses did not record exactly how he was enslaved, only that he was captured—which could mean kidnapped—and sold into slavery when he was a young man. There are later examples from the area of slaves who worked along the coast and rivers being kidnapped, and historian George Brooks noted that "African groups along both banks of the Gambia River were riven by chronic warfare, slave raiding, and kidnapping." Pharaoh Sack N'Jaie's name suggests that he was Mandinka and Muslim, which may offer a clue into his status among the Christians at Gorée. He was forced to leave behind his wife, his daughter Mary, and his son Sack N'Jaie. Moses did not give the date of his enslavement, but he was born in 1771, and he was a young married man with two children. There is a gap in imports of slaves from Senegambia into Charleston between 1785 and 1803 when the African slave trade was closed. South Carolina reopened the trade in late

1803 in a desperate attempt to import as many slaves as possible before the African slave trade closed in 1808. Between 1804 and 1808, thirty-six slave ships arrived in Charleston from the Senegambia region, fourteen from Gorée, and Pharaoh Sack N'Jaie was almost certainly on one of them.[22]

He was purchased by a Jewish merchant whom he referred to as Miah Moses (probably Jeremiah or Nehemiah), and he took his master's surname. Pharaoh became a skilled artisan, a stone mason, and Miah Moses allowed Pharaoh to hire out his time. He saved enough to purchase his own freedom as well as that of his new African American wife, Sylvia, his son Anthony, and his daughter Rachel. Many free blacks worked as masons; in fact, it was the third most common occupation for free blacks in Charleston after carpenters and tailors. He joined a large and successful community of skilled free blacks in the city. Free people of color were more successful in the Lower South ports including Charleston than in the Upper South. In fact, free blacks in Charleston were more skilled than most whites and controlled a much higher proportion of the skilled trades than free blacks in Richmond, for instance, a situation that brought a steady stream of complaints from skilled white workers in the city. Moses's ability to purchase not only his own freedom but that of his entire family deserves emphasis. Recall the difficulties Dimmock Charlton faced in his efforts to purchase freedom for himself and other family members and the many times he was cheated by unscrupulous masters. No doubt Miah Moses's fair treatment was one of the reasons Pharaoh respected and trusted him. But even when masters dealt fairly with them, slaves and free blacks had a hard time saving enough money to self-purchase or purchase family members. Skilled slaves could rarely hire themselves out for more than a couple of hundred dollars annually, from which the hired slave had to pay his master and support himself and perhaps his family. Moses's self-purchase and the purchase of his entire family, then, is evidence of years of hard work, tremendous self-discipline, and scraping by in order to save every penny.[23]

Pharaoh decided to return with his family to the colony of Liberia, established by the American Colonization Society in 1820 as a haven for free blacks and manumitted slaves. He attended an 1832 meeting of potential emigrants held in Charleston at the home of Titus Gregoire where the speakers advocated emigration as a Christian duty. Junius

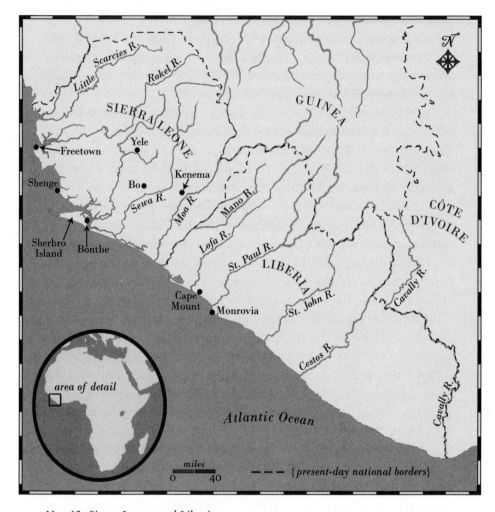

Map 15. Sierra Leone and Liberia

Eden, elected chairman of the meeting, expressed that sentiment when
he said, "The inhabitants invite us to come and possess it, and to assist
them to infuse into the natives the notions of pure morality, and to
erect temples dedicated to the worship of Jehovah." After several similar speeches, Pharaoh Moses rose to speak; he said that he was at a loss
for words. As the only native African in the group, he had a unique
perspective. He said, "If you, who are natives of this country, and have
never seen Africa, speak so highly of her, what must I say who have trod
the soil—the soil which gave me birth, and where yet live my relations

and kindred, from whom by the hand of violence I was torn away and deprived of freedom, which, thanks be to God, I have again obtained, and not only mine but I have obtained also the liberty of the companion of my life, and that of two children." At that point, he was so overcome by emotion that he could not continue, and as he sat down he said, "I go with you, my brethren. It is a good land." His entire family departed from Savannah on the bark *Hercules* on December 11, 1832, with 160 other emigrants headed for Liberia.[24]

The *Hercules* arrived in Monrovia in January 1833, and Pharaoh Moses once again set foot on African soil. He had been away for at least twenty-four years, and perhaps even longer. He told his friends in Charleston that his relatives still lived, but he could not have known which of his family members still survived. Remarkably, he found his son, Sack N'Jaie, and his daughter, Mary Sack N'Jaie, and reunited with them. It is important to emphasize how exceptional it was for an enslaved African to free himself and his second family, to return to Africa, and to reunite with the family he had left behind long ago. Disease devastated the new immigrants from Charleston; thirty-four of them died shortly after their arrival. Conditions were so bad that thirteen of the survivors returned to the United States, and another twenty-four—including the Moses family—migrated to Sierra Leone in 1836. It is unclear whether Sack N'Jaie was already in Sierra Leone or if Pharaoh brought his entire family together there. It is impossible to imagine Pharaoh's sorrow to learn in 1838 that, after having struggled for years to free his family from slavery in South Carolina and to return his family to freedom in Africa, his African son was now enslaved on a plantation in Alabama. Pharaoh's efforts to free his son, then, had a special urgency. He appealed to British authorities for help: "I therefore most respectfully and earnestly pray and solicit the interference of Her Majesty's Government, that such measures may be taken as will lead to Sack N'Jaie's being liberated and restored to his afflicted wife, children and family."[25]

British authorities in Sierra Leone were eager to help. H. W. Macaulay, British Commissioner there, urged action. He wrote to the Governor in Chief Richard Doherty, "He was much esteemed by all who knew him, and by none more than myself; and I cannot but believe, that the British Government will consider this a case, in which it may properly exert itself to restore so valuable a man to his afflicted wife and family, and to the Colony." Macaulay offered to bear any expense that might be associated with his return, and he expressed his confidence that Sack "would himself joyfully repay to me the price of his freedom."[26] When Doherty passed that information along to Lord Glenelg, Secretary of State for War and the Colonies, he informed him that "his case excites great interest." As we have seen, the Foreign Office wrote U.S. officials in August demanding a "searching inquiry" of the matter. Henry S. Fox sent all the documentation to U.S. Secretary of State John Forsyth, whose reply was less than encouraging. Forsyth complained that Smith's affidavit "is defective, and in some instances, entirely silent as to names, dates, and other statements essential to a successful prosecution of the inquiry. This circumstance, taken in connextion [*sic*] with the improbable character of the whole transaction, is calculated to create some doubt as to the veracity of the deponent." Forsyth cleverly shifted the investigation from whether or not Sack N'Jaie was lying in chains on a plantation outside Mobile to an effort to prove or disprove every facet of Smith's statement.[27]

The State Department demanded that the British provide verification of Smith's protection issued by the British consul in New York, evidence from British authorities in St. John's of the voyage Smith took there, and information from the consulate in Mobile of a ship under the command of Captain Freebody as well as of the *Sarah Nixon* of Sunderland's voyage to Liverpool and Smith's service on board the ship. They also requested that U.S. officials in the various cities investigate. Problems arose almost immediately. As we have seen already, James Buchanan, British consul in New York City, could not confirm the details of Smith's stay in New York City, and he had no record of a protection issued to him. H. Bowyer Smith, Collector of the Port in St. John's, could not find any evidence of an American vessel commanded by a man named Parker having arrived there in 1838, or any record of a ship departing that port for Mobile, nor any records of a Charles Smith. The American consul in St. John's had no evidence to support any of these topics either. H. A. Schroeder, British Pro-Consul in Mobile, replied that he could find no record of a Captain Freebody and no record of a ship called the *Sarah Nixon*, and added that no British vessel had been at the wharves of Mobile during the past four years (though shipping records show regular traffic between Mobile and Liverpool).

B. F. Butler, U.S. Attorney in New York City, investigated the matter on Forsyth's instructions and he found the *William and Robert*, but no record of a Charles Smith on board, and he could find no record of an American vessel commanded by Parker leaving New York for St. John's, or of a ship called the *Sarah Nixon*. A. B. Thurston, Inspector of the Port of Mobile, replied that he could not find that any Portuguese vessel had arrived there, he could not identify a Captain Freebody, and he could not find a ship called the *Sarah Nixon*. American officials tallied up these gaps and used them to discredit Smith's narrative. After investigating Smith's deposition, J. B. Hogan, Collector of the Port of Mobile, wrote, "I have no hesitation in saying that in my opinion the whole story is what sailors call 'a yarn,' and originates in the fertile brain of Charles Smith." No case involving Smith had ever come before him, there was no cotton plantation within sixty miles of Mobile, and the racial mores Smith described in Mobile were inaccurate. He concluded, "The fact is the whole story is full of falsehoods, and I do not believe there is one particle of truth in any part of his statement." John Searvele, the U.S. Attorney for South Alabama, also concluded that Smith "has chosen to fabricate in story what he never witnessed."[28]

With all that documentation in hand, Forsyth wrote a gloating letter to Fox. "As the tenor of those papers leaves no room to doubt that the colonial officials in Sierra Leone had been imposed upon, and that the affidavit upon which their belief was founded is totally destitute of truth, it appears unnecessary to longer delay this communication," he wrote.[29] This case was a part of the ongoing diplomatic wrangling between the United States and Great Britain over the former's involvement in the illegal slave trade, which explains Forsyth's attitude. The United States had joined the British in outlawing the trade in 1808, and U.S. laws against the trade were the world's most stringent, but the laws were poorly enforced. The British had long pushed the American government to allow them the Right of Search, the only way to really police the trade. The United States adamantly refused to allow the British to stop, board, and search U.S. ships, and, as a result, slavers from other countries used the U.S. flag as a cover and U.S. shippers also engaged in the trade. So long as those slavers were carrying their cargos to Cuba and Brazil and not to its shores, the U.S. government showed a lack of zeal in prosecuting them. As Secretary of State, Forsyth made it clear

that the United States would not compromise with Britain on these issues, and, as a slave owner himself, he was dedicated to the institution
and eager to defend it.[30]

But was Forsyth correct? Was Smith's account nothing more than a
sailor's yarn? It is important to further interrogate the inconsistencies
in Smith's account to answer that question. In fact, James Buchanan,
British consul in New York City, verified much of Smith's story. Bu-
chanan verified the arrival of the *William and Robert*, and he recalled
that the crew of the ship had only signed up for the voyage to New York
City. He observed that six men were discharged: William Moore,
J. Robinson, Benjamin Smart, Lewis Waters, James Lougan, and Charles
Foster. According to his records, there was no sailor named Charles
Smith on board the ship, but he acknowledged that "sailors are much in
the habit of changing their names," and he speculated that perhaps
Charles Foster was, in fact, Smith.

Smith also claimed to have received a Seaman's Protection Certificate, but Buchanan had no record of issuing such a document, though
he acknowledged that he may have done so. Introduced in the late
eighteenth century, Seaman's Protection Certificates were issued to
sailors to certify citizenship, and black sailors often relied on these documents to protect them in southern ports. It is likely that Smith took
his certificate under another name and nationality. Charles Rockwell,
an American sailor, described how often sailors changed their names
and identities and commonly acquired forged certificates:

> In a crew . . . one meets with seamen of every class and condition, and
> almost every nation under heaven. More common, sailors are of no na-
> tion, but change from the employ of one to that of another, just as con-
> venience, or caprice, or higher wages may induce them to do so. . . .
> That by desertion or otherwise, men are constantly passing from one
> service to the other, is well known. As those who ship seamen often
> receive so much a head for all they furnish, no very close inquiries are
> made as to whether a seaman's protection, as it is called, that is, the
> legal paper that certifies to which nation he belongs, tells the truth
> about him or not; for aside from false swearing, at which few common
> sailors would hesitate, there are other ways which seamen obtain new
> papers and a new name.

He described sailing with a Swede or Dane who spoke broken English
and who claimed to be an American named John Cole. Rockwell asked

him why he had such a "Yankee" name, and Cole explained that he paid his landlord in Portland fifty cents for the certificate with his new name, but added, "I've got most sick of it, and shall change it for another before long." Rockwell observed, "Thus it is often true, that sailor-landlords sell the papers of seamen who have died in their houses, or have gone to sea leaving them behind. Many of the seamen in our navy, ship by a new name almost every cruise."[31]

Smith could have easily learned about these subterfuges from his fellow sailors or from his landlord in New York City, and for Africans like him, a name change was nothing new. Smith did not record his birth name or when and where he took the name Charles Smith. While it was common for the Liberated Africans in Sierra Leone to take English names, it is unclear whether those names were assigned to them on board the slave ships, given to them by the Liberated African Department, given to them in the missionary schools or when they were baptized as Christians, or if they simply chose them themselves. Whatever the case may be, Africans who traveled the Atlantic World were well practiced in changing their names and identities.

My search of shipping records failed to turn up a ship with a Captain Parker from New York to St. John's or Mobile in the first half of 1838 but, since Smith indicated that Parker could have been master and not captain, the lack of such a record is not conclusive. On the other hand, there were many departures from New York City to both St. John's and Mobile in the first six months of 1838, and either of Smith's accounts could be accurate. A route from St. John's to Mobile would have been a highly unusual one, and the Mobile shipping records do not reveal the arrival of a ship from St. John's in 1838, but if the ship stopped along the way, at Boston, New York or Baltimore, for example, as would have been likely, then the records would record the ship as coming from those ports and not St. John's. H. Bowyer Smith, Collector of the Port in St. John's, offered one possible match for Smith's ship. He told the British that a ship called the *Derigo*, Thomas M. Parker, Captain, arrived there from East Port, Maine, on February 25, 1839 and cleared on the 27th for Lubec, Maine. While that date is too late for Smith's 1838 voyage, a ship by that name arrived in New York from Frenchman's Bay, Maine, in May 1838 and could have been the same ship. If Smith was employed on that ship, it was probably through friends who were on the *William and Robert* which was a St. John's vessel.

Another glaring gap in Smith's account was the fact that no ship called the *Sarah Nixon* from Sunderland, the ship that took Smith to Liverpool, could be found in the records. That ship could not be found because of a slip in Smith's memory or a problem with the men who took his deposition. The ship was the *Sarah Nicholson* of Sunderland, and it arrived in New York City on April 20, sailed from New York City for Liverpool on May 22, and arrived in Liverpool on June 22, 1838. That date also makes it possible for Smith to have walked to London and sailed on the *Lord Wellington* with Captain Tate which left London for Sierra Leone on November 16, 1838. There is no evidence, however, that the *Sarah Nicholson* sailed to Mobile. It might have been just possible for the ship to sail to Mobile and back between April 20 and May 22, a voyage that took anywhere from six to twenty-four days each way, but typically American newspapers reported every leg of a merchant ship's voyage. So, New York newspapers would report the ship's departure to Mobile, Mobile newspapers would report its arrival and departure, and the New York newspapers would report its return. It would be highly improbable that the press missed every leg of such a voyage. Smith also reported seeing a Captain Freebody in Mobile whom he had known on the West Coast of Africa. The newspapers reported the name of the ship and its captain in the "Shipping News," and there is no mention of a Captain Freebody in Mobile in 1838. Freebody was based in Cape Coast Castle on the Gold Coast, and he was in Baltimore and Charleston in 1835, so a voyage to Mobile is not far-fetched. Unless he was there in a capacity other than captain, however, his absence from the newspapers is troubling.[32]

As compelling and convincing as aspects of Smith's description of his time in Mobile are, it is not possible to verify any aspect of his story about what happened there with certainty. There is no question that he was in New York, and that he arrived on the *William and Robert* in April 1838 and departed on the *Sarah Nicholson* in May 1838. What happened in between, however, remains speculative. What we do have is his sworn deposition given to officials in Sierra Leone after a herculean effort to inform Pharaoh Moses of his son's whereabouts. His role was the same as John Alford's in Jamaica, another sailor who went to great lengths to inform the authorities of the whereabouts of Wellington, kidnapped into slavery in Cuba. When it comes to his story of Sack N'Jaie, we are left with two possibilities: either Smith's story is true or, as the American officials contended, it is nothing more than a sailor's yarn. While there were compelling reasons for Dimmock Charlton to fabricate service in the British Navy, if he did so, there is no obvious motivation for Smith to make up the story of Sack N'Jaie's plight, to get back to Sierra Leone, to go immediately to Pharaoh Moses with the news of his son, and to make depositions before British officials to try to help rescue him. It is one thing to make up a good story to share with sailors to pass the time on a long voyage, and quite another to embark on an Atlantic quest to help free a fellow African from illegal enslavement and to raise the hopes of a devastated family who had lost a beloved son, husband, and father. Sack N'Jaie disappeared in July 1837 and Smith left the Gambia in December 1838, so he could have known about N'Jaie's disappearance before he left West Africa. Certainly, everyone in Sierra Leone believed Smith. Sack N'Jaie's family may have been so desperate that they would have grasped at any hope that he was alive, though British officials who interviewed Smith in person and were also convinced of the truth of his statements were far less personally invested.

There is one other possibility, that keeping Sack N'Jaie alive somehow worked to the advantage of Pharaoh Moses and the N'Jaie family, and they colluded with Smith to convince British authorities that he was enslaved in Alabama. Sack N'Jaie owned considerable property in Freetown—two houses and a ship—and it could be that keeping the estate unsettled may have somehow benefitted the N'Jaies. Did Pharaoh Moses, as family patriarch, have some control over the estate that he might lose to Sack N'Jaie's widow were the estate to be settled? Did he convince Smith to engage in such an elaborate subterfuge after Smith's return to Sierra Leone from the United States presented him with such an opportunity? If so, then they expertly manipulated the colonial authorities, but there is insufficient evidence to take such a scenario any further. If Smith's account was truthful, then Sack N'Jaie probably spent the remainder of his life enslaved in Alabama. His family had the comfort of knowing that he was alive, and Pharaoh Moses, whose experience mirrored that of his son, would have known that his son could carve out a life for himself in the plantation South.

Yet, this case dramatically illustrates the remarkably intricate webs, the "complex mesh of networks," that crisscrossed the Atlantic. Through a most unlikely series of chance encounters and a web of personal relationships among Africans around the Atlantic and the Gulf, word of Sack N'Jaie's plight reached his family in Sierra Leone, and Moses's complaint set off an investigation that swept around the Atlantic World.

Conclusion

THE LIFE NARRATIVES presented here demonstrate the remarkable diversity, mobility, and resourcefulness that characterized the lives of Africans in the Old South. One overarching conclusion to be drawn from the cases is that it is difficult to generalize about any common experience among them. The diverse experiences of these extraordinary individuals highlight the difficulties—and pitfalls—of trying to characterize an "African" identity in the Old South. Yet, their narratives do suggest the possibility for and value in mapping individual narratives of Africans across the Atlantic World, even if in fragments, as they do share some important links, connections, and life strategies. One feature common to all of them is the malleability of their identities. Their self-identification was both situational and relational as circumstances demanded. We see individual identities shaped by changing locales as these Africans moved through the Atlantic World. Elizabeth Cleveland's positions as a member of an elite Anglo-African slave trading family on the Banana Islands, as a student at a Liverpool boarding school, and as a wife and widowed member of the South Carolina planter elite demonstrate the intimate connection between self and place and between race, class, and gender. Catherine Cleveland's position changed dramatically when she stepped off the *Queen of Bara* in Charleston and into the role of a free person of color; when in Africa her position had been the same as her aunt's. Another family of Anglo-African slave traders, the Holmans, arriving twenty-five years later than the Clevelands, negotiated the Atlantic World's complex racial dynamics as they moved back and forth between South Carolina and the Rio Pongo. They joined the ranks of the elite free people of color in the Lowcountry but operated as members of the Anglo-African merchant elite in Africa. Charlton went from a boy in the Kissi nation, to a Liberated African, to John Bull, a crewman on board a British warship, to Dimmock Charlton enslaved in Savannah, to John Bull / Dimmock Charlton as a free man in the North and in Britain.

The concept of "life geographies" is useful when mapping the lives of individuals whose lives were shaped by mobility and who were positioned in a complex interplay of states, nations, and boundaries.[1] For all of the Africans here, the most important boundary separated slavery from freedom, and this boundary shifted dramatically from the eighteenth to the nineteenth centuries. Slavery began to disappear from the northern states in the wake of the American Revolution. Liberia and Sierra Leone arose as states opposed to the slave trade in West Africa, and both the United States and Britain and then other European nations outlawed the African slave trade. But despite those efforts, the African slave trade proved to be remarkably resilient; British abolitionist Thomas Clarkson wrote that "the Slave-trade may be considered, like the fabulous hydra, to have had a hundred heads, every one of which it was necessary to cut off before it could be subdued."[2] The British assumed the role of the enforcers of the ban on the Atlantic Ocean, and the line between slavery and freedom moved with the British naval squadrons enforcing the ban on the Atlantic slave trade. Africans quickly understood how to manipulate these new realities. The Clevelands and Holmans sought to position themselves as slaveowners within a slaveholding society, while the others sought to escape to freedom. The narratives suggest that the boundary between slavery and freedom was malleable, and the dangers of re-enslavement varied even between supposedly free zones. Dimmock Charlton sent his granddaughter to Canada to put her as far from those dangers as he could. Pharaoh Moses took his family to the free colony of Sierra Leone, but saw his son kidnapped into the illegal slave trade.

Members of two prominent Anglo-African slave trading families from the Rio Pongo-Rio Nunez region put down roots in South Carolina. Two of the Africans here were children from the Kissi nation who were shipped off the West African coast from the Sierra Leone region, others from Old Calabar. These commonalities reflect important slave trade routes in the late eighteenth century and into the nineteenth century. Once the British outlawed the trade, it shifted to the north, to the Sierra Leone region, and to the south in the Bight of Biafra. Those networks help explain what appear to be the remarkable coincidences in finding Elizabeth Cleveland having the Holmans as neighbors, or in Charles Smith's finding two Africans he knew on a plantation outside Mobile. Both Dimmock Charlton and Sack N'Jaie arrived in the South through the illegal slave trade, and their cases serve as a reminder that the trade did not actually stop in 1808.

Overlay the maps that outline the travels of each of the Africans profiled here and a remarkably complex network—that webbed spatiality—that defined the eighteenth- and nineteenth-century Atlantic World comes into view. Scholars of the Atlantic World have generally seen 1815 as the cutoff date for that field, though there is no compelling reason for such a constricted chronology. The life narratives presented here make a case for extending the Atlantic World chronology well into the nineteenth century. As some of these narratives suggest, the illegal slave trade continued (at rates nearly equal to the eighteenth century), and the trade networks crisscrossing the Atlantic Basin multiplied as did the volume of traffic.

These life narratives challenge the view of enslaved Africans brought into the South as provincial, ignorant of the Atlantic and its complexities, and lacking in linguistic skills and cultural adaptability. This generalization might apply—in part—to the Africans picked up by the *Aurora,* but their repeated escapes from enslavement and their eventual return to West Africa show them to be more resilient than might be expected given their circumstances. Certainly, the Clevelands and Holmans, members of mixed-race, cosmopolitan slave-trading dynasties whose very existence and livelihood was intimately connected to the Atlantic World, could not be characterized as provincial or ignorant of that world. All the enslaved Africans here may have been enslaved in the interior of Africa, but they were hardly provincial. They quickly learned English, had families, and over time, accumulated money, freed themselves, and, in the case of Pharaoh Moses, freed his entire family. They understood American and Atlantic jurisprudence and the boundaries between slave and free territories in the United States, North America, and the Atlantic World. They knew that the British could offer protection and freedom, and that the American Colonization Society offered a path back to Africa. They did not make the same choices: Dimmock Charlton made his way to Britain and sought to immigrate to Canada, Robert Johnson put down roots in Boston, while Pharaoh Moses returned to Africa with his American family. They understood, and manipulated, the "legal geography" of the Atlantic World with radically different outcomes in view.

These Africans, apart from those on the *Aurora,* shared another important geographical characteristic—they all lived in southern port cities. Dimmock Charlton and Pharaoh Moses were skilled slaves who hired out their time in urban environments which enabled them to save enough money to buy themselves out of slavery. Their residence in urban ports certainly played an important role in shaping their identities and opening many doors. Had they been isolated on a rural plantation, as the vast majority of Africans were, those opportunities would not have been as readily available to them. They understood that as well; Charlton reported that he withheld his claim to British protection for years for fear that if he had revealed it then he would have been sold into the rural plantation South.

Historians of slavery in the antebellum South have shown little interest in the African presence, and given the rapid growth of a native-born, creole slave population, that focus is understandable. Those demographics certainly play a part in the acculturation of Moses, Charlton, Johnson, and other Africans who arrived in the late eighteenth and early nineteenth centuries. They did not enter a predominantly African slave community, perhaps with others from their homeland, but rather lived in a heavily creolized community that encouraged a more rapid acculturation. Given these demographics, histories of African enslavement in the American South have focused on the colonial and early national periods, but these narratives demonstrate that it is important to carry the story of African enslavement in the South into the nineteenth century.

Anyone who has taken the London Underground has heard that familiar warning, "mind the gap." I thought of it often as I combed through the British National Archives in an attempt to further verify various aspects of the narratives presented here, a search that all too often ended in disappointment. My inability to verify important parts of these narratives forced me to consider the nature of historical evidence, the problem of the archives, and the very nature of "truth" in history. Of the six life narratives of Africans presented here, only two—those of Elizabeth Cleveland Hardcastle and the Holman family—can be veri-

fied beyond any shadow of doubt and without glaring gaps. That is not
so surprising when we consider that Elizabeth lived her life as a member
of South Carolina's white planter elite, a group most likely to leave their
mark in the historical record, and the Holmans, though free people of
color, were wealthy enough to leave their mark in the historical record
on both sides of the Atlantic. Archives are a reflection of power, and
those whose voices are most likely to be preserved in them had wealth,
position, and influence. Even today, archives like the South Carolina
Historical Society or the Georgia Historical Society stand as monu-
ments to those elites, built and maintained by their descendants down
to the present. Subalterns, and particularly enslaved Africans, are most
likely to appear in the records as they related to those with power—as
an enumeration on a slave list, in a transfer of property or in a record
of manumission—their own voices usually silenced. Free blacks, as
owners of property and heads of households, might leave a marginally
better trace in the public records—enumerated in census returns and
recorded as property owners and taxpayers. Some archival silences
have a different source; one group of records I wanted to consult at
Kew—the Custom's records from Liverpool for the 1830s—were "destroyed by enemy actions in the Second World War." But even so, major
questions loom over these life narratives: did Dimmock Charlton serve
on board the *Peacock?* Was Delia's throat slashed by John McIntosh? Did
Sack N'Jaie live out his life on a cotton plantation outside Mobile?

The gaps in the historical record raise important questions about
evidence and the very nature of the archives that shape historical
research. In 1994 Jacques Derrida presented an influential lecture,
later published in book form, called "Mal d'archive: une impression
freudienne"—translated as "Archive fever"—in which he traced the origins of archives back to the *arkhe,* the house occupied by the archons or
chief magistrates of ancient Greek city-states. He explored the fundamental link between power, authority, and control over the historical
record and concluded that "there is no political power without control
of the archive." The link between the state and the archive posed a
real threat to historians who could fall victim to the state power represented *by* and *in* the archive. Anthropologist Ann Laura Stoler challenged scholars to identify "the conditions of possibility that shaped
what could be written, what warranted repetition, what competencies
were rewarded in archival writing, what stories could be told, and what

could not be said." All of these considerations, she argued, created a "hierarchy of credibility" and require scholars to weigh evidence on the "scales of trust." Given the nature of archives and the larger historical record, there are certain kinds of records one should not expect to find—like records relating to Delia's murder—and records that one might reasonably expect to find—like the voyage of the *Sarah Nicholson* to Mobile or Dimmock Charlton's service on board the *Peacock* (where anyone who received a wage or ate food on board the ship was to be recorded in the ship's manifests).[3]

The claims that Charlton, Smith, and Johnson made cannot be completely verified by the accepted standards of historical research—the gaps in the historical record are simply too great. In large part, these gaps are a result of the very nature and purpose of archives, of what sort of information was thought worthy of preservation, or what Jacques Derrida called the "politics of the archive."[4] Since they were created as an apparatus of the state, Sonia Combe warned that historians could be entrapped by the archives and fall victim to that state power and the limitations it imposed on their scholarship. Trouillot reminds us that archives are created, that mentions and silences in the archives are active, ongoing, and significant, and "that some peoples and things are absent in history, and that this absence itself is constitutive of the process of historical production," all of which remind us of the need to be vigilant in the use of archives.[5]

French historian Arlette Farge, in her elegant meditation on the pleasures and pitfalls of the archives, asks, "How can we rescue from oblivion those lives that were never made note of even when they were alive (or if they were recognized it was only in order to punish them)?" It is a crucial question for scholars who work with individuals and groups whose voices are seldom heard or filtered. Fortunately for the practitioners of microhistory, these silences were seldom complete, and subaltern voices can be heard in the archives, often as fragments, often filtered through the pens of elite record keepers. Historian Saidiya V. Hartman contends that "there is no access to the subaltern consciousness outside dominant representations or elite documents," and it is certainly true that the unfiltered voices of subalterns are extremely rare in the historical record.[6] Rebecca J. Scott and Jean M. Hebrard make the very important observation that subalterns, in this case enslaved blacks and free people of color, consciously resisted the silence of the archives and intentionally wrote themselves into the historical record at every opportunity. In their sweeping Atlantic history of the Tinchant family, they wrote:

> The family emerges as one with a tenacious commitment to claiming dignity and respect. Members of each generation, moreover, showed an awareness of the crucial role of documents in making such claims, as they arranged for papers to be brought into being—sacramental records when taking a child to be baptized, notarial records when registering a contract, letters to the editor when engaging in public debate, private correspondence when conveying news to each other. For many members of the family, individual nationality and formal citizenship were not clearly defined, but a person could still make things happen by putting words on paper. The manumission documents drafted to protect the members of the first generations from slavery to reenslavement, for example, turn out to be highly complex creations with a power both more fragile and more real than one might imagine.[7]

Theirs is a crucial insight that speaks directly to the efforts of Johnson, Charlton, and Moses not only to claim dignity and respect, but to write themselves and their families and personal histories into the record. It is these fragments, and especially those created by subalterns with some intentionality, that we must attend to most carefully and employ critically to assemble their life narratives. These vitally important sources cannot be dismissed simply because they cannot be documented through other sources, otherwise we fall victim to the power of the archives, to Derrida's *mal d'archive*.

None of the individuals here wrote an autobiography. In some cases the archival record is substantial enough to create a full biography—from cradle to grave—but in other cases the records are fragmentary, so much so that not even their names have been recorded. The very nature of archives makes it impossible to verify some of the key elements of these narratives. That uncertainty raises important questions about subaltern voices and how we weigh their testimony in the scales of credibility in the absence of corroborating evidence. That does not mean that we should read them uncritically, but it does mean that, whether we think of them as fragments or disabled histories, we must be aware that we may not be able to fully verify the narratives through outside sources. That these narratives survived at all, that these Africans found ways to inscribe their narratives into the historical record despite efforts of southern slaveholders to silence African and enslaved voices, demands that they be heard. In one sense, this book is narrowly focused on the lives of a few individuals, on the backside of history, with the larger history of slavery and the slave trade on the obverse. I hope that the broad contours of that larger history become visible, that through these extraordinary lives the terror, the violence, the heartrending separations, and the life-affirming struggles of the enslaved come into sharper focus. Their lives are reminders of just how pervasive and extensive the institution of slavery was, just how vicious that many-headed hydra appeared, and how large it loomed over the lives of individuals caught up in its tentacles.

NOTES

ACKNOWLEDGMENTS

INDEX

Notes

Introduction

1. These estimates are drawn from The Trans-Atlantic Slave Trade Database at http://www.slavevoyages.org/tast/assessment/estimates (accessed June 11, 2015).
2. For a useful overview of the field of microhistory, see Sigurður Gylfi Magnússon and István M. Szijártó, *What is Microhistory? Theory and Practice* (London: Routledge, 2013).
3. For an overview of the scholarship on the Black Atlantic, see Philip D. Morgan, "Africa and the Atlantic, c. 1450 to c. 1820," in Jack P. Greene and Morgan, eds., *Atlantic History: A Critical Appraisal* (Oxford: Oxford University Press, 2009), 223–248. Their introduction reviews the major criticisms of the field of Atlantic History.
4. Carlo Ginzburg, *The Cheese and the Worms: The Cosmos of a Sixteenth-Century Miller* (New York: Penguin Books, 1982), xx.
5. Joseph C. Miller, "A Historical Appreciation of the Biographical Turn," in Lisa A. Lindsay and John Wood Sweet, eds., *Biography and the Black Atlantic* (Philadelphia: University of Pennsylvania Press, 2014), 19 (quotation). For examples of monographs that have taken a biographical approach to Africans and Atlantic history, see Robin Law and Paul E. Lovejoy, *The Biography of Mahommah Gardo Baquaqua: His Passage from Slavery to Freedom in Africa and America* (Princeton, NJ: Markus Wiener, 2001); Randy J. Sparks, *The Two Princes of Calabar: An Eighteenth-Century Atlantic Odyssey* (Cambridge, MA: Harvard University Press, 2003); Vincent Carretta, *Equiano, The African: Biography of a Self-Made Man* (Athens: University of Georgia Press, 2005); Jon F. Sensbach, *Rebecca's Revival: Creating Black Christianity in the Atlantic World* (Cambridge, MA: Harvard University Press, 2005); Clifton Crais and Pamela Scully, *Sara Baartman and the Hottentot Venus: A Ghost Story and a Biography* (Princeton, NJ: Princeton University Press, 2009); Sandra E. Greene, *West African Narratives of Slavery: Texts from Late Nineteenth- and Early*

Twentieth-Century Ghana (Bloomington: Indiana University Press, 2011); James H. Sweet, *Domingos Álvares, African Healing, and the Intellectual History of the Atlantic World* (Chapel Hill: The University of North Carolina Press, 2011); and Benjamin N. Lawrance, *Amistad's Orphans: An Atlantic Story of Children, Slavery, and Smuggling* (New Haven, CT: Yale University Press, 2015). See also Paul E. Lovejoy, "Biography as a Source Material: Towards a Biographical Archive of Enslaved Africans," in *Source Material for Studying the Slave Trade and the African Diaspora: Papers from a Conference of the Centre of Commonwealth Studies, University of Stirling, April 1996,* Robin Law, ed. (Stirling, UK: University of Stirling, 1997), 119–140. On the SHADD project, see http://www.tubmaninstitute.ca/shadd.

6. Georgia Writer's Project, *Drums and Shadows: Survival Studies Among the Georgia Coastal Negroes* (Athens: University of Georgia Press, 1940), 8, 18, 31, 67, 79 (first quotation), 96, 101, 139, 147, 150 (second quotation); Harold Courlander, *A Treasury of Afro-American Folklore: The Oral Literature, Traditions, Recollections, Legends, Tales, Songs, Religious Beliefs, Customs, Sayings and Humor of Peoples of African Descent in the Americas* (New York: Da Capo Press, 2002), 286 (third and fourth quotations); Russell Duncan, *Freedom's Shore: Tunis Campbell and the Georgia Freedmen* (Athens: University of Georgia Press, 1986), 4, 28; Michael A. Gomez, *Exchanging Our Country Marks: The Transformation of African Identities in the Colonial and Antebellum South* (Chapel Hill: The University of North Carolina Press, 1998), 117–120. Gomez argues that these tales of flight may refer to suicides.

7. Ira Berlin, *Many Thousands Gone: The First Two Centuries of Slavery in North America* (Cambridge, MA: Harvard University Press, 1998), 103 (first quotation). For his discussion of Atlantic Creoles, see pp. 17–28; on the Charter Generations, see Part I, pp. 15–92.

8. Philip D. Morgan, *Slave Counterpoint: Black Culture in the Eighteenth-Century Chesapeake & Lowcountry* (Chapel Hill: The University of North Carolina Press, 1998), 95; Gomez, *Exchanging Our Country Marks,* 20.

9. Berlin, *Many Thousands Gone,* 95, 102–103 (first and second quotations on p. 102).

10. Ginzburg and Poni quoted in Magnússon and Szijártó, *What is Microhistory?,* 7.

11. For useful introductions to subaltern studies and the subaltern voice, see the forum in *American Historical Review* 99 (December 1994): 1475–1545, and David Ludden, ed., *Reading Subaltern Studies: Critical History, Contested Meaning and the Globalization of South Asia* (London: Anthem Press, 2002).

12. Ann Laura Stoler reviews the debate over the nature of archives in *Along the Archival Grain: Epistemic Anxieties and Colonial Common Sense* (Princeton, NJ: Princeton University Press, 2009), 17–53.

13. Michel-Rolph Trouillot, *Silencing the Past: Power and the Production of History* (Boston: Beacon Press, 1995), 26 (second quotation), 48, 99 (first quotation).

14. Stoler, *Along the Archival Grain,* 3 (first quotation), 20 (second quotation).

15. For a useful review of the literature on African identity formation in the Americas, see Philip D. Morgan, "Africa and the Atlantic, c. 1450 to c. 1820" in Greene and Morgan, eds., *Atlantic History,* 235–241.

16. Miller, "Historical Appreciation," 41, 46 (quotation).

17. Gomez, *Exchanging Our Country Marks,* 14; Lindsay, "Remembering His Country Marks: A Nigerian American Family and Its 'African' Ancestor," in Lindsay and J. W. Sweet, *Biography and the Black Atlantic,* 194 (first quotation), 206 (second quotation); J. H. Sweet, *Domingos Álvares,* 230 (third and fourth quotations).

18. Frederick Cooper, *Colonialism in Question: Theory, Knowledge, History* (Berkeley: University of California Press, 2005), 7.

19. Trouillot, *Silencing the Past,* 23–24 (quotations on p. 23).

20. My understanding of the relationship between geography and identity has been influenced in part by the creative work of scholars of the Indian Ocean, most especially in Clare Anderson, *Subaltern Lives: Biographies of Colonialism in the Indian Ocean World, 1790–1920* (Cambridge: Cambridge University Press, 2012). See also Ann Laura Stoler, *Along the Archival Grain;* David Ludden, ed., *Reading Subaltern Studies;* Judith M. Brown, " 'Life Histories' and the History of Modern South Asia," *American Historical Review* 114, no. 3 (2009): 587–595. On "life geographies" see Alan Lester, "Relational Space and Life Geographies in Imperial History: George Arthur and Humanitarian Governance," *Journal of the Canadian Historical Association / Revue de la Société historique du Canada* 21, no. 2 (2010): 29–46; Stephen Daniels and Catherine Nash, "Life Paths: Geography and Biography," *Journal of Historical Geography* 30 (2004): 449–458; Miles Ogborn, *Global Lives: Britain and the World, 1550–1800* (Cambridge: Cambridge University Press, 2008); and David Lambert and Alan Lester, eds., *Colonial Lives Across the British Empire: Imperial Careering in the Long Nineteenth Century* (Cambridge: Cambridge University Press, 2006).

21. Tony Ballantyne, *Orientalism and Race: Aryanism in the British Empire* (Basingstoke, UK: Palgrave Macmillan, 2002), 45–46 (quotation on p. 46).

22. Lambert and Lester, *Colonial Lives,* 13 (quotation), 26.

23. Stoler, "Tense and Tender Ties," *Journal of American History* 88, no. 3 (2004): 862; Gomez, *Exchanging Our Country Marks,* 194–195, 217.

24. Salman Rushdie, *Imaginary Homelands: Essays and Criticism, 1981–1991* (London: Granta Books, 1991), 210 (fourth quotation), 394 (third quotation).

25. Daniels and Nash, "Life Paths," 449–458.

26. I have relied heavily on the in-depth genealogical research conducted by a descendant of the Cleveland family, E. Louise, who published her findings in *Elizabeth Clevland Hardcastle, 1741–1808: A Lady of Color in the South Carolina Low Country* (Columbia, SC: Phoenix Publishers, 2001).

1. Anglo-African Women Join a Plantation Society

1. Lopez quoted in Robert Olwell, *Masters, Slaves, and Subjects: The Culture of Power in the South Carolina Low Country, 1740–1790* (Ithaca, NY, and London: Cornell University Press, 1998), n. 72, pp. 35–36. On Charleston's growth and trade in the period, see R. C. Nash, "The Organization of Trade and Finance in the Atlantic Economy: Britain and South Carolina, 1670–1775," in Jack P. Greene, Rosemary Brana-Shute, and Randy J. Sparks, eds., *Money, Trade and Power: The Evolution of Colonial South Carolina's Plantation Society* (Columbia: University of South Carolina Press, 2001), 74–107. For details on the *Queen of Barra* see The Trans-Atlantic Slave Trade Database, Voyage 76050 (http://www.slavevoyages.org/tast/index.faces).

2. Philip D. Morgan, *Slave Counterpoint: Black Culture in the Eighteenth-Century Chesapeake & Lowcountry* (Chapel Hill: The University of North Carolina Press, 1998), 59, 61, 63, 74, 75, 95 (quotations), 97.

3. Walter Rodney, *A History of the Upper Guinea Coast, 1545–1800* (Oxford: Clarendon Press, 1970), 216–218.

4. Nicholas Owen, *Journal of a Slave-Dealer,* Eveline Martin, ed. (Boston and New York: Houghton Mifflin Co., 1930), 76.

5. Two of his voyages appear in The Trans-Atlantic Slave Trade Database, Voyages 27191 and 77582 (accessed October 15, 2013).

6. E. Louise, *Elizabeth Clevland Hardcastle, 1741–1808: A Lady of Color in the South Carolina Low Country* (Columbia, SC: Phoenix Publishers, 2001), 28.

7. The Liverpool Directory for 1766 lists two boarding schools run by women, but there were probably more in the city. George T. Shaw and Isabella Shaw, comps., *Liverpool's First Directory: A Reprint of the Names and Addresses From Gore's Directory for 1766* (Liverpool: Henry and Young, 1907), 4, 30, 46. In 1837 there were over 240 Dame Schools in that city. *The Penny Magazine of the Society for the Diffusion of Useful Knowledge,* 4 February 1837, 43.

8. William Woodfall, *An Impartial Report of the Debates that Occur in the Two Houses of Parliament, In the Course of the Second Session of the Eighteenth Parliament of Great Britain* (London: T. Chapman, 1798), 256; Rodney, *Upper Guinea Coast,* 218; George E. Brooks, *Eurafricans in Western Africa: Commerce, Social Status, Gender, and Religious Observance from the Sixteenth to the Eighteenth Century* (Athens: Ohio University Press, 2003), 244–246.

9. Sandcasters were described as "a kind of conjurer who pretends to the power of discovering by throwing handfuls of sand on the ground." African Institution, *Sixth Report of the Directors of the African Institution* (London: Ellerton and Henderson, 1812), 129; House of Commons, Reports of Committees, Report on the Lords of Trade of the Slave Trade, Part 1, vol. 69, *Report Of The Lords of the Committee of Council appointed for the Consideration of all Matters relating to Trade and Foreign Plantations; Submitting To His Majesty's Consideration The Evidence and Information they have collected in consequence of*

his Majesty's Order in Council, dated the 11th of February 1788, concerning the present State of the Trade to Africa, and particularly the Trade in Slaves; and concerning the Effects and Consequences of this Trade, as well in Africa and the West Indies, as to the general Commerce of this Kingdom (London: Board of Trade, 1789), 85.

10. In 1860 Catherine's great-grandson Andrew Dibble recorded in his certificate of freedom that Elizabeth and Catherine arrived in Charleston on board the *Queen of Barra* captained by Alexander Taylor and consigned to Henry Laurens. All of these details about the ship are accurate. The Trans-Atlantic Slave Trade Database, Voyage 76050; Henry Laurens, *The Papers of Henry Laurens*, vol. 4, *September 1, 1763–August 31, 1765* (Columbia: University of South Carolina Press, 1974), 457, 459, 466.

11. Louise, *Elizabeth Clevland Hardcastle*, 63, 65, 170–171. Despite considerable digging, E. Louise was unable to verify the exact kinship between Elizabeth's father, William Cleveland, and John Cleland. Some of the South Carolina Clelands later suggested that William and John were brothers, and while William did have a brother named John, he did not move to South Carolina. Louise suggests, without evidence, that William's father must have had a son by a previous and unrecorded marriage, a son who appears nowhere in the records. Since John Cleland was a native of Scotland, the Clevelands and Clelands must be more distantly related than she suggests. George C. Rogers, *Charleston in the Age of the Pickneys* (Columbia: University of South Carolina Press, 1980), 5.

12. David Dobson, *Scottish Emigration to Colonial America, 1607–1785* (Athens: University of Georgia Press, 1994), 107–108; Clara A. Langley, South Carolina deed abstracts, 1719–1772, vol. 4 (Easley, SC: 1983), 77, 227; *South-Carolina Gazette*, 16 May 1761, 25 September 1762, 3 October 1768 (quotation); *South-Carolina Gazette*, 5 March 1771; Laurens, *Papers of Henry Laurens*, vol. 5, *September 1, 1765–July 31, 1768* (Columbia: University of South Carolina Press, 1976), 335; Frederick Augustus Porcher and Samuel Gaillard Stoney, "The Memoirs of Frederick Augustus Porcher," *South Carolina Historical and Genealogical Magazine* 44 (April 1943): 67; Samuel DuBose, "Reminiscences of St. Stephen's Parish, Craven County and Notices of Her Old Homesteads," in Samuel DuBose and Frederick A. Porcher, *A Contribution to the History of the Huguenots of South Carolina Consisting of Pamphlets* (New York: G. P. Putnam's Sons, 1887), 36–85 (first quotation on p. 37, second quotation on p. 38).

13. Paul Richards, "Culture and Community Values in the Selection and Maintenance of African Rice," in Stephen B. Brush, Doreen Stabinsky, eds., *Valuing Local Knowledge: Indigenous People and Intellectual Property Rights* (Washington, DC: Island Press, 1996), 217.

14. Olwell, *Masters, Slaves, and Subjects*, 104; Frederick Dalcho, *An Historical Account of the Protestant Episcopal Church in South Carolina* (Charleston, SC: E. Thayer, 1820), 264–274. Catherine recorded her baptism by Hockley who was only at the church between those years. Louise, *Elizabeth Clevland Hardcastle*, 425.

15. Porcher and Stoney, "Memoirs" 44 (July 1943): 140. Porcher, the author of the memoirs, heard the stories about Elizabeth secondhand from his elderly friends and relations. He claimed that Elizabeth visited Keithfield as a child, and that Mrs. Porcher played with her then, a version that E. Louise also accepts. There is no evidence that Elizabeth visited South Carolina as a child, no evidence that her father traded for slaves there, and it is difficult to imagine how, why, or when she would have done so. I therefore conclude that the mulatto girl at Keithfield was Catherine, not Elizabeth. Louise, *Elizabeth Clevland Hardcastle*, 61–62. Olwell, *Masters, Slaves, and Subjects*, 54.

16. The sale was delayed at least once, perhaps to give Cleveland time to arrange for funds. *South-Carolina Gazette*, 28 February 1771, 5 March 1771, 11 March 1771. Loocock was a physician and colleague of Hardcastle. A Dr. William Clarkson also appears in the records. *South-Carolina Gazette*, 16 November 1773, 12 May 1775, 16 May 1775.

17. Elizabeth Hardcastle to Charles Mill, Release of Inheritance, and Charles Mill to John Cleveland, Deed of Trust, reproduced in Louise, *Elizabeth Clevland Hardcastle*, 387–392, 75–76; in 1772 William Moultrie advertised for a spaniel that had been lost by "curling" through Dr. Hardcastle's plantation near Monck's Corner. *South-Carolina Gazette*, 23 June 1772, 29 April 1774.

18. Porcher and Stoney, "Memoirs," 139; Louise, *Elizabeth Clevland Hardcastle*, 75–77.

19. His estate inventory, along with other materials related to his death, is reproduced in Louise, *Elizabeth Clevland Hardcastle*, 399–401. Seven "valuable Negroes" belonging to Hardcastle were sold by the sheriff in 1774, suggesting that he may have been in financial difficulty. *South Carolina and American General Gazette*, 29 April 1774. Olwell, *Masters, Slaves, and Subjects*, 34.

20. DuBose, "Reminiscences," 40–41, 51–56, 59, 63 (quotation), 66.

21. Ibid., 40–41, 51–56, 59, 63, 66; Olwell, *Masters, Slaves, and Subjects*, 229 (quotation), 245–270; Edward Ball, *Slaves in the Family* (New York: Farrar, Strauss & Giroux, 1998), 221–236.

22. DuBose, "Reminiscences," 56, 67.

23. Ibid., 68.

24. Tucker Plantation is described in the advertisement for its sale following her death and the settlement of her estate. *Charleston City Gazette and Commercial Daily Advertiser*, 4 January 1822.

25. DuBose and Porcher, *A Contribution*, 21 (quotation); Louise, *Elizabeth Clevland Hardcastle*, 150, 152, 186–188.

26. "Report from the committee on the petition of the Court of Directors of the Sierra Leone Company, Select Committee on Petition of Court of Directors of Sierra Leone Company: Report, Appendix," in House of Commons, Reports of Committees, vol. 81, pp. 57, 57, 58, House of Commons Parliamentary Papers Database, available at http://gateway.proquest.com/openurl?url

_ver=Z39.88-2004&res_dat=xri:hcpp-us&rft_dat=xri:hcpp:rec:1803-000497 (accessed October 14, 2015).

27. Louise, *Elizabeth Clevland Hardcastle,* 150, 152, 186–188.

28. *Charleston City Gazette and Commercial Daily Advertiser,* 23 April 1821.

29. "Dr. Wm. Chisolm Deposition" in Louise, *Elizabeth Clevland Hardcastle,* 195.

30. Ibid., "Archibald Kenedy's answers to cross interrogatories," 186.

31. Ibid., "Maurice H. Cooper Answers," 188.

32. Ibid., "Letter of John and Betty Kirkwood," 5 April 1796, 182.

33. Ibid., "Elizabeth Hardcastle's Alleged Will of 1784 annexed to Thomas Scouler's Petition," 164, 315.

34. Testimony in the dispute over her will from Connor and others shows that they were on intimate terms. Ibid., 132–134, 137.

35. Ibid., 133 (quotation), 360–367.

36. Ibid., 142 (first quotation); "Catherine Cleveland's Certificate of Freedom," Elizabeth Hardcastle to Catherine Clevland, Deed of Gift, ibid., 98, 403; Frederick A. Porcher, "Upper Beat of St.John's, Berkeley: A Memoir," *Transactions of the Huguenot Society* 13 (1906): 31–78 (second quotation on p. 36).

37. Louise, *Elizabeth Clevland Hardcastle,* 122 (first quotation), 127.

38. Ibid., 122, 125–126 (first and second quotations on p. 126), 128.

39. Ibid., 123 (third quotation), 127 (fourth and fifth quotations), 135, 136 (first quotation), 137, 138 (second quotation).

40. Ibid., 124, 128 (first quotation), 129–130.

41. *Carolina Gazette,* 6 January 1809; *Charleston City Gazette and Commercial Daily Advertiser,* 4 January, 10 January 1809; *Charleston Courier,* 4 January 1809.

42. Louise, *Elizabeth Clevland Hardcastle,* 150–152; David Raizman, *History of Modern Design: Graphics and Products Since the Industrial Revolution* (London: Laurence King Publishing, 2003), 28 (quotation); Jennifer L. Anderson, *Mahogany: The Costs of Luxury in Early America* (Cambridge, MA: Harvard University Press, 2012), 16, 32, 37, 38, 51, 93, 134, 147, 150, 200.

43. "Thomas Scouler, nephew of Jasper Scouler, Petition to Senate" in Louise, *Elizabeth Clevland Hardcastle,* 162–163 (first quotation on p. 163), 276–277; "Committee Report on Thomas Scouler Petition to the Senate," ibid., 165; Thomas Cooper, ed., *The Statutes at Large of South Carolina: Containing the acts from 1786,* vol. 5 (Columbia, SC: A. S. Johnston, 1839), 46–49 (second quotation on p. 47).

44. "Equity Bill 40" in Louise, *Elizabeth Clevland Hardcastle,* 206–210, 260–261, 327; *Charleston City Gazette and Commercial Daily Advertiser,* 23 March 1821.

45. "Equity Bill 66," in Louise, *Elizabeth Clevland Hardcastle,* 211–212 (second and third quotations), 323; Porcher, "Memoirs," 139 (first quotation).

46. Louise, *Elizabeth Clevland Hardcastle,* 285–286.

47. "The Real Estate of Mrs. Hardcastle ads. Isaac Porcher, Escheator for Pineville Academy," William Harper, ed., *Report of Cases Determined in the Constitutional*

Court of South Carolina (Charleston: Black and Sweeny, 1860), 317–322; Louise, *Elizabeth Clevland Hardcastle*, 287.

48. "Mary Hillen and Charles Mayrant Petitions" in Louise, *Elizabeth Clevland Hardcastle*, 168–170.

49. David McCord, ed., *The Statutes at Large of South Carolina*, vol. 6 (Columbia, SC: A. S. Johnston, 1839), 385–386.

50. Louise, *Elizabeth Clevland Hardcastle*, 198.

51. Ibid., 123, 124, 125–126, 127, 128–129 (first quotation), 132 (second, third, and fourth quotations), 133 (fifth quotation), 142 (sixth quotation).

52. Ibid., 125, 127, 326, 366. During her final illness, Elizabeth reportedly said that she declined to leave twenty-two shares of bank stock to Catherine outright for fear that "her sons might deprive her of it." (p. 127). David Ramsay, *History of South Carolina from Its First Settlement in 1670, to the Year 1808* (Charleston, SC: David Longworth, 1809), 2: 569.

53. Michael P. Johnson and James L. Roark, *Black Masters: A Free Family of Color in the Old South* (New York: W. W. Norton & Co., 1984), 36 (quotation), 37, 43–45; Louise, *Elizabeth Clevland Hardcastle*, 420–427.

54. Johnson and Roark, *Black Masters*, 52–61, 96–97, 185 (quotation on p. 97); Louise, *Elizabeth Clevland Hardcastle*, 326.

55. Louise, *Elizabeth Clevland Hardcastle*, 326–327, 412; *Charleston Courier*, 8 June, 1835; *Charleston Mercury*, 3 February 1859; Johnson and Roark, *Black Masters*, 204–205. Minda or Mindah is an African "homeland" name sometimes given to creoles in the South Carolina Lowcountry. See Morgan, *Slave Counterpoint*, 454.

56. Louise, *Elizabeth Clevland Hardcastle*, 372–373.

57. James Sidbury and Jorge Cañizares-Esguerra, "Mapping Ethnogenesis in the Early Modern Atlantic," *William and Mary Quarterly* 68 (April 2011): 182–183.

58. Brooks, *Eurafricans in Western Africa*, 267.

59. Elizabeth M. Pruden, "Investing Widows: Autonomy in a Nascent Capitalist Society," in Jack P. Greene, Rosemary Brana-Shute, and Randy J. Sparks, eds., *Money, Trade and Power: The Evolution of Colonial South Carolina's Plantation Society* (Columbia: University of South Carolina Press, 2001), 345–346.

60. Ira Berlin, *Slaves Without Masters: The Free Negro in the Antebellum South* (New York: Pantheon, 1974), 97–99.

61. Olwell, *Masters, Slaves, and Subjects*, 50–51; Jordan, *White Over Black*, 144–150, 173–178.

62. Maurie D. McInnis, *The Politics of Taste in Antebellum Charleston* (Chapel Hill: The University of North Carolina Press, 2005), 5 (first quotation), 24; Porcher, "Memoirs," 139 (first and third quotations).

63. Porcher, "Memoirs," 139 (first quotation); Louise, *Elizabeth Clevland Hardcastle*, 186 (second quotation), 187 (third and fourth quotations), 193 (fifth quotation).

64. Porcher, "Memoirs," 139 (first quotation); Richard Waterhouse, *A New World Gentry: The Making of a Merchant and Planter Class in South Carolina, 1670–1770* (Charleston, SC: The History Press, 2005), 75, 100 (second quotation).
65. Porcher, "Memoirs," 140 (first quotation); Kate Masur, *An Example for All the Land: Emancipation and the Struggle Over Equality in Washington, D.C.* (Chapel Hill: The University of North Carolina Press, 2010), 192 (second quotation); McInnis, *Politics of Taste*, 286–287.
66. Markus Vink, "Indian Ocean Studies and the 'New Thalassology,'" *Journal of Global History* 2 (2007): 41–62 (first quotation on p. 52). John Thornton has emphasized the importance of recognizing class in Africa and in the conduct of the slave trade in "African Political Ethics and the Slave Trade" in *Abolitionism and Imperialism in Britain, Africa, and the Atlantic*, Derek R. Peterson, ed. (Athens, OH: Ohio University Press, 2010), 38–62; Frederick Cooper, *Colonialism in Question: Theory, Knowledge, History* (Berkeley: University of California Press, 2005), 72 (second quotation).

2. Finding a Transatlantic Middle Ground between Black and White

1. Larry Koger, *Black Slaveowners: Free Black Slave Masters in South Carolina, 1790–1860* (Columbia: University of South Carolina Press, 1985), 110–113; Henry Laurens, *The Papers of Henry Laurens*, vol. 7, *Aug. 1, 1769–Oct. 9, 1771*, George C. Rogers, Jr. and David R. Chesnutt, eds. (Columbia: University of South Carolina Press, 1979), 344–345 (first and second quotations); Race and Slavery Petitions Project, "Holman Petition to the South Carolina Senate," January 12, 1791, Petition 11379101, http://library.uncg.edu/slavery/petitions /results.aspx?s=3&sid=293&lRec=11378602&lastset=25&perpag=25 (accessed February 19, 2015) (third and fourth quotations).
2. *Dispatch* (1787), Voyages: The Trans-Atlantic Slave Trade Database, Voyage 25613, http://slavevoyages.org/tast/database/search.faces (accessed February 19, 2015); Laurens to Clay, 21 April 1791 (first, second, and third quotations), at http://www.worthpoint.com/worthopedia/1789-slave-slavery-stampless -folded-480077575 (accessed February 19, 2015); "Holman Petition to the South Carolina Senate" (fourth, fifth, and sixth quotations). On Laurens's political career, see Daniel J. McDonough, *Christopher Gadsden and Henry Laurens: The Parallel Lives of Two American Patriots* (Selinsgrove, PA: Susquehanna University Press, 2000).
3. "An Act to Permit John Holman to come with his Negro slaves into and to remain with them in this state, February 19, 1791," *Act of the General Assembly of the State of South Carolina from February, 1791, To December, 1794, Both Inclusive* (Columbia, SC: D. & J. J. Faust, 1808), 135–136. Laurens's support was probably crucial. Richard Johnson made the same case claiming that he intended his shipment of 50 slaves for use on his plantation and that the South Carolina ban was passed while he was engaged on the slave-trading

voyage from Charleston to Sierra Leone and back, but his petition was rejected. Petition of Richard Johnson, August 31, 1787, "Petition of Richard Johnson, August 31, 1787" in Adele Stanton Edwards, ed., *State Records of South Carolina: Journals of the Privy Council, 1783–1789* (Columbia: University of South Carolina Press, 1971), 206–208. A 1789 voyage for the *Eliza* with Olderman as captain appears in the Voyages database, but not a 1790 voyage. See Voyage 37032. The Savannah newspaper recorded a June 18, 1789 departure of the *Eliza* with Olderman as captain from Charleston (*Georgia Gazette,* June 18, 1789), and a December 2, 1790 departure of the *Eliza* from that port bound for Africa, which indicates that the voyage that brought Holman first to Charleston and then to Savannah is missing from the database. *Savannah City Gazette, or the Daily Advertiser,* December 2, 1790. The ship sank on that voyage. Voyages Database, Voyage 25405. "John Holman to South Carolina House, 1791," in Loren Schweninger, *The Southern Debate Over Slavery: Petitions to Southern Legislatures, 1778–1864,* vol. 1 (Urbana: University of Illinois Press, 2001), 13–14. On Laurens's complex and conflicted relationship with the slave trade, see James A. Rawley, *London: Metropolis of the Slave Trade* (Columbia: University of Missouri Press, 2003), chapter 5; Egerton Leigh, *The Man Unmasked; or, The World Undeceived: In the Author of a Late Pamphlet, Intitled, "Extracts from the Proceedings of the High Court of Vice-Admiralty in Charlestown, South-Carolina," &c. With Suitable Remarks on that Masterly Performance* (Charleston, SC: Peter Timothy, 1769), 144.

4. David Northrup, *Africa's Discovery of Europe: 1450–1850* (Oxford: Oxford University Press, 2009), 71 (quotation); George E. Brooks, *Eurafricans in Western Africa: Commerce, Social Status, Gender, and Religious Observance from the Sixteenth to the Eighteenth Century* (Athens: Ohio University Press, 2003), 44–56, 200–201; Bruce L. Mouser, *American Colony on the Rio Pongo: The War of 1812, The Slave Trade, and the Proposed Settlement of African Americans, 1810–1830* (Trenton, NJ: Africa World Press, 2013), 6–7; Bruce L. Mouser, "Trade and Politics in the Nunez and Pongo Rivers, 1790–1865" (PhD diss., Indiana University, 1971), 1–6, 15–21; Paul E. Lovejoy, *Transformations in Slavery: A History of Slavery in Africa* (Cambridge: Cambridge University Press, 2000), 49, 60–61, 75, 93, 118, 120, 127.

5. Brooks, *Eurafricans in Western Africa,* 44–56, 200–201; Mouser, *American Colony on the Rio Pongo,* 5–9; Mouser, "Trade and Politics in the Nunez and Pongo Rivers," 1–6, 15–21; Lovejoy, *Transformations in Slavery,* 49, 60–61, 75, 93, 118, 120, 127.

6. John Thornton, *Africa and Africans in the Making of the Atlantic World, 1400–1680* (Cambridge: Cambridge University Press, 1992), 60–63, 187–189, 231; Brooks, *Eurafricans in Western Africa,* 50–63; Mouser, "Trade and Politics in the Nunez and Pongo Rivers," 15–22; Boubacar Barry, *Senegambia and the Atlantic Slave Trade* (Cambridge: Cambridge University Press, 1998), 17, 19, 27; Mouser, *American Colony of the Rio Pongo,* 20.

7. Brooks, *Eurafricans in Western Africa,* 198–201, 293; Mouser, "Trade and Politics in the Nunez and Pongo Rivers," 24–26; Barry, *Senegambia and the Atlantic Slave Trade,* 20–36, 50, 61–65, 72–79; Philip J. Havik, *Silences and Soundbites: The Gendered Dynamics of Trade and Brokerage in the Pre-Colonial Guinea-Bissau Region* (Munster, Germany: Lit Verlag Munster, 2004), 130–131.

8. Schweninger, *The Southern Debate Over Slavery,* 1:13; Mouser, *American Colony on the Rio Pongo,* 44; Brooks, *Eurafricans in Western Africa,* 301; John Mathews, *A Voyage to the River Sierra-Leone on the Coast of Africa* (London: B. White and Son, 1788), 14–15; Lovejoy, *Transformations in Slavery,* 60–61, 75, 93, 118, 120, 127.

9. Bruce L. Mouser, "Trade, Coasters, and Conflict in the Rio Pongo from 1790 to 1808," *Journal of African History* 14, no. 1 (1973), 45–64; Mouser, *American Colony on the Rio Pongo,* 43–44; Kenneth G. Kelly, "Preliminary Archaeological Reconnaissance of Sites Related to the Slave Trade Era along the Upper Rio Pongo, Guinea," available at http://www.academia .edu/986975/ (accessed March 1, 2015); Barry, *Senegambia and the Atlantic Slave Trade,* 64, 78–79, 116–118; Koger, *Black Slaveowners,* 110; Christopher McKee, *A Gentlemanly and Honorable Profession: The Creation of the U.S. Naval Officer Corps, 1794–1815* (Annapolis, MD: United States Naval Institute, 1991), 191–193.

10. Leigh, *The Man Unmasked,* 7 (first quotation); Laurens to Holman, 8 September 1770, Laurens, *Papers of Henry Laurens,* 7:344–345 (remaining quotations); Laurens to John Lewis Gervais, 23 January 1773, Laurens, *Papers of Henry Laurens,* vol. 8 (Columbia: University of South Carolina Press, 1980), 538–539.

11. Laurens to Holman, 8 September 1770, Laurens, *Papers of Henry Laurens,* 7:344 (first and second quotations); Laurens to John Lewis Gervais, 23 January 1773, Laurens, *Papers of Henry Laurens,* 8:538–539; David Hancock, *Citizens of the World: London Merchants and the Integration of the British Atlantic Community, 1735–1785* (Cambridge: Cambridge University Press, 1995), 389.

12. Mouser, *American Colony on the Rio Pongo,* 44–45; Barry, *Senegambia and the Atlantic Slave Trade,* 79.

13. Barry, *Senegambia and the Atlantic Slave Trade,* 122–123; Mathews, *A Voyage to the River Sierra-Leone,* 150 (quotation); Mouser, "Rebellion, Marronage and Jihād: Strategies of Resistance to Slavery on the Sierra Leone Coast, c. 1783–1796," *Journal of African History* 48, no. 1 (2007): 27–44.

14. *Osborne's New-Hampshire Spy,* May 22, 1790; *The Herald of Freedom,* Boston, May 18, 1790; *Newport Herald,* Newport, RI, June 10, 1790; Voyage 32782, Voyages Database (accessed March 2, 2015); Mouser, "Rebellion, Marronage and Jihād," 38–44.

15. Robin Law and Kristin Mann, "West Africa in the Atlantic Community: The Case of the Slave Coast," *William and Mary Quarterly* 56, no. 2 (April 1999): 307–334; Mouser, *American Colony on the Rio Pongo,* 26–28; Mouser,

"The Baltimore/Pongo Connection: American Entrepreneurism, Colonial Expansionism, or African Opportunism?," *International Journal of African Historical Studies* 33, no. 2 (2000): 319; Daniel L. Schafer, "Zephaniah Kingsley's Laurel Grove Plantation, 1803–1813" in Jane Landers, ed., *Colonial Plantations and Economy in Florida* (Gainesville: University Press of Florida, 2000), 101; Schafer, "Ties that Bind: Anglo-African Slave Traders in Africa and Florida, John Fraser and His Descendants," *Slavery and Abolition* 20 (December 1999): 1–21; Schafer, *Zephaniah Kingsley, Jr. and the Atlantic World: Slave Trader, Plantation Owner, Emancipator* (Gainesville: University Press of Florida, 2013), 70, 105, 114, 117–119, 143, 168, 204–205, 228–229.

16. Philip D. Morgan, *Slave Counterpoint: Black Culture in the Eighteenth-Century Chesapeake & Lowcountry* (Chapel Hill: The University of North Carolina Press, 1998), 61; John Holman Estate, Inventories, vol. C, 1793–1800, Charleston County, 8–9.

17. Will of John Holman, Record of Wills, Charleston County, SC, vol. 24, 1786–1793, pp. 1076–1078; Koger, *Black Slaveowners*, 115.

18. Over one-third of the slaves manumitted in the decades following the Revolution purchased their freedom. John Boles, *Black Southerners, 1619–1869* (Lexington: University Press of Kentucky, 1984), 134–135; Michael P. Johnson and James L. Roark, *Black Masters: A Free Family of Color in the Old South* (New York: W. W. Norton & Co., 1984), 32–34, 36, 205–206; Ira Berlin, *Many Thousands Gone: The First Two Centuries of Slavery in North America* (Cambridge, MA: Belknap Press, 1998), 224–227, 282–289, 319–326; Koger, *Black Slaveowners*, 20, 22, 118–119.

19. Will of Robert Collins, Probate Records, 1799, South Carolina Probate Index, p. 552, available at http://search.ancestrylibrary.com (accessed March 3, 2014).

20. Johnson and Roark, *Black Masters*, 212–227 (first quotation on p. 212, second quotation on p. 215); Koger, *Black Slaveowners*, 99, 167–172.

21. See entries for Elias Collins, Georgetown, SC, U.S. Censuses of 1800, 1810, 1820, and 1840, available at http://search.ancestrylibrary.com (accessed March 3, 2015). He does not appear in the 1830 Census, but Elizabeth Collins is listed as head of a household with ten slaves. See Elizabeth Collins, Georgetown, SC, http://search.ancestrylibrary.com (accessed March 3, 2015).

22. Koger, *Black Slaveowners*, 104, 112, 114–115, 119, 125–127; Esther Holman, St. James Santee, South Carolina, Census of 1820, available at http://search.ancestrylibrary.com (accessed March 3, 2015); Johnson and Roark, *Black Masters*, 62–63.

23. Loren Schweninger, Marguerite Ross Howell, Nicole Marcon Mazgaj, eds., *The Southern Debate Over Slavery*, vol. 2, *Petitions to Southern County Courts, 1775–1867* (Urbana: University of Illinois Press, 2008), 68–70 (first and second quotations); Petition 21380303, "To the Honorable Hugh Rutledge and William

Marshall Esquires Judges of the Court of Equity," January 14, 1803, Race and Slavery Petitions Project, http://library.uncg.edu/slavery/petitions /details.aspx?pid=13366 (accessed March 4, 2015) (third quotation).

24. James A. McMillan, *Final Victims: Foreign Slave Trade to North America, 1783– 1810* (Columbia: University of South Carolina Press, 2004), 88; Adam Afzelius, *Sierra Leone Journal, 1795–1796,* Alexander Peter Kup, ed. (Uppsala: Almqvist & Wikells, 1967), 105–106 (first quotation), 108–109 (second quotation on p. 108), 137 (third quotation); Zachary Macaulay, *Life and Letters of Zachary Macaulay* (London: Edward Arnold, 1900), 125, 126–127 (quotation), 212; Theodore Canot, *Adventures of an African Slave Trader* (Mineola, NY: Dover Publications, 2002), 87; Mouser, *American Colony on the Rio Pongo,* 46.

25. McMillan, *Final Victims,* 88; Mouser, *American Colony on the Rio Pongo,* 30, 46; Afzelius, *Sierra Leone Journal,* 105–106 (first quotation), 108–109 (second quotation on p. 108), 137 (third quotation); Tavel was listed as the owner of an 1806 Charleston slave ship that brought a cargo of 105 enslaved Africans from the Rio Pongo to Charleston, and he was one of several owners of the same ship that carried slaves from the Rio Pongo to Barbados. Voyage 25530, *Tartar* (1806), Voyage 7501, *Tartar* (1808), Voyages Database, http:// slavevoyages.org/ (accessed March 4, 2015). Jellorum Harrison was not a slave trader but a missionary educated in Scotland whose travels took him to Asia, the United States, and the Caribbean before his return to the Rio Pongo region to teach in a mission school.

26. Koger, *Black Slaveowners,* 116–117; McMillan, *Final Victims,* 88, 93; Anthony Chanet against George Parker, South Carolina Constitutional Court of Appeals, *Reports of Judicial Decisions in the Constitutional Court of South Carolina Held at Charleston and Columbia in 1817, 1818,* vol. 1 (Charleston, SC: John Mill, 1819), 333; John Taylor against Samuel Holman, South Carolina Constitutional Court of Appeals, *Reports of Judicial Decisions,* 1:172–177; Henry William De Saussure, *Reports of Cases Argued and Determined in the Court of Chancery of the State of South Carolina, From the Revolution, to December, 1813, Inclusive,* vol. 3 (Philadelphia: Robert H. Small, 1854), 209–211 (second and third quotations on p. 211); Petitions 21380802, 21381413 (first quotation), 21381421, Race and Slavery Petitions Project, http://library.uncg.edu/slavery /petitions/details.aspx?pid=13366 (accessed March 5, 2015).

27. *Charleston Southern Evangelical Intelligencer,* April 3, 1819; *The Missionary Register* (London: L. B. Seeley, 1816), 357; Gregory and Fitzgerald to Marquess of Londonderry, September 20, 1822, *Sierra Leone. Papers Presented to Both Houses of Parliament by Command of His Majesty April 1823* (London: R. G. Clarke, 1823), 324; Suzanne Schwarz, "Commerce, Civilization and Christianity: The Origins of the Sierra Leone Company," in David Richardson, Suzanne Schwarz, and Anthony Tibbles, eds., *Liverpool and Transatlantic Slavery* (Liverpool: Liverpool University Press, 2007), 265–266; Macaulay, *Life and Letters,* 127, 130, 165, 174, 205, 209; Iain Whyte, *Zachary Macaulay*

1768–1838: The Steadfast Scot in the British Anti-Slavery Movement (Liverpool: Liverpool University Press, 2011), 39–47; Mouser, "Trade and Politics," 156–157; Louise, *Elizabeth Clevland Hardcastle, 1741–1808: A Lady of Color in the South Carolina Low Country* (Columbia, SC: Phoenix Publishers, 2001), 31–33. For a comprehensive overview of the history of Sierra Leone see John Peterson, *Province of Freedom: A History of Sierra Leone, 1787–1870* (Evanston, IL: Northwestern University Press, 1969).

28. Three slave traders, Malcolm Brodie, George Cooke, and James Dunbar, were captured by the British in the 1814 raid on the Rio Pongo, tried in Sierra Leone, convicted, and sentenced to be transported to Botany Bay for a penal term of fourteen years. They were taken to Portsmouth and loaded onto a ship for transport, but they appealed that decision, and the British courts overturned it on the grounds that Maxwell had no jurisdiction on the Rio Pongo. George Cooke, the American, sued and was awarded $20,000 in damages. Gregory and Fitzgerald to Marquess of Londonderry, September 20, 1822, 324; "Slave Trade and Slave Registry Question," *British Review, and London Critical Journal* 8 (London: Baldwin, Craddock and Joy, 1816): 232–233; John Joseph Crooks, *History of the Colony of Sierra Leone, Western Africa: With Maps and Appendices* (Dublin: Browne and Nolan, 1903), 89; Mouser, "Trade and Politics," 160–169, 194–199.

29. Will of John Holman, Record of Wills, Charleston County, SC, vol. 36, 1818–1826, pp. 920–921. Bruce Mouser observed that keeping track of the Holmans in Africa was complicated by the repetition of the names John and Samuel, and who his nephew's parents were is unclear. Mouser, *American Colony on the Rio Pongo*, 24, 28, 46, 50, 99, 100. Lightbourn was lost at sea on his way to attend a brother's funeral in Savannah, Georgia, in 1833. *Columbia Star,* June 23, 1833.

30. Hugh Thomas, *The Slave Trade: The Story of the Atlantic Slave Trade, 1440–1870* (New York: Simon & Schuster, 1997), 616.

3. From Manservant to Abolitionist and Physician

1. Massachusetts Anti-Slavery Society, *Fifth Annual Report of the Board of Managers of the New-England Anti-Slavery Society, Presented January 9, 1837* (Boston: Isaac Knapp, 1837), xxvi (quotations).

2. Andreas Massing, "A Segmentary Lineage Society Between Colonial Frontiers: The Kissi of Liberia, Sierra Leone, and Guinea, 1892–1913," *Liberian Studies Journal* 9 (1980): 1–12; Yves Person, "Ethnic Movements and Acculturation in Upper Guinea Since the Fifteenth Century," *African Historical Studies* 4 (1971): 669–690; George Tucker Childs, *A Grammar of Kisi: A Southern Atlantic Language* (Berlin: Walter de Gruyter, 1995), 3–5; Benjamin N. Lawrance, *Amistad's Orphans: An Atlantic Story of Children, Slavery, and Smuggling* (New Haven, CT: Yale University Press, 2015), 82–83; Philip Misevich, "The Origins of Slaves Leaving the Upper Guinea Coast in the Nineteenth

Century," in David Eltis and David Richardson, eds., *Extending the Frontiers: Essays on the New Transatlantic Slave Trade Database* (New Haven, CT: Yale University Press, 2008), 166–168.

3. *Liberator,* February 4, 1837 (quotation); James H. Sweet, *Domingos Álvares, African Healing, and the Intellectual History of the Atlantic World* (Chapel Hill: The University of North Carolina Press, 2011), 230–233.

4. Elizabeth Isichei, *A History of African Societies to 1870* (Cambridge: Cambridge University Press, 1997), 386; Johannes Postma, *The Dutch in the Atlantic Slave Trade, 1600–1815* (Cambridge: Cambridge University Press, 2008), 121–122; Stephen D. Behrendt, *The British Slave Trade, 1785–1807: Profitability, and Mortality,* vol. 1 (Madison: University of Wisconsin Press, 1993), 116 (last quote); Lawrance, *Amistad's Orphans,* 77, 98–99.

5. Francis B. Spilsbury, *Account of a Voyage to the Western Coast of Africa; Performed by His Majesty's Sloop Favourite, in the Year 1805* (London: Richard Phillips, 1807), 32–33 (quotation); Lawrance, *Amistad's Orphans,* 160–67, 268–271.

6. *Liberator,* 4 February 1837; Transatlantic Slave Trade Database, Voyages 36622 (1795), 36661 (1797), http://www.slavevoyages.org/tast/index.faces (accessed July 10, 2015); James A. McMillin, *The Final Victims: Foreign Slave Trade to North America, 1783–1810,* vol. 2, (Columbia: University of South Carolina Press, 2004), 50, 63–64, 86; *Columbian Museum & Savannah Advertiser,* 9 September 1796, 15 August 1797. Neither the Slave Trade Database nor the Savannah newspapers show a slave ship called the *Hunter* in this period. The only ship listed in the Savannah papers called the *Hunter* was a New York brig carrying a wide array of merchandise. *Georgia Gazette,* 11 December 1800.

7. Bowen's son and namesake who lived in Rhode Island inherited his father's extensive landholdings in Georgia and sold 4,000 acres of land to Jabez Bowen following his father's death. Jabez sold that property in 1813. William J. Northern, *Men of Mark in Georgia: A Complete and Elaborate History of the State from Its Settlement to the Present Time, Chiefly Told in Biographies and Autobiographies of the Most Eminent Men of Each Period of Georgia's Progress and Development,* vol. 1 (Atlanta: A. B. Caldwell, 1907), 15–18; http://genforum .genealogy.com/bowen/messages/568.html (accessed June 5, 2014); Eugene Genovese, *Roll, Jordan, Roll: The World the Slaves Made* (New York: Vintage Books, 1974), 232–234. In his Coffin interview, Johnson dated the McIntosh dinner party "about the year 1802," but it must have occurred after Bowen's appointment to the bench in 1804.

8. *Liberator,* 4 February 1837.

9. Daniel L. Schafer, "A Class of People Neither Freemen nor Slaves: From Spanish to American Race Relations in Florida, 1821–1861," *Journal of Social History* 26 (Spring, 1993): 587–590; Frank Marotti, *The Cana Sanctuary: History, Diplomacy, and Black Catholic Marriage in Antebellum St. Augustine, Florida* (Tuscaloosa: University of Alabama Press, 2012), 9–28; Rembert

W. Patrick, *Florida Fiasco: Rampant Rebels on the Georgia-Florida Border, 1810–1815* (Athens: University of Georgia Press, 1954), 56, 83–84, 98, 101, 155–56. Lachland McIntosh lived until 1806, but would have been too old to be the person Johnson described, and he did not live in St. Mary's. Zephaniah Kingsley, *Balancing Evils Judiciously: The Proslavery Writings of Zephaniah Kingsley,* Daniel W. Stowell, ed. (Gainesville: University of Florida Press, 2000); Jane Landers, *Black Society in Spanish Florida* (Champaign: University of Illinois Press, 1999), 91, 99, 152–153, 167–171; Mark A. McDonough, *The Francis Richard Family: From French Nobility to Florida Pioneer* (lulu.com, 2010), 45–46; Julie Winch, *Between Slavery and Freedom: Free People of Color in America From Settlement to the Civil War* (Lanham, MD: Rowman and Littlefield, 2014), 2, 40; Marotti, *Heaven's Soldiers: Free People of Color and the Spanish Legacy in Antebellum Florida* (Tuscaloosa: University of Alabama Press, 2013), 28–29. McIntosh met his wife through a cousin, William Houstoun, who had moved to New York and married Mary Bayard, Eliza's sister. They brought Eliza to Savannah on a visit. Julius Goebel, Jr. and Joseph H. Smith, eds., *The Law Practice of Alexander Hamilton: Documents and Commentary,* vol. 5 (New York: Columbia University Press, 1981), 47; Edith Duncan Johnson, *The Houstouns of Georgia* (Athens: University of Georgia Press, 1950), 337.

10. *Augusta Chronicle,* 7 November 1807. Flournoy must have been there before that date since the Georgia Legislature appointed him in January 1807 as one of two commissioners to mark the dividing line between Georgia and North Carolina. John Preston Arthur, *Western North Carolina: A History* (Raleigh, NC: Edwards & Broughton, 1914), 34; William O. Foster, *James Jackson: Duelist and Militant Statesman, 1757–1806* (Athens: University of Georgia Press, 1960), 169; William R. Bagnall, *The Textile Industries of the United States: Including Sketches and Notices of Cotton, Woolen, Silk and Linen Manufactures in the Colonial Period,* vol. 1 (Cambridge, MA: Riverside Press, 1893), 394–395. The senior Christopher Olney was one of the commissioners to the Chickasaw nation and was present when a treaty was signed with them in July 1805 which would have put him in the Deep South. The only evidence of a visit from one of the Christopher Olneys to the Lowcountry is a notice for a letter waiting for him in Charleston in 1803. *City-Gazette and Daily Advertiser,* 18 January 1803; Donald B. Ricky, *Encyclopedia of Florida Indians,* vol. 1 (St. Clair Shores, MI: Somerset Publishers, 1998), 70–71; *The Freemason's Repository,* 12 (October 1882): 132. For an example of Sea Island cotton for sale in Rhode Island, see *The Providence United States Chronicle,* 13 May 1802.

11. Massachusetts Anti-Slavery Society, *Fifth Annual,* 72.

12. Genovese, *Roll, Jordan, Roll,* 333; Elizabeth Fox-Genovese, *Within the Plantation Household: Black and White Women of the Old South* (Chapel Hill: The University of North Carolina Press, 1988), 140–144, 308–314 (quotations on p. 308), 325–333.

13. Walter G. Charlton, "A Judge and a Grand Jury," Orville A. Park, ed., *Report of the Thirty-First Annual Session of the Georgia Bar Association* (Marion, GA: J. W. Burke Co., 1914), 206–210.

14. Ibid., 211–212.

15. *New York Chronicle Express,* 10 May 1804.

16. Charlton, "A Judge and a Grand Jury," 208.

17. Massachusetts Anti-Slavery Society, *Fifth Annual,* xxviii.

18. *Albany Gazette* (New York), 14 May 1804.

19. Ibid. (first quotation); *Washington Federalist,* 14 May 1804 (second quotation).

20. *Albany Gazette* (New York), 14 May 1804. Bowen's annual salary was $1500. *Providence Phoenix,* 4 December 1802.

21. John Quincy Adams, *Writings of John Quincy Adams,* Worthington Chauncey Ford, ed., vol. 3 (New York: Macmillan Co., 1914), 41 (first and second quotations); *Augusta Chronicle,* 2 June 1804; *Providence Gazette,* 21 July 1804 (third and fourth quotations); *Providence Patriot & Columbian Phoenix,* 17 August 1816 (fifth quotation); Charles C. Jones, *History of Savannah, Ga. From Its Settlement to the Close of the Eighteenth Century* (Savannah, GA: O. F. Vidder and Frank Weldon, 1890), 424. See, for example, the *New York Morning Chronicle,* 9 May 1804; *Philadelphia Aurora General Advertiser,* 11 May 1804; *Georgetown Washington Federalist,* 14 May 1804; *Wilmington (DE) Mirror of The Times, and General Advertiser,* 16 May 1804. The elder Bowen wrote the Providence Town Council in April 1806, "I am contemplating a Voige [voyage] to Georgia on Business of much importance to me and my Family," probably to settle his son's affairs there. Bowen to Town Council / Court of Probate, April 7, 1806, Providence, Rhode Island, City Archives.

22. "Manumission of Robert, Jabez Bowen, Jun., 22 August 1808," Deed Book 30, p. 432, Providence City Archives. Bowen's file in the Providence City Archives is labelled 1807, although the only documents it contains date from 1815 which suggests that he was placed under guardianship in 1807 and 1815. His first guardian was his father, Jabez Brown, but after his father's death in 1815, Thomas Arnold, another prominent Providence businessman related to the Bowens by marriage, was appointed guardian. Guardianship Bond, June 5, 1815, Providence City Archives (# A 3853). Henry Chapin, *Address Delivered at the Unitarian Church, in Uxbridge, Mass., in 1864* (Worcester, MA: Press of Charles Hamilton, 1881), 53–54 (first quotation on p. 54); Benjamin Bowen Carter, "The John Carter Family," *Publications of the Rhode Island Historical Society,* New Series, 2 (January 1895): 249 (second quotation); Massachusetts Anti-Slavery Society, *Annual Report,* 72; *Providence Gazette,* Aug. 9, 1816.

23. Stanley C. Harold, Jr., "The Southern Strategy of the Liberty Party," in John R. McKivigan, ed., *Abolitionism and American Politics and Government* (London: Taylor & Francis, 1999), 33–34; George William Van Cleve, *A Slaveholder's Union: Slavery, Politics, and the Constitution in the Early American Republic* (Chicago: University of Chicago Press, 2010), 94, 206–266.

24. William J. Brown, *The Life of William J. Brown of Providence, R.I.: With Personal Recollections of Incidents in Rhode Island* (Lebanon: University of New Hampshire Press, 2006), xxiv-xxvi, 86–88; Providence City Directory, 1836/37, 131; Providence death records noted as "col'd" John, 60 years, July 31, 1849, and Joseph I., 60 years, January 26, 1846. Records of Births, Deaths, and Marriages, 1636–1850, Providence City Archives; "To the General Assembly of the State of Rhode Island at Their June Term, A.D. 1833," Petitions to the General Assembly, June Term 1833, Rhode Island State Archives, Providence, Rhode Island. There were 108 slaves in Rhode Island in 1810, 49 in 1820, 15 in 1830, and 5 in 1840. Under Rhode Island law, anyone born there on or after March 1, 1784, was born free.

25. W. Caleb McDaniel, *The Problem of Democracy in the Age of Slavery: Garrisonian Abolitionists and Transatlantic Reform* (Baton Rouge: Louisiana State University Press, 2013), 53–56, 66–75; Dorothy Porter Wesley and Constance Porter Uzelac, eds., *William Cooper Nell: Selected Writings, 1832–1874* (Baltimore: Black Classic Press, 2002), 68 (first and second quotations); Massachusetts Anti-Slavery Society, *Fifth Annual Report*, xxviii (third and fourth quotations).

26. Jeffrey R. Kerr-Ritchie, *Rites of August First: Emancipation Day in the Black Atlantic World* (Baton Rouge: Louisiana State University Press, 2007), 84–86, 89, 170; *The Boston Directory* (Boston: John Norman, 1807), 4; Debra Gold Hansen, *Strained Sisterhood: Gender and Class in the Boston Female Antislavery Society* (Boston: University of Massachusetts Press, 2009), 37–38, 81; Wesley and Uzelac, *William Cooper Nell*, 30. For a full discussion of the creation of "African" institutions, their significance, and change over time, see James Sidbury, *Becoming African in America: Race and Nation in the Early Black Atlantic* (Oxford: Oxford University Press, 2007), 67–68, 72–73, 131–144, 157–202.

27. *The Liberator,* 18 August 1848; Julie Winch, *Between Slavery and Freedom: Free People of Color in America from Settlement to the Civil War* (London: Rowan and Littlefield, 2014), 79–80; James Brewer Stewart, *Abolitionist Politics and the Coming of the Civil War* (Boston: University of Massachusetts Press, 2008), 61–88.

28. *The Liberator,* 5 April 1850 (quotations); Robert V. Remini, *Daniel Webster: The Man and His Time* (New York: W. W. Norton, 1997), 192, 673–680; Margaret Garb, *Freedom's Ballot: African American Political Struggles in Chicago from Abolition to the Great Migration* (Chicago: University of Chicago Press, 2014), 29–34.

29. Wesley and Uzelac, *William Cooper Nell*, 270–276.

30. Ibid., 257; *The Liberator,* 5 April 1850; John W. Blassingame, *Slave Testimony: Two Centuries of Letters, Speeches, Interviews, and Autobiographies* (Baton Rouge: Louisiana State University Press, 1977), 124, n. 2.

31. *The Liberator,* 15 November 1850 (first quotation); Wesley and Uzelac, *William Cooper Nell*, 532; David Grimsted, *American Mobbing, 1828–1861: Toward*

Civil War (Oxford: Oxford University Press, 1998), 38; State Street Trust Company, *Mayors of Boston* (Boston: State Street Trust Co., 1914), 21; Margaret Washington, *Sojourner Truth's America* (Urbana-Champaign: University of Illinois Press, 2009), 207 (second quotation).

32. Frederick Cooper, *Colonialism in Question: Theory, Knowledge, History* (Berkeley: University of California Press, 2005), 76; Charles Tilly, "Models and Realities of Popular Collective Action," *Social Research* 52 (Winter 1985): 717–748.

33. *The Liberator,* 4 February 1837 (quotation); Adelaide M. Cromwell, "The Black Presence in the West End of Boston, 1800–1864: A Demographic Map," in Donald M. Jacobs, ed., *Courage and Conscience: Black and White Abolitionists in Boston* (Bloomington: Indiana University Press, 1993), 157; Thomas Neville Bonner, *Becoming a Physician: Medical Education in Great Britain, France, Germany and the United States, 1750–1945* (Oxford: Oxford University Press, 1995), 208; Massachusetts State Census, 1855 [database online], Ancestry.com, 2014; Massachusetts 1855–1865 State Census [microform], reel 25, vol. 34, household 1011, New England Historic Genealogical Society, Boston; Massachusetts Death Records, 1841–1915, 1861: Massachusetts Death Records, 1841–1915 [database online], Ancestry.com, 2013 (Original: Massachusetts Vital Records, 1840–1911, New England Historic Genealogical Society, Boston); Massachusetts Town and Vital Records, 1620–1988, Ancestry.com, 2011. The U.S. Census of 1850 for Ashburnham, Massachusetts, located fifty miles from Boston near the border with New Hampshire, lists a Robert Johnson, aged 74, a black laborer, whose household included his 52-year-old black wife, Vina, a native of New Hampshire, and three children: Robert and Vina, both aged 15, and a son Harkless, aged 10 (probably Hercules). The ages do not quite match since Robert was listed as aged 89 only 11 years later, but this could be the same Robert Johnson. U.S. Federal Census, 1850, Massachusetts, Roll M432_340, p. 10B, Image 26.

34. Frederick Cooper, *Colonialism in Question: Theory, Knowledge, History* (Berkeley: University of California Press, 2005), 23 (quotation).

35. Anthony W. Marx, "The Dynamics of Racial Identity and Social Movements," in Charles Tilly, ed., *Citizenship, Identity and Social History* (Cambridge: Cambridge University Press, 1996), 162–164 (quotation on p. 163).

36. Aime Cesaire described colonialism's power to corrupt the colonizer and colonized, an insight I have adapted here. Cooper, *Colonialism in Question,* 41 (quotations).

37. Ibid.; Eugene D. Genovese and Elizabeth Fox-Genovese, *The Mind of the Master Class: History and Faith in the Southern Slaveholder's Worldview* (Cambridge and other cities: Cambridge University Press, 2005), 375 (first quotation); Genovese, *Roll, Jordan, Roll,* 37–44 (second quotation on p. 39); Anthony W. Neal, *Unburdened by Conscience: A Black People's Collective Account of America's Ante-Bellum South and the Aftermath* (Lanham, MD: University Press of

America, 2010), 37; Thomas D. Morris, *Southern Slavery and the Law, 1619–1860* (Chapel Hill: The University of North Carolina Press, 1996), 161–181 (third quotation on p. 172); Glen McNair, *Criminal Injustice: Slaves and Free Blacks in Georgia's Criminal Justice System* (Charlottesville: University of Virginia Press, 2009), 55 (fourth quotation), 168.

38. Morris, *Southern Slavery,* 168–169, 179–181; Donald Lee Grant, *The Way It Was in the South: The Black Experience in Georgia* (Athens: University of Georgia Press, 1993), 55–56; Ariela Gross, *Double Character: Slavery and Mastery in the Antebellum Southern Courtroom* (Athens: University of Georgia Press, 2006), 112, 116, 121 (quotation); Carolyn J. Powell, "In Remembrance of Mira: Reflections on the Death of a Slave Woman," in Patricia Morton, ed., *Discovering the Women in Slavery: Emancipating Perspectives on the American Past in Slavery* (Athens: University of Georgia Press, 1996), 49–50.

39. *The Liberator,* 4 February 1837 (quotation); Blassingame, *Slave Testimony,* 127; Sidbury, *Becoming African,* 201–202.

4. Navigating a Way to Freedom

1. *Albany Journal,* July 10, 1857.

2. Jay served as President of the Continental Congress, wrote several of the Federalist Papers, and served as the first Chief Justice of the Supreme Court. He freed his slaves only after he judged their labor had provided a "modest compensation" for the funds he had expended to support them and when he judged them able to support themselves as free men. Jay was a founder and president of the New York Manumission Society, and as governor he supported and signed the 1799 emancipation bill that ended slavery in New York. The New York Manumission Society has been viewed both as a high-minded enterprise inspired by the noblest ideals of the Revolution and as a conservative organization intent on controlling the free black population of the city and seeing that the voluntary end of slavery occurred with as little disruption as possible. Shane White, *Somewhat More Independent: The End of Slavery in New York City, 1770–1810* (Athens and London: University of Georgia Press, 2012), 56, 82 (quotation), 86. *New-York Daily Tribune,* August 13, 1857.

3. As early as 1826 he helped free Gilbert Horton, a free black man from Westchester County, who traveled to Washington, DC and was arrested there as a fugitive slave. William withdrew from the American Anti-Slavery Society in 1840 in part because women were allowed to serve on committees without the consent or presence of their husbands. He published a number of important anti-slavery pamphlets before his death in 1858. Robert A. Trendel, *William Jay: Churchman, Public Servant, and Reformer* (New York: Arno Press, 1982); J. Thomas Sharf, *History of Westchester County, New York,* vol. 1 (Philadelphia: L. E. Preston & Co., 1886), 529; *Hudson River Chronicle,* August 4,1840. Jay's $1,000 bequest would be worth about $390,000 today (income

value calculated at http://www.measuringworth.com/uscompare/relative value.php, accessed May 14, 2014).

4. Robert Trendel, "John Jay II: Antislavery Conscience of the Episcopal Church," *Historical Magazine of the Protestant Episcopal Church* 45 (September 1976): 237–252. St. Philip's was established in 1818 and in 1839 decided to seek admission to the governing body of the church. B. F. De Costa, *Three Score and Ten: The Story of St. Philip's Church, New York City. A Discourse Delivered in the New Church, West Twenty-Fifth Street At Its Opening, Sunday Morning, February 17, 1889* (New York: By the Parish, 1889); Craig D. Townsend, *Faith in Their Own Color: Black Episcopalians in Antebellum New York City* (New York: Columbia University Press, 2005); Graham Russell Hodges, *Studies in African American History and Culture* (New York: Garland, 2000), 32–34, 60–65; Paul Finkelman, *Slavery in the Courtroom: An Annotated Bibliography of American Cases* (Washington, DC: Library of Congress, 1985), 75–77; Samuel May, *The Fugitive Slave Law and Its Victims* (New York: American Anti-Slavery Society, 1861), 24.

5. Shirley Lindefjeld Blanco and John Stockbridge, *Bedford* (Portsmouth, NH: Arcadia Publishing, 2004), 103; Chauncey M. Depew, *My Memories of Eighty Years* (New York: Charles Scribner's Sons, 1921), 60 (first quotation); Henry T. Smith, *Westchester County in History, Manual and Civil List, Past and Present*, vol. 2 (White Plains, NY: Henry T. Smith, 1912), 251 (second and third quotations).

6. J. Thomas Scharf, *History of Westchester County, New York*, vol. 2 (Philadelphia: L. E. Preston and Co., 1886), 359, 488; *The Hudson River Chronicle*, 2 January 1838, 16 May 1843, 6 November, 27 November, 18 December 1838, 1 January, 4 June 1839 (first quotation), 24 May 1842, 4 August 1850 (second quotation). The *Chronicle* called the *Westchester Herald* and the *Peekskill Democrat* "abolitionist papers."

7. Virtual Historic Savannah Project (vsav.scad.edu/vhs/old_resources/, accessed May 14, 2014).

8. Ibid.; *Anti-Slavery Reporter*, January 1, 1858. Deborah Gray White, *Arn't I A Woman?: Female Slaves in the Plantation South* (New York: W. W. Norton & Co., 1999), 37–38, 53–54 (quotation on p. 53); Brenda Stevenson, *Life in Black and White: Family and Community in the Slave South* (Oxford: Oxford University Press, 1996), 196–205, 223–225, 249–250.

9. *New-York Daily Tribune*, 13 August 1857; John W. Blassingame, *Slave Testimony: Two Centuries of Letters, Speeches, Interviews, and Autobiographies* (Baton Rouge: Louisiana State University Press, 1977), 336 (final quotation).

10. *Albany Journal*, July 10, 1857; *New-York Daily Tribune*, 13 August 1857; Dimmock Charlton, *Narrative of Dimmock Charlton, A British Subject, Taken from the Brig "Peacock" by the U.S. Sloop "Hornet," Enslaved while a Prisoner of War, and Retained Forty-Five Years in Bondage* (Philadelphia: n.p., 1859), 1–2, 13 (quotation).

11. *New York Times*, 23 July 1857.

12. *London Anti-Slavery Reporter,* 1 January 1858; Philip Misevich, "The Origins of Slaves Leaving the Upper Guinea Coast in the Nineteenth Century," in David Eltis and David Richardson, *Extending the Frontiers: Essays on the New Transatlantic Slave Trade Database* (New Haven, CT and London: Yale University Press, 2008), 155–175; Oscar Grandio Moraguez, "The African Origins of Slaves Arriving in Cuba, 1789–1865," in ibid., 189–190. Misevich notes that names from the Sierra Leone region typically end in vowels, so "Tallen" is an unlikely name (Misevich to the author, personal email, May 21, 2014). A search on the African Origins database of African names from the slave trade shows two examples of Tali/Tilly from the Sierra Leone region in this period: Voyages 2420 (Tali), 500052 (Tilly), http://www.african-origins .com/african-data/ (accessed May 21, 2014). Voyage 2420 is a Spanish vessel, the *Primera,* which left the Gallinas in 1831. Lawrance, *Amistad's Orphans,* 100–102 (quotation on p. 100); Augustine Konneh, *Religion, Commerce, and the Integration of the Mandingo in Liberia* (Lanham, MD: University Press of America, 1996); Hugh Thomas, *The Slave Trade: The Story of the Atlantic Slave Trade, 1440–1870* (New York: Simon & Schuster, 1997), 681; Rosalind Shaw, *Memories of the Slave Trade: Ritual and the Historical Imagination in Sierra Leone* (Chicago: University of Chicago Press, 2002), 33–35; Carol P. MacCormack, "Wono: Institutionalized Dependency in Sherbro Descent Groups," in Suzanne Miers and Igor Kopytoff, eds., *Slavery in Africa: Historical and Anthropological Perspectives* (Madison: University of Wisconsin Press, 1977), 183–184; Boubacar Barry, *Senegambia and the Atlantic Slave Trade* (Cambridge: Cambridge University Press, 1998), 22–25, 42, 64–65, 76, 111, 118, 122.

13. The Portuguese predominated in the trade carrying an estimated 516,854 slaves. Eltis and Richardson, "A New Assessment of the Transatlantic Slave Trade," in Eltis and Richardson, *Extending the Frontiers,* 34–38, 44–47.

14. Charlton, *Narrative,* 4 (quotations); Transatlantic Slave Trade Database, 7951 *(San Jose y Animas),* 14554 *(S Isabel);* "African Institution: Substance of the XVth Report of the African Institution," *The Annual Register, or a View of the History, Politics and Literature of the Year 1821* (London: Baldwin, Craddock and Joy, 1822), 556. Charlton claimed that the captives and crew from the Spanish slaver were taken to Britain where he and several of the Spanish prisoners were transferred to the *Peacock,* but that version of events is highly unlikely.

15. "African Institution," 560.

16. Blassingame, *Slave Testimony,* 327 (quotation in n. 12).

17. Denver Alexander Brunsman, *The Evil Necessity: British Naval Impressment in the Eighteenth-century Atlantic World* (Charlottesville: University of Virginia Press, 2013), 3–15, 91–136 (quotation on p. 14); "Uncovering Hidden Lives: Developing a Database of Mariners in the Black Atlantic," *Common-place* 9 (Jan. 2009):1, www.common-place.org.

18. Theodore Roosevelt, *The Naval War of 1812* (New York and London: G. P. Putnam's Sons, 1900), 1:5 (first quotation), 160, 172, 175, 209 (second quotation).

19. Seymour Drescher, *Econocide: British Slavery in the Era of Abolition* (Chapel Hill: The University of North Carolina Press, 2010), 66, 77; Blassingame, *Slave Testimony,* 327 (quotation).

20. Roosevelt, *Naval War,* 1:211–216 (quotations on pp. 214, 216).

21. The given name is also spelled "Demook." Dimmock as a surname appeared in antebellum Savannah.

22. Blassingame, *Slave Testimony,* 328.

23. American Anti-Slavery Society, *Slavery and the Internal Slave Trade in the United States of North America; Being Replies to Questions Transmitted By the Committee of the British and Foreign Anti-Slavery Society for the Abolition of Slavery and the Slave Trade Throughout the World* (London: Thomas Ward & Co., 1841), 19 (quotation), 20; Religious Society of Friends, *A View of the Present State of the African Slave Trade* (Philadelphia: William Brown, 1824), 33, 43–48; James A. McMillin, *The Final Victims: Foreign Slave Trade to North America, 1783–1810* (Columbia: University of South Carolina Press, 2004).

24. J. P. Setze placed an advertisement in a Savannah newspaper in 1820 asking that his customers follow him to his new establishment. *Savannah Republican,* March 11, 1820. *Albany Evening Journal,* July 10, 1857. J. P. Setze appears in the Augusta city directory for 1841 as an "importer and dealer in dry goods." *The Augusta Directory and City Advertiser for 1841* (Augusta, 1841), 73. John P. Setze, ID I12600, at http://wc.rootsweb.ancestry.com/cgi -bin/igm.cgi?op=GET&db=jimpetty&id=I12600 (accessed May 20, 1814).

25. *Georgian* (Savannah), February 24, 1824; *Daily Georgian* (Savannah), October 5, 1826 (quotations), January 12, February 6, 1827. Captain Dubois died in the famous explosion of the *Pulaski* in 1838. See Bob Brooke, *Shipwrecks and Lost Treasures: Outer Banks: Legends and Lore, Pirates and More!* (Guilford, CT: Globe Pequot, 2007), 29–35.

26. James Dunwoody Brownson DeBow, *The Industrial Resources, Etc., of the Southern and Western States: Embracing a View of Their Commerce, Agriculture, Manufactures, Internal Improvements, Slave and Free Labor, Slavery Institutions, Products, Etc., of the South . . .* (New York: Appleton, 1853), 3:144–145.

27. *Albany Evening Journal,* July 10, 1857; Richard C. Wade, *Slavery in the Cities: The South, 1820–1860* (Oxford: Oxford University Press, 1964), 51–52 (quotation on p. 52); Jonathan D. Martin, *Divided Mastery: Slave Hiring in the American South* (Cambridge and London: Cambridge University Press, 2009), 173–174.

28. For example, the British sloop *Widow's Son* stopped in Savannah in 1822 with a cargo of turtles, fruits, vegetables, salt, and passengers on board, including William Martin, the island's attorney general. *Charleston Courier,* 30 November 1822. Paul L. Adderley, *The Bahamas in the Mid-Nineteenth Century, 1850–1869* (Nassau: Department of Archives, Ministry of Education

1988), 22; Gerald Horne, *The Deepest South: The United States, Brazil, and the African Slave Trade* (New York: New York University Press, 2007), 284, n.73; Roscoe R. Oglesby, *Internal War and the Search for Normative Order* (The Hague: Martinus Nijhoff, 1971), 72, n.1.

29. In an 1825 advertisement for a Sheriff's slave, two enslaved women owned by Nathaniel F. Pratt and two enslaved men owned by Abraham Pratt were to be sold to satisfy debts. *Georgian* (Savannah), January 3, 1825.

30. *Albany Evening Journal,* July 10, 1857. Molyneaux was appointed in May 1826. *Daily Georgian,* May 19, 1826. For an advertisement from Chandler and Davidson with liquor for sale, see *Georgian,* May 4, 1830.

31. The *Alabama* was a sidewheel steamer built in New York City and delivered to the New York and Savannah Steam Navigation Co. for commercial service in January 1851. http://www.navsource.org/archives/09/86/86101 .htm (accessed March 31, 2014). Charlotte Forten Grimké, *The Journals of Charlotte Forten Grimké,* Brenda Stevenson, ed. (Oxford and New York: Oxford University Press, 1988), 345 (first quotation); Charlton, *Narrative,* 1–2; *National Anti-Slavery Standard,* 27 November 1858 (second, third, fourth, and fifth quotations); freepages.genealogy.rootsweb.ancestry.com /~edbradford/ed/additional/hansell/sarah.pdf (accessed May 28, 2014). Both Susan and Mary Cox spoke at the 1854 Women's Rights Convention in Philadelphia where Sarah Cox denounced the Fugitive Slave Act. *Brooklyn Daily Eagle,* 23 October 1854.

32. "Introduction to the Cropper Family of Dingle Bank," Adam Mathew Publications, http://www.ampltd.co.uk/digital_guides/abolition_emancipation _part_2_3/introduction%20to%20the%20cropper%20family%20of%20 dingle%20bank.aspx (accessed May 28, 2014).

33. Douglas A. Lorimer, *Colour, Class and the Victorians: English Attitudes to the Negro in the Mid-Nineteenth Century* (Leicester, UK: Leicester University Press, 1978), 220–221; *Anti-Slavery Reporter,* 1 January 1858.

5. Unidentified Africans Seek British Protection

1. James Baker to John Bidwell, 7 April 1832, The National Archives of the UK (hereinafter cited as TNA), FO 5/276 (quotation); "Explanatory Remarks accompanying Consul Baker's Accounts," 1 January 1833, TNA, FO 5/285.

2. Charles Bankhead to Lord Palmerston, 21 April 1832, TNA, FO 115/54; James Baker to Charles Bankhead, 7 April 1832, TNA, FO 5/272.

3. Baker to Bankhead, 7 April 1832 (quotation).

4. Ibid.; R. L. Crawford to Baker, 6 April 1832 (first quotation); Baker to R. L. Crawford, 9 April 1832; Edward Livingston to Baker, 24 March 1832; and Baker to Livingston, 19 April 1832, TNA, FO 5/272; "Explanatory Remarks" (second and third quotations).

5. Records of the Boards of Customs, Excise, and Customs and Excise, and HM Revenue and Customs, Board of Customs: Board and Secretariat: Minute Books, 1 July 1832, TNA, CUST 28/97.

6. Paul E. Lovejoy, *Transformations in Slavery: A History of Slavery in Africa* (Cambridge: Cambridge University Press, 2000), 145, 148–149.

7. Christopher Knight to J. W. Croker, 5 August 1821; Knight to Captain Kelly, 7 August 1821; *Journals of the House of Commons, Appendices, From February the 5th, 1822, in the Third Year of the Reign of King George the Fourth, to January the 2nd, 1823, in the Third Year of the Reign of King George the Fourth*, p. 717, House of Commons Parliamentary Papers Database, available at http://gateway.proquest.com/openurl?url_ver=Z39.88-2004&res_dat=xri:hcpp-us&rft_dat=xri:hcpp:fulltext:jhc-016651:51 (accessed March 13, 2015); Lovejoy, *Transformations in Slavery*, 148–149.

8. Jamie Bruce Lockhart, "Journals or Journalism?: The Landers' Niger Journal (1834)," The Harriet Tubman Institute, York University, available at http://www.tubmaninstitute.ca/documents_relating_to_the_lander_brothers_niger_expedition_of_1830 (accessed August 13, 2014).

9. Thomas Fowell Buxton, *The Remedy: Being a Sequel to the African Slave Trade* (Cambridge: Cambridge University Press, 2010), 65–70, 255, 263–265; Robin Hallett, ed., *The Niger Journal of Richard and John Lander* (Abingdon, UK: Routledge, 2004), 292–296; I. K. Sundiata, *From Slaving to Neoslavery: The Bight of Biafra and Fernando Po in the Era of Abolition, 1827–1930* (Madison: University of Wisconsin Press, 1996), 42–45.

10. Hallett, ed., *Niger Journal*, 292–296; Robert Huish, *Lander's Travels: The Travels of Richard Lander into the Interior of Africa* (London: John Saunders, 1836), Chapter LXIII, available at Project Guttenberg, http://www.gutenberg.org/cache/epub/12667/pg12667.html (accessed on March 13, 2015).

11. H. L. Fox to Palmerston, 5 October 1839; Sir William Colbrooke to Fox, 18 June 1839; Testimony of Jane McMillan, 31 May 1839; Affidavit to John Shiell given to Police, 30 May 1839; Fox to Colbrooke, 20 July 1839; William Gray to Fox, 13 August 1839; Gray to Fox, 25 September 1839; and Fox to Colbrooke, 30 September 1839, TNA, FO 5/333; Great Britain, Emigration Commission, *Correspondence with Spain, Portugal, Brazil, The Netherlands, Sweden, and the Argentine Confederation Relative to the Slave Trade from January 1 to December 31, 1841 Inclusive* (London: William Clowes and Sons, 1842), 167–172.

12. Anderson to R. S. Lambert, 13 July 1841, Emigration Commission, *Correspondence with Spain, Portugal, Brazil, The Netherlands, Sweden, and the Argentine Confederation Relative to the Slave Trade*, 169.

13. Ibid.

14. Hardy to Sir Lionel Smith, 20 October 1838, Parliamentary Papers, House of Commons, *Correspondence with Spain, Portugal and Brazil, Relative to the Slave Trade, From February 2, 1839, to May 31, 1839* (London: William Clowes

and Sons, 1839), 23; Earl of Aberdeen to Charles Clarke, 1 February 1842, and Joseph T. Crawford to the Earl of Aberdeen, 7 May 1843, Parliamentary Papers, House of Commons, *Correspondence on the Slave Trade with Foreign Powers, Parties to Treaties, Under Which Captured Vessels Are to be Tried by Mixed Tribunals* (London: William Clowes and Sons, 1844), 38, 69.

15. H. J. Ricketts to R. W. Hay, 22 May 1829; Alexander Findlay to Hay, 30 June 1830 (second quotation); and Findlay to Hay, 17 July 1830 (first quotation), 4 August 1830, 29 November 1830, 30 October 1830, 25 December 1830, 1 February 1831, 11 November 1831, 16 December 1831, 20 March 1832, TNA, CO 268/10; Findlay to Hay, 19 January 1832, 15 April 1833, and 9 May 1833, TNA, CO 268/11; Viscount Goderich to Lieutenant Governor of Sierra Leone, 18 January 1832, TNA, CO 268/30.

16. Matthew Mason, "The Battle of the Slaveholding Liberators: Great Britain, the United States, and Slavery in the Early Nineteenth Century," *William and Mary Quarterly*, 3rd Series, 59 (July 2002): 665–696; Joseph C. Miller, "Atlantic Ambiguities of British and American Abolition," *William and Mary Quarterly*, 3rd Series, 66 (October 2009): 677–714; Randy J. Sparks, "Micro-Diplomacy and the Illegal Slave Trade: Individuals, States, and Illegal Enslavement" (conference paper presented at "A Crime Against Humanity: Slavery and International Law, Past and Present," Stanford Law School, Stanford University, Stanford, CA, May 15, 2015); Christopher Leslie Brown, *Moral Capital: Foundations of British Abolitionism* (Chapel Hill: The University of North Carolina Press, 2006), 451–462.

6. Caught in the Illegal Slave Trade

1. Viscount Palmerston to Mr. Fox, August 14, 1839, *The Sessional Papers Printed by Order of the House of Lords, or Presented by Royal Command, in the Session 1820*, vol. 19, Class B, "Correspondence with Foreign Powers Relating to the Slave Trade" (London: William Clowes and Sons, 1840), 140.

2. John Morley, *The Life of William Ewart Gladstone*, vol. 2 (London: Macmillan and Co., 1904), 45 (quotation); Leslie Bethell, *The Abolition of the Brazilian Slave Trade: Britain, Brazil and the Slave Trade Question* (Cambridge: Cambridge University Press, 2009), 93–118; Christopher Lloyd, *The Navy and the Slave Trade: The Suppression of the African Slave Trade in the Nineteenth Century* (London and New York: Routledge, 2012), 40–49, 139–149.

3. Mr. Cole to Governor Doherty, 2 February 1839, 1840 [268], Class D, *Correspondence with Foreign Powers, Not Parties to Conventions Giving Right of Search of Vessels Suspected of the Slave Trade. From June 1st to December 31st, 1839, Inclusive*, 142, House of Commons Parliamentary Papers Database, available at http://gateway.proquest.com/openurl?url_ver=Z39.88–2004&res_dat=xri:hcpp-us&rft_dat=xri:hcpp:fulltext:1840–019393:154 (accessed March 18, 2015).

4. The *Fama da Cuba* (Spain) was captured February 7, 1827, with 100 enslaved Africans on board. The *Silvenhina* (Brazil) was captured March 12, 1827,

with 266 Africans on board. The *Creola* (Brazil) was captured April 8, 1827, carrying 309 Africans. The *Musquito* (Spain) was captured April 14, 1827, with 126 Africans on board. "Extract of a Letter from Commodore Charles Bullen, C. B., to J. W. Croker, Esq. Dates on Board His Majesty's Ship Maidstone, Entrance to Sierra Leone River, 22 May 1827," *Papers Relating to the Slave Trade: Viz. Copies and Extracts of the Correspondence between the Admiralty and Naval Officers, since 1st January 1826, Not Already Laid before the House of Commons, Relative to the Suppression of the Slave Trade: November 1825–July 1827* (London: House of Commons, 1828), 16, 22; Correspondence with the British commissioners, Sierra Leone, 22, 83 (first quotation), http://gateway .aa1.proquest.com/openurl?url_ver=Z39.88–2004&res_dat=xri:hcpp-us &rft_dat=xri:hcpp:rec:1828–011324; Class A, Correspondence with the British commissioners, at Sierra Leone, the Havana, Rio De Janeiro, and Surinam, relative to the slave trade, 1828, 22, 23, http://gateway.aa1.proquest.com /openurl?url_ver=Z39.88–2004&res_dat=xri:hcpp-us&rft_dat=xri:hcpp:fu lltext:1829–011694:3 (accessed June 23, 2014); Knight to J. W. Croker, 5 August 1821 (second quotation), *Journals of the House of Commons, Appendices, From February the 5th, 1822, in the Third Year of the Reign of King George the Fourth, to January the 2nd, 1823, in the Third Year of the Reign of King George the Fourth*, p. 717, House of Commons Parliamentary Papers Database, http:// gateway.proquest.com/openurl?url_ver=Z39.88–2004&res_dat=xri:hcpp-us &rft_dat=xri:hcpp:rec:jhc-016651 (accessed March 13, 2015).

5. Mary Church, *Sierra Leone, Or, The Liberated Africans: In a Series of Letters from a Young Lady to Her Sister in 1833 & 34* (London: Longman and Co., 1835), 6 (first and second quotations), 19 (third quotation), 29–31, 38, 48 (fourth quotation); D. Denham to R. W. Hay, 14 May 1828, The National Archives of the UK (hereinafter cited as TNA), CO 268/10 (fifth quotation); H. J. Ricketts to R. W. Hay, 20 November 1828, TNA, CO 268/10.

6. In 1848, census records showed 1,231 Liberated Africans from the Bight of Biafra where Old Calabar was located. Antonio McDaniel, *Swing Low, Sweet Chariot: The Mortality Cost of Colonizing Liberia in the Nineteenth Century* (Chicago: University of Chicago Press, 1995), 32–36. Between 1808 and 1833, over 55,000 Liberated Africans were resettled in Sierra Leone, 65 percent were male and 35 percent were children. Bronwen Everill, *Abolition and Empire in Sierra Leone and Liberia* (London: Palgrave Macmillan, 2013), 21–22, 34, 38.

7. R. W. Hay to J. K. Stewart, 20 November 1831 (first and second quotations), G. Randall to R W. Hay, 20 July 1832 (third quotation), Hay to Stewart, 12 October 1832, Rear Ad. Warren to Sir James Graham, 21 January 1832, T1/3774, Treasury Board Papers and In-Letters, Treasury Long Bundles, Long Papers, Bundle 308: Gambia: Liberated Africans, TNA; Findlay to Hay, 2 February 1832, TNA, CO 268/10.

8. Numbers compiled from "Return Showing the Number of Liberated Africans at the Gambia," "Africans Gambia, 17701/33," TNA, T1/3774. The 1833 figures cover the period from January to March.

9. Peter Leonard, *Journal of an Officer Under Captain Owen, Records of a Voyage in the Ship Dryad in 1830, 1831 and 1832* (Philadelphia: Edward C. Mielke, 1833), 176 (first, second, and third quotations); "Return Showing the Number of Liberated Africans at the Gambia," TNA, T1/3774; Parliament, House of Commons, *Report from the Select Committee on the West Coast of Africa; Together with the Minutes of Evidence, Appendix, and Index*, part 2 (London: House of Commons, 1842), 187 (fifth quotation), 508 (fourth quotation).

10. Charles Smith Deposition, 31 January 1839, Class D, *Correspondence with Foreign Powers, Not Parties to Conventions Giving Right of Search of Vessels Suspected of the Slave Trade. From June 1st to December 31st, 1839, Inclusive*, 143–144, House of Commons Parliamentary Papers Database, available at http://gateway.proquest.com/openurl?url_ver=Z39.88–2004&res_dat =xri:hcpp-us&rft_dat=xri:hcpp:fulltext:1840–019393:157 (accessed June 20, 2014); "Return of the British Trade at the Principal Ports within the Consulate of New York during the Year Ending 31st December 1838," TNA, FO 5/336.

11. Population of the 100 Largest Urban Places: 1840, http://www.census.gov /population/www/documentation/twps0027/tab07.txt (accessed June 24, 2014); Charles Smith Deposition, 143–144; James Silk Buchanan, *The Slave States of America*, vol. 1 (London: Fisher, Son, and Co., 1842), 287 (third and fourth quotations), 288 (second quotation), 293 (first quotation).

12. Pharoah Moses to Mr. Cole, 7 January 1839; and Smith Affidavit, 31 January 1839, *Sessional Papers*, 143–144.

13. "Appendix No. 9, Observations Upon the Report of the Commissioner of Inquiry on the Western Coast of Africa," 31 July 1841, *Report from the Select Committee on the West Coast of Africa*, 224–228; Pharoah Moses to Mr. Cole, 7 January 1839, *Sessional Papers*, 143. Booray (and many other phonetic variations of that name) was a common one on ships seized in the Gallinas and Rio Pongo. See the African Origins database at http://www.african -origins.com.

14. Third Enclosure in No. 142, Macaulay to Doherty, 4 April 1839, in Boubacar Barry, *Senegambia and the Atlantic Slave Trade* (Cambridge: Cambridge University Press, 1998), 143; George E. Brooks, *Western Africa and Cabo Verde, 1790s-1830s: Symbiosis of Slave and Legitimate Trades* (Bloomington, IN: AuthorHouse, 2010), 124; Bruce Mouser, "Accommodation and Assimilation in the Landlord-Stranger Relationship," in B. K. Swartz, Raymond E. Dumett, eds., *West African Culture Dynamics: Archaeological and Historical Perspectives* (The Hague: Mouton Publishers, 1980) 506; Bruce Mouser, "The Nunez Affair," www.tubmaninstitute.ca/sites/default/files/file/Nunez_Affair .pdf (accessed June 25, 2014), 701; Barry, *Senegambia and the Atlantic Slave Trade*, 130, 142–143.

15. William Whitaker Shreeve, *Sierra Leone: The Principal British Colony on the Western Coast of Africa* (London: Simmonds and Co., 1817), 21 (first quotation);

Maryland Colonization Journal, 15 March 1842 (second quotation); Charles Smith Deposition, Sixth Enclosure in No. 142, 115.

16. Brooks, *Western Africa and Cabo Verde,* 43–45, 85, 108–109, 134, 222. In 1840 the U.S. imported 596,302 bushels of salt from Portugal, and 3,381,980 bushels from England. *Hunt's Merchant's Magazine and Commercial Review* 8 (March 1843): 358.

17. For an account of smuggling of enslaved Africans near Mobile in 1821, see *Alabama Republican,* 18 May 1821. The United States owned schooner *Alerina* or *Merino,* took 19 slaves aboard in Havana, then brought them into the Port of Mobile in 1818. See U.S. v. William Robertson, 1818, Case No. 87, Box 4, U.S. District Court for the Southern District of Alabama (Mobile). At least 2 slaves were brought to Mobile from the Florida territory in 1836. U.S. v. Steamboat Merchant, 1836, Case No. 1736, Box 46, U.S. District Court for the Southern District of Alabama (Mobile). Five slaves were transported from Pensacola to Mobile aboard the ship *Davy Crockett* in 1843. U.S. v. J. D. Jarvis, 1843, Case No. 2320, Box 55, U.S. District Court for the Southern District of Alabama (Mobile). National Archives and Records Administration Southeast Region, Atlanta, GA. On Cape Verde as a depot for illegal slave ships, see E. W. Schenley to Palmerston, 30 July 1836, TNA, FO 313/14.

18. *London Morning Chronicle,* 27 January 1857.

19. The *Lord Wellington,* Captain Tate, left London for Sierra Leone on November 16, 1838. *London Morning Post,* 17 November 1838.

20. Pharaoh Moses to Mr. Cole, 7 January 1839.

21. David Geggus, "The French Slave Trade: An Overview," *William and Mary Quarterly,* 3rd Series, 58 (January 2001): 119–138; Trevor R. Getz, *Slavery and Reform in West Africa: Toward Emancipation in Nineteenth-Century Senegal and the Gold Coast* (Athens: Ohio University Press, 2004), 33; Martin A. Klein, *Slavery and Colonial Rule in French West Africa* (Cambridge: Cambridge University Press, 1998), 22–23; Hilary Jones, *The Metis of Senegal: Urban Life and Politics in French West Africa* (Bloomington: Indiana University Press, 2013), 19–50; Donald R. Wright, *The World and a Very Small Place in Africa* (Armonk, NY: M. E. Sharp, Inc., 1997), 99–104.

22. Brooks, *Western Africa and Cabo Verde,* 1–27, 129 (quotation); Barry, *Senegambia,* 256. Transatlantic Slave Trade Database, Voyage Identification Numbers 25392, 25416, 25417, 25420, 25422, 25425, 25432, 25438, 25449, 25463, 25473, 25480, 25484, 25491, 25493, 25510, 25521, 25523, 25524, 25551, 25564, 25567, 25608, 36810, 36812, 36893, 36902, 36917, 36921, 36925, 37105, 37122, 37137, 82446, 82479. Only 3,864 of the 50,814 enslaved Africans who arrived in South Carolina between 1803 and 1808 came from the Senegambia. I am grateful to Paul Lovejoy who suggested that Sack N'Jaie was likely Muslim and Mandinka. Communication with the author, June 30, 2014.

23. Jonathan D. Martin, *Divided Mastery: Slave Hiring in the American South* (Cambridge, MA: Harvard University Press, 2009), 19, 20–28, 32, 166, 168, 173–174, 180–184; Ira Berlin, *Slaves Without Masters: The Free Negro in the Antebellum South* (New York: New Press, 1974), 219–221, 236–238.

24. *Philadelphia National Gazette,* December 25, 1832. A list of the passengers on the *Hercules* can be found on Christine's Genealogical Website, http://www .ccharity.com/contents/roll-emigrants-have-been-sent-colony-liberia -western-africa/emigrants-to-liberia-ship-lists/shipherculess1833/ (accessed June 26, 2014); *The Friend: A Religious and Literary Journal,* June 16, 1832 (quotations).

25. Charles Smith Deposition, Sixth Enclosure in No. 142, 145. The American Colonization Society began to send African Americans to Africa in 1820, and several separate colonies were established by various colonization societies. These were brought together to form Liberia in 1838. Tom W. Shick, *Behold the Promised Land: A History of Afro-American Settler Society in Nineteenth-Century Liberia* (Baltimore: The Johns Hopkins University Press, 1980); James Wesley Smith, *In Search of Freedom: The Settlement of Liberia by Black Americans* (Lanham, MD: University Press of America, 1987), 116–117.

26. Macaulay to Doherty, 4 April 1839, 141–142.

27. Doherty to Lord Glenelg, 5 April 1839, *Correspondence with Spain, Portugal, Brazil, The Netherlands, and Sweden Relative to the Slave Trade, from January 1, 1840 to May 10, 1840* (London: William Cowles and Sons, 1840), 141 (first quotation); Palmerston to Fox, 14 August 1839, *Correspondence with Spain,* 146 (second quotation); Mr. Fox to Mr. Forsyth, 22 October 1839, *Correspondence with Spain,* 180.

28. Forsyth to Fox, 30 October 1839, *Sessional Papers,* 180–181; Fox to Forsyth, 3 November 1839, *Sessional Papers,* 181; Mr. Buchanan to Mr. Fox, 7 November 1839, and Mr. Schroeder to Mr. H. S. Fox, 23 November 1839, *Sessional Papers,* 52; Mr. Butler to Mr. Forsyth, 8 December 1839, *Sessional Papers,* 53; Mr. Thurston to Mr. J. B. Hogan, 13 November 1839, *Correspondence with Spain,* 53–54; John Searvele to Mr. Forsyth, 16 November 1839, *Correspondence with Spain,* 54. To cite one of many examples, the *Tuskin* left Mobile for Liverpool on April 13, 1838. *Commercial Advertiser,* 20 April 1838.

29. Mr. Forsyth to Mr. Fox, 12 December 1839, *Correspondence with Spain,* 52–53.

30. Lonnie Burnett, *The Pen Makes a Good Sword: John Forsyth of the Mobile Register* (Tuscaloosa: University of Alabama Press, 2006), 9; Alvin Laroy Duckett, *John Forsyth: Political Tactician* (Athens: University of Georgia Press, 2010), 33–34, 182–185.

31. Charles Rockwell, *Sketches of Foreign Travel and Life at Sea* (Bedford, MA: Applewood Books, 2009), 387–388.

32. *Charleston Courier,* 28 May, 1838; *London Morning Post,* 25 June 1838, 17 November 1838. The *Sarah Nicholson* sailed from Liverpool to Charleston in

1843 on another voyage carrying cotton from southern ports to Liverpool. *Charleston Courier,* 23 June 1843. On Freebody, see *Baltimore Gazette and Daily Advertiser,* 8 April 1835, *London Shipping Gazette,* 22 June 1837.

Conclusion

1. On "life geographies" see Alan Lester, "Relational Space and Life Geographies in Imperial History: George Arthur and Humanitarian Governance," *Journal of the Canadian Historical Association / Revue de la Société historique du Canada* 21, no. 2 (2010): 29–46; Stephen Daniels and Catherine Nash, "Life Paths: Geography and Biography," *Journal of Historical Geography* 30 (2004): 449–458; Miles Ogborn, *Global Lives: Britain and the World, 1550–1800* (Cambridge: Cambridge University Press, 2009); and Alan Lester and David Lambert, *Colonial Lives Across the British Empire: Imperial Careering in the Long Nineteenth Century* (Cambridge: Cambridge University Press, 2006).

2. Thomas Clarkson, *Abolition of the African Slave-Trade, By the British Parliament,* vol. 1 (Augusta, ME: P. A. Brinsmade, 1830), 19–20.

3. Jacques Derrida, *Archive Fever: A Freudian Impression,* trans. Eric Penowitz (Chicago: University of Chicago Press, 1996), 4, n.1 (first quotation); Sonia Combe, *Archives interdites. Les peurs françaises face à l'histoire contemporaine* (Paris: Albin Michel, 1994), 321; Carolyn Steedman, *Dust: The Archive and Cultural History* (New Brunswick, NJ: Rutgers University Press, 2002); Ann Laura Stoler, "Colonial Archives and the Arts of Governance," *Archival Science* 2 (2002): 87–109 (second quotation on p. 91); Stoler, *Along the Archival Grain: Epistemic Anxieties and Colonial Common Sense* (Princeton, NJ: Princeton University Press, 2009), 23 (third and fourth quotations).

4. Derrida, *Archive Fever,* 4, 7.

5. Combe, *Archives interdites,* 318–321; Jacques Le Goff, *History and Memory* (New York: Columbia University Press, 1977); Carolyn Steedman, "The Space of Memory: In An Archive," *History of the Human Sciences* 11, no. 4 (1998): 65–83; Steedman, *Dust: The Archive.* On colonial archives and their links to imperial power, see Christopher Bayley, *Empire and Information: Intelligence Gathering and Social Communication in India, 1780–1870* (Cambridge: Cambridge University Press, 1996); Indrani Chatterjee, "Testing the Local Against the Colonial Archives," *History Workshop* 44 (1997): 215–224; Richard Thomas, *The Imperial Archive: Knowledge and the Fantasy of Empire* (London: Verso, 1990); Michel-Rolph Trouillot, *Silencing the Past: Power and the Production of History* (Boston: Beacon Press, 1995), 48–49, 52–53, 58–59 (quotation on p. 49).

6. Arlette Farge, *The Allure of the Archives,* trans. Thomas Scott-Railton (New Haven, CT: Yale University Press, 2013), 6 (first quotation); Saidiya V. Hartman, *Scenes of Subjection: Terror, Slavery, and Self-Making in Nineteenth-Century America* (Oxford: Oxford University Press, 1997), 10–12 (second

quotation on p. 10). Hartman is drawing on the influential concepts of Gayatri Chakravorty Spivak. For a thoughtful assessment of his treatment of subaltern voices, see Rosalind Morris, *Can the Subaltern Speak? Reflections on the History of an Idea* (New York: Columbia University Press, 2010).

7. Rebecca J. Scott and Jean M. Hébrard, *Freedom Papers: An Atlantic Odyssey in the Age of Emancipation* (Cambridge, MA: Harvard University Press, 2012), 3.

Acknowledgments

Like all historians, I have accumulated heavy debts in the course of my work, and I am happy to acknowledge those debts here, even if I cannot fully repay them. Archives and archivists make our work possible, and I have benefitted greatly from the help of those experts, particularly at the National Archives of the UK in Kew. I am especially grateful for the research assistance provided by Betsy Cazden in Rhode Island whose knowledge of the archives there was invaluable, and to Leah Worthington in Charleston who tracked down documents for me there. The maps are an essential component of this work, and I am fortunate to have Rebecca Wren as the cartographer. Thanks to the Department of History, the Lurcy Fund, the Executive Committee of the School of Liberal Arts, and the New Orleans Gulf South Humanities Center at Tulane University for their support of my research.

I presented aspects of this work at Cambridge University and Texas A&M University, at the Non-Traditional Slaveholding in the Atlantic World Conference, Senate House, London, in July 2014, at the 2015 American Historical Association meeting, and at the Tulane History Department's Faculty Seminar. I benefitted from the useful comments and questions from commenters and the audiences in those venues. I am grateful to the Harvard University Press's anonymous readers whose insights and suggestions have been most helpful, and to Joyce Seltzer and Brian Distelberg at HUP for their continued encouragement. Sylvia Frey and James Sidbury generously read the entire manuscript, and their insights have greatly improved it, though I alone am responsible for its shortcomings. My dear friend Judith Hunt also read the manuscript, as she has most of my work over the long years I have imposed it on her, and I am happy to recognize that support by dedicating this book to her. It is poor repayment for the riches she has brought into my life in over twenty-five years of friendship.

Index

abolition: of the slave trade, 15, 80, 85, 120, 134, 151; of slavery, 13, 14, 81, 89–91, 92, 93, 94, 97, 98, 99, 101, 102, 104, 105, 106, 108, 110, 114, 118, 119, 186n2

American Anti-Slavery Society, 104, 106, 186n2

American Colonization Society, 15, 96, 101, 147, 159, 196n25

American Revolution, 28–30, 31, 50, 52, 59, 71, 85, 86, 97, 139, 158

Anderson, James, 72, 73

archives, 7–8, 15, 101, 160–163

Atlantic World, 12, 16, 49, 55, 79, 133, 159; Africans in, 1, 2–4, 6, 12, 15, 79, 119, 121, 130, 133, 144, 145, 153, 157, 159, 160

Bahamas, 111, 117, 189n28

Baker, James, 123, 125, 127, 130

Banana Islands, 21, 22, 28, 31, 110, 157

Black Loyalists, 29, 77, 138, 139

Boston, 72, 81, 92, 93, 94, 95, 96, 98, 101, 102, 160

Bowen, Jabez, 13, 85, 87, 92, 181n7, 183nn21–22

Bowen, Jabez, Jr., 87, 89, 90, 91, 92–93, 98

Brazil, 69, 80, 134, 136, 151

Brown Fellowship Society, 72–73

Bulloch, William Bellinger, 87, 91

Canot, Theodore, 75, 132

Charleston, SC, 38, 48, 116, 149; colonial, 17, 18; free blacks in, 48, 72–74; Revolution and, 29; slave trade in, 13, 15, 17, 18, 19, 23, 55, 57, 58, 65, 69, 72, 76, 78, 79, 114, 143, 146–147, 149, 157

Charlton, Dimmock, 14, 132, 163; in Britain, 119–121; in the British Navy, 111–113, 120–121, 155, 160, 161, 162, 188n14; court case involving, 103, 105, 107, 108, 109; enslavement, 109–111, 113–118, 119, 121, 122; family, 103, 107–108, 117; hiring out, 116, 117, 160; self-purchase, 116–117, 118, 160

Charlton, Ellen, 103, 106, 107, 117, 118

Charlton, Thomas, 113, 114, 115

Cleland, John, 24, 27, 171n11

Cleveland, Catherine: arrival in South Carolina, 12, 17, 23–24, 48, 52, 55, 157; baptism, 27, 171n14; early life, 11–12, 17, 19, 23; family, 19, 35, 36, 44–48, 54, 174n52; property, 35, 36, 40, 41, 43, 44–47, 174n52; race, 19, 35, 41–42, 44–45, 50–52, 54–56, 157

Cleveland, Elizabeth (Hardcastle), 159, 160, 172n15; arrival in South Carolina, 17–19, 23–24, 48, 52, 55, 171n10; early life, 11–12, 21–23, 157; education, 21, 23, 52–53, 54, 70, 79, 157; family, 12, 19–21, 24, 28, 31, 33, 35, 36–37, 40, 41–42, 43, 44, 45, 49, 51, 52, 55, 70, 79, 110, 157, 159, 171n11, 174n52; healing skills, 28; illness and death, 34–38, 174n52; marriage and relationships, 27, 33, 34, 50, 53, 157; property, 12, 24–26, 27–28, 29, 30–31, 32, 33, 34, 35, 36, 38–41, 43–44, 46, 49, 50, 52, 54–55, 74, 161, 174n52; race, 11–12, 19, 23, 34, 41–43, 44, 45, 49, 50–52, 53–54, 55, 56, 70, 161; religion, 27, 33, 34, 54; as a slave owner, 12, 28, 31–32, 36, 47, 55, 158, 159